Cold War Dixie

COLD WAR DIXIE

Militarization and Modernization in the American South

KARI FREDERICKSON

The University of Georgia Press *Athens and London*

© 2013 by the University of Georgia Press
Athens, Georgia 30602
www.ugapress.org
All rights reserved
Set in Minion Pro by Graphic Composition, Inc., Bogart, Georgia

Printed digitally

Library of Congress Cataloging-in-Publication Data

Frederickson, Kari A.
 Cold War Dixie : militarization and modernization in the American
South / Kari Frederickson.
       pages cm. — (Politics and culture in the twentieth-century South)
   Includes bibliographical references and index.
   ISBN-13: 978-0-8203-4519-2 (hardcover : alkaline paper)
   ISBN-10: 0-8203-4519-9 (hardcover : alkaline paper)
   ISBN-13: 978-0-8203-4520-8 (paperback : alkaline paper)
   ISBN-10: 0-8203-4520-2 (paperback : alkaline paper)
   1. Savannah River Valley (Ga. and S.C.)—History—20th century.
2. Savannah River Valley (Ga. and S.C.)—Social conditions—20th
century. 3. Savannah River Valley (Ga. and S.C.)—Economic
conditions—20th century. 4. Cold War—Social aspects—Savannah
River Valley (Ga. and S.C.) 5. Nuclear weapons industry—Social
aspects—Savannah River Valley (Ga. and S.C.)—History—20th
century. 6. Savannah River Plant (E.I. du Pont de Nemours &
Company)—History. 7. Militarism—Savannah River Valley (Ga. and
S.C.)—History—20th century. 8. Social change—Savannah River
Valley (Ga. and S.C.)—History—20th century. 9. Aiken (S.C.)—
Social conditions—20th century. 10. Aiken (S.C.)—Economic
conditions—20th century. I. Title.
   F277.S3F74 2013
   975'.043—dc23   2012048326

British Library Cataloging-in-Publication Data available

FOR OLIVIA AND REBECCA

CONTENTS

ILLUSTRATIONS

ACKNOWLEDGMENTS

One does not successfully conclude a twelve-year scholarly journey without racking up a lot of debts. So it is with this project. First and foremost, this book would not have been possible without the generosity of the former employees of the Savannah River Plant/Site and of the residents of Aiken and Graniteville who shared their insights with me about the impact of the Cold War on their communities. I am especially grateful to Dr. Walter Joseph and Mr. Willar Hightower, who spent many hours talking with me and who served as particularly perceptive guides to the region and its transformation.

I was fortunate to have had the expert assistance of many archivists, fellow historians, and other history professionals along the way, including Stan Price at the Gregg-Graniteville Library; James Farmer Jr., who pointed me in the direction of the John Shaw Billings Collection; Elliot Levy, Brenda Baratto, and Mary White of the Aiken County Historical Society; Allan Riddick; Henry Fulmer, Beth Bilderbeck, and Herb Hartsook at the South Caroliniana Library; Jon M. Williams of the Hagley Museum and Library; George Wingard Jr. of the Savannah River Archaeological Research Project; Mary Beth Reed of New South Associates; Caroline Bradford of the Savannah River Site Cold War Historic Preservation Program; and James E. Cross, archivist of the Strom Thurmond Collection at Clemson University. Grants from the National Endowment for the Humanities and the Institute for Southern Studies at the University of South Carolina helped get this project off the ground.

Colleagues, staff, and students at the University of Alabama, especially Larry Clayton, Lisa Dorr, John Giggie, Andrew Huebner, Howard Jones, Larry Kohl, Michael Mendle, George Rable, and Josh Rothman provided and continue to provide a great support network. Two years ago, I took on the duties of department chair. Our wonderful staff—Kay Branyon, Christina Kircharr, Ellen Pledger, and Fay Wheat—made transitioning to a twelve-month position incredibly easy. I am grateful to Dean Robert Olin and Associate Dean Carmen Burkhalter of the College of Arts and Sciences for granting me a sabbatical to work on this book but mostly for their patience as I struggled to balance my duties as department chair with the demands of finishing a book. Undergraduate student Nick Theodore contributed careful research from the U.S. Census. Graduate student Joseph Pearson read an entire draft of the manuscript and offered useful suggestions at a critical juncture in the project. Eric Rose, a history graduate student from the University of South Carolina, conducted research for me when I could not get to Columbia.

My greatest debt goes to my family—immediate and extended. My in-laws, Otis and Esther Melton, shared their memories of growing up in Graniteville and provided me a place to stay while I conducted my research. My husband, Jeff, gave me the idea for the book and remained enthusiastic about the project for more than a decade. He read each chapter more than once and often brought his considerable literary skills to bear. I have dedicated this book to my daughters, Olivia and Rebecca. Although their arrivals greatly delayed the completion of this book, I would not have had it any other way.

Open any South Carolina highway map and you will find standard features— blue highways and roads, black railroad lines, dotted lines denoting county boundaries, red flags marking schools and hospitals, green parks and golf courses. Near the state's western border, though, is a massive blank space labeled "The Savannah River Site—U.S. Department of Energy." Covering approximately 20 percent of Aiken County, 30 percent of Barnwell County, and 10 percent of Allendale, the Savannah River Site is rendered featureless on most maps, a vast expanse of federal white space that is devoid of traditional cartographic characteristics. Built in the early 1950s amid the escalating tensions and threats of the Cold War, the Savannah River Plant (as it was known until the 1980s) was an Atomic Energy Commission (AEC) facility operated by the Du Pont Corporation and dedicated to producing plutonium, tritium, deuterium, and heavy water for the hydrogen bomb. In size and scope, the Savannah River Plant (SRP) was a technological and engineering marvel—the most expansive federal project ever undertaken. Its five nuclear reactors and more than two hundred other industrial and administrative buildings were spread across more than three hundred square miles—an area roughly the size of Washington, D.C. Built to meet the needs of a new kind of war—a war with no end in sight—the SRP imprinted the modern military state on the southern landscape, transforming not only the space within its boundaries but the surrounding communities.

As the AEC's largest installation, the experiences and problems encountered in the development of the SRP provided a blueprint for future Cold War communities across the nation. The changes that unfolded in this mostly rural section of South Carolina reflected the intersection of national policy and priorities with complex local realities. The SRP was the first AEC installation

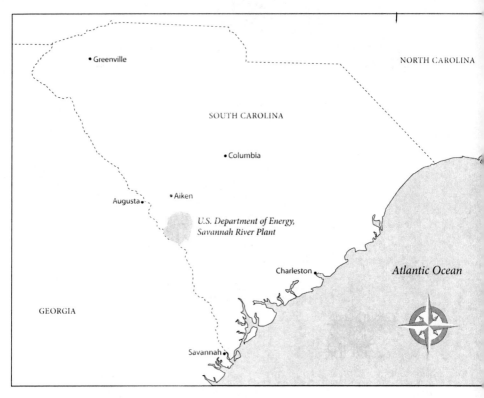

Map 1. The Savannah River Plant, South Carolina.

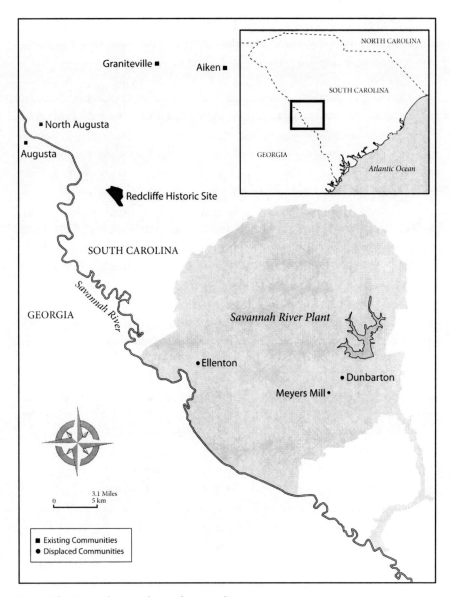

Map 2. The Savannah River Plant and surrounding area.

created without an adjoining company town. Seeking to avoid the implementation of excessive governmental controls and planning that are fundamental to a garrison state, the Truman administration chose instead to rely on existing infrastructure and private enterprise to prepare the country for and maintain a permanent state of war readiness. The needs of the expanding national security state, filtered through the specific culture of Du Pont Corporation, transformed the area's economy, landscape, social relations, and politics, precipitating and shaping the rapid modernization of this largely undeveloped corner of the state. A region that in 1950 had been primarily poor, uneducated, rural, and staunchly Democratic by the mid-1960s boasted the most PhDs per capita of any South Carolina region and had become increasingly middle class, suburban, consumption oriented, and Republican. The story of the impact of the SRP and the dawn of the Cold War in the South is ultimately a story of the rapid process of modernization. A deep investigation of a small place, this book places America's longest war at the center of regional change. With particular emphasis on the critical 1950–70 period, this study captures the dynamic social, political, and cultural transformations that unfolded in this part of the South as the military-industrial complex took hold.

Beginning in the late 1940s and continuing until the end of the 1980s, the American South became an increasingly attractive location for the many and varied institutions—military, aeronautical, industrial, scientific—that rose to meet the nation's expanding Cold War needs. Although the West (in particular, Southern California) emerged as the largest beneficiary in terms of total defense dollars received, the South surpassed the national average in terms of its dependence on the defense establishment for both employment and income. Historians have only just begun to examine the Cold War's impact on the region and how specific Cold War facilities shaped individual communities. Published in 1994, Bruce Schulman's *From Cotton Belt to Sunbelt* remains the definitive work for those seeking to understand how federal policy—including military spending—shaped the South. "In 1973," Schulman writes, "more southerners worked in defense-related industries than in textiles, synthetics, and apparel combined. Defense dollars permeated nearly every town in the region."[1] But subsequent historical inquiry into the complex nature of this dependency and its effects on southern development has lagged behind studies of the Cold War's impact on the American West. Studies by Roger Lotchin,

Gerald Nash, Kevin Fernlund, Bruce Hevly and John M. Findlay, and Lisa Mc-Girr, among others, explore how defense industries and military bases were integral to that region's economic, political, and cultural development.[2] Among the Manhattan Project facilities, the Hanford Engineering Works and Los Alamos National Laboratory have been the subjects of numerous historical studies and memoirs, while Oak Ridge National Laboratory and its effect on the surrounding Tennessee communities remains understudied.[3] Among defense-related installations in the South, military bases have received the greatest attention from historians. This makes perfect sense, for as Schulman notes, "the region remained the nation's boot camp throughout the postwar era."[4] But scores of facilities, plants, and research parks dependent on defense spending, each with its own distinct population, mission, and culture, await historians.

To explain postwar change, historians have looked elsewhere, particularly to the civil rights movement.[5] Scholars have begun to move away from straight movement histories to look at other forces, such as suburbanization, to help explain regional change in the 1960s and 1970s.[6] In these works, the Cold War serves mostly as a chronological frame rather than as a national undertaking that set in motion interlocking forces with explanatory powers of their own. Those historians interested in the effect of the Cold War specifically on the South have largely focused on the complex impact of anticommunism on southern politics and the budding civil rights movement. Anticommunism poisoned the liberal political well and fueled the Massive Resistance movement, making even the most tepid statement on racial progress by an elected official a sure road to political oblivion. The nation's concurrent struggle against communism gave civil rights activists some leverage in pushing political leaders to give substance to America's democratic principles.[7] This study does not seek so much to supplant this narrative as to broaden the story of postwar change and the consequences of the Cold War beyond the political ramifications of a toxic anticommunism. It does so by highlighting the ways in which Cold War imperatives transformed the economy, social structure, and culture of a particular community, thus ultimately shaping the way in which the civil rights movement unfolded in this corner of the South.

In 1950, the tricounty region out of which the SRP was carved was a diverse mixture of charming small towns, textile mill villages, and struggling rural areas. Some of the country's wealthiest owners of racehorses set up their winter training quarters in the city of Aiken, in Aiken County, and built magnificent homes they referred to as their winter "cottages." Over the next ten years, thousands of highly skilled and educated scientists and engineers recruited by the AEC and Du Pont from across the nation poured into this region, and the majority of them settled in and around Aiken. At the height of its productivity, the SRP and its affiliated industries employed more than twenty-five thousand people in what eventually became known as the Central Savannah River Area. Scores of suburban subdivisions and national retail outlets served the housing and lifestyle needs of these new white-collar residents and offered new opportunities to longtime residents. For residents of the mill villages in nearby Horse Creek Valley and the outlying rural communities, the SRP was an economic godsend, enabling many of them to enter the middle class and giving them new opportunities to participate in the region's expanding mass consumer culture. Most native South Carolinians as well as newcomers proudly embraced their new roles in the nation's Cold War weapons program.

This burgeoning middle class, the influx of national retail establishments and a flourishing consumer culture, and mass suburbanization introduced a larger culture heralding efficiency, rationality, consumption, technological innovation, and progress—all components of the process of modernization—that threatened to displace the region's older rural and leisure culture. Much of this impact drew from the influence of the Du Pont Corporation. The changes that befell the communities surrounding the SRP reflected the needs of the national security state as they were filtered through and shaped by Du Pont's specific corporate culture. Du Pont arrived in South Carolina prepared to do battle in the Cold War. Although the company's origins lay in the production of gunpowder, by the mid-twentieth century, Du Pont boasted a long line of consumer products with nylon—the "miracle fiber"—in the forefront. With its focus on the production of both fissile materials and consumer goods, Du Pont represented the new orientation of postwar America, in which corporations became central to the nation's security and prosperity. With its thousands of employees in South Carolina, Du Pont fostered a local culture that privileged modernization, innovation, efficiency, consumption, and civic involvement as indispensable components in the Cold War battle with communism. By the 1960s, Du Pont and AEC employees constituted roughly one-third of the region's population. Riding the crest of the "scientists movement"—a broad popular belief that students of science were particularly well positioned to weigh in on a whole host of public policy issues—the SRP employees moved confidently into positions of power and influence in their communities, leaving a lasting imprint on the development of those communities.

The region's new emphasis on modernization and efficiency had wide-ranging cultural, social, racial, and political consequences. The creation of the SRP profoundly changed the region's landscape. This study follows closely historian Mart Stewart's definition of landscape as "land shaped by human hands."[8] Furthermore, Stewart argues, "humans create landscapes in accordance with both aesthetic and social values or in order to facilitate certain kinds of production."[9] The confiscation of hundreds of thousands of acres of land for the development of a sprawling Cold War complex decisively reordered the area's traditional rural landscape, not only within the plant boundaries but also through the institution of newly built structures such as suburban tract housing and the creation of new commercial outlets. An emphasis on efficiency and security likewise blurred traditional geographic boundaries and introduced a new understanding of land and space defined by Cold War needs. In a region where the relationship between town and country had once been relatively fluid, planners of the military-industrial complex introduced modern concepts of boundaries and land use that rendered the environment subordinate to technology and security. The town of Aiken, South Carolina, where most new plant personnel lived, exhibited growth patterns that resulted in part from population expansion but were also shaped by Du Pont's specific corporate culture and the nature of the work undertaken at the plant.

The Cold War and civil rights movement dawned simultaneously in South Carolina. African Americans saw in the SRP an opportunity for advancement and hoped to use the Cold War crisis to their economic advantage—that is, as a means of prying open a calcified labor market that offered few opportunities for advancement and economic security. Led by national civil rights organizations and putting their faith in federal antidiscrimination employment policies, local blacks looked cautiously to the plant for economic salvation. Civil rights leaders couched their demands in the new language of national security, arguing that the failure to use African American workers at a moment of national emergency not only violated federal policy but was dangerous, was irresponsible, and made for poor publicity abroad.

Civil rights advocates' demands, however, were trumped by the arguments put forth by Du Pont Corporation. A profoundly conservative industrial behemoth that saw its history and that of the nation as forever linked, Du Pont used the project's urgency as an argument against changing social patterns.

The speed with which the plant had to be built permitted the federal government to give lip service to antidiscrimination provisions and to rely on Du Pont's tepid assurances of fair hiring practices. Whereas existing and new government statutes might have been enforced, thus opening the door wide for African American advancement, the Cold War emergency allowed Du Pont's corporate culture to predominate and to blunt most of the plant's opportunities and potential for promoting rapid and meaningful social change.

The political changes that befell the region in the 1950s and 1960s were shaped first by the Cold War and Du Pont's specific corporate culture. The region surrounding the SRP, especially Aiken County, was among the first in the state to support Republican candidates at the presidential level. More significant, though, Aiken Republicans were the first to organize at the local level. By the late 1950s, Republican candidates, many of them plant employees, were vying for municipal and county offices. Growing out of local civic associations, the local Republican Party recruited support in part by appealing to issues that resonated with conservatives across the nation but, more important, by arguing that a two-party system promoted transparency and efficiency—in effect, a modern political system. This study does not dispute the importance of the civil rights movement in generating a conservative backlash that ultimately led many white southerners to vote Republican in national elections but does contend that the roots of this Republican resurgence lay in the 1950s and were directly tied to changes wrought by the Cold War.[10]

The region that would play host to the SRP boasted some of the worst racial violence of the Reconstruction and New South eras and spawned politicians— among them Benjamin Tillman, Cole Blease, and Strom Thurmond—who dedicated much of their public lives to the preservation of the color line. It is perhaps surprising, then, that the civil rights revolution unfolded relatively quietly in the communities surrounding the plant. Those readers looking for a traditional civil rights narrative will find a different story in these pages. Race was and remains today an important factor in the region's development; nevertheless, a comprehensive and nuanced rendering of the history of this region in the 1950s and 1960s requires placing the Cold War at the center. The area's profound demographic shift of the 1950s—a direct result of the creation of the SRP; the impact of Du Pont's particular modernizing impulse; the existence of well-respected black educational institutions; and the peculiar historic social and economic relations within the city of Aiken—shaped whites' ideas about African American culture and responses to racial change. These factors likewise affected the lengths to which African Americans would go to demand change. Although whites in Aiken and the surrounding communities were certainly not in the forefront of groups demanding change, they also did not put up significant resistance when integration finally came. In no way discounting the horrors visited on movement participants and the African American community generally in Birmingham, the Mississippi Delta, or elsewhere, this particular story of begrudging but nonviolent acquiescence to social change is perhaps more typical of southern communities transformed a decade earlier by forces accompanying the Cold War.

And so we return to the map. The large, seemingly blank expanse of federal space masks an impact that was highly textured and far-reaching. Increasingly in the post–World War II era, federal installations—many of them operated by huge corporations—dotted the southern landscape, and private industries in southern cities and towns grew fat on military contracts. The formidable presence of the military-industrial complex in the region demands that historians begin to craft a new narrative of the postwar South that takes into consideration the myriad forces that swept over the region in the late 1940s and early 1950s and that helped define the modern South.

CHAPTER ONE

"This Most Essential Task"
The Decision to Build the Super

It was routine. On September 3, 1949, a U.S. Air Force WB-29 flying east of the Kamchatka Peninsula in the Soviet Union on a secret detection flight picked up radioactivity in its filters. The suspect sample was sent to Tracerlab at the University of California at Berkeley, which confirmed a man-made device. For the following two weeks, American scientists tracked the radioactive air mass as it drifted across the Pacific Ocean and blew across the United States. One Tracerlab physicist recalled that during that tense period, "I didn't sleep more than four hours a day. Our little group was working around the clock." British sniffer flights sent north from Scotland and along the Norwegian coast confirmed the presence of radioactivity. Tracerlab estimated that the device was Soviet in origin and that the explosion had taken place on August 29, 1949. On the morning of September 23, armed with scientific data from American and British experts, a somber President Harry Truman informed the nation that the Soviets had exploded an atomic bomb, ultimately nicknamed Joe 1. America's nuclear monopoly had lasted just four years. The world had become a much more dangerous place.[1]

Unaware of the radioactive cloud drifting thousands of miles above them, the residents of Aiken County in western South Carolina busied themselves with more parochial concerns during the late summer of 1949. Locals eagerly anticipated the opening of the second annual Aiken Cotton Festival. The brainchild of local merchants seeking to capitalize on postwar prosperity and escalating consumer demand, the Cotton Festival was a three-day event designed to lure working-class and rural consumers from the county's textile mill villages and farms to the town of Aiken, the county seat, to shop. The festival featured time-honored and folksy rural traditions. Patrons could peruse exhibits constructed by the Future Farmers of America, attend demonstrations of the latest farm equipment, and enjoy barbecue, which, the local paper assured its white readers, was "served to white and colored [patrons] in separate lines." The festival concluded with the coronation of Queen Cotton at the Cotton Ball gala.[2] Even as town leaders sought to capitalize on the postwar consumption desires of area residents as a way to boost local business, they did so with a distinctly backward glance by drawing on the practices and folkways of the region's rural past.

The realization that the Soviets possessed atomic capabilities escalated the international arms race and brought about a collision of national defense priorities and local concerns. By the end of January 1950, the Truman administration decided to proceed with the development of the hydrogen bomb. The production of materials for the "super," as it was commonly called, required a new facility. The particular demands involved in developing such a plant to produce the necessary amounts of plutonium and tritium were numerous and complicated, requiring the planners to consider a range of factors from climate to prevailing wage scales. By the end of the year, residents of Aiken and two neighboring counties in western South Carolina learned that they would play host to a sprawling Cold War weapons complex. Locals who a year earlier had enjoyed the comfortable anonymity and relative predictability shared by thousands of inhabitants of small towns and rural communities across the nation suddenly found themselves thrust into the national spotlight, their fate intimately and at times frighteningly entwined with the nation's Cold War fortunes and ambitions.

The detonation of two atomic bombs in Japan in 1945 had not only brought an end to World War II but also fundamentally changed the balance of power between the United States and the Soviet Union. Schooled in the means of power and intimidation, the Soviets understood this development. "The bombs dropped on Japan were not aimed at Japan but rather at the Soviet Union," former deputy prime minister and foreign minister Vyacheslav Molotov recalled. "They said, bear in mind you don't have an atomic bomb and we do, and this is what the consequences will be like if you make a wrong move!" The Soviets immediately designed a strategy to counter any American attempts at atomic diplomacy, undertaking a massive program to develop their own nuclear device.[3]

Stalin's fears of nuclear intimidation were misplaced, however, because the Truman administration never transformed the nation's atomic monopoly into an effective instrument of peacetime coercion.[4] For several years following those fateful days in August 1945, the administration followed a policy that discouraged the exploration of atomic diplomacy and instead chose to pursue a rather optimistic vision for the peacetime development of atomic science and technology. President Truman signed the Atomic Energy Act on August 1, 1946, creating a five-member Atomic Energy Commission (AEC) to take over the nation's nuclear programs, which had been administered by the Manhattan District of the U.S. Corps of Engineers. The nation's nuclear program would come under civilian rather than military control. Responding to pressure from scientists, public opinion, and allies, the United States also sought international control of atomic energy, a plan that ultimately failed.[5] With U.S. efforts directed elsewhere, historian John Lewis Gaddis notes, "the production of atomic weapons [between 1945 and 1949] proceeded at what seems in retrospect a remarkably relaxed pace, so that at the time he proclaimed the Truman Doctrine in March 1947, the President understood there to be only fourteen bombs in the American arsenal." According to Gaddis, Truman's commitment to civilian control of the nuclear arsenal was such that he "denied the Pentagon the most basic information about how many atomic bombs were available, or on what their effects would be if employed."[6]

The administration's policies were designed with the assumption that America could enjoy its atomic monopoly for six to eight years, although scientists had long said that five years was a more probable timeline. Soviet atomic success came about much more quickly than politicians and the public had predicted, changing the defense equation. If Truman had been ambivalent about U.S. atomic policies, he had no hesitation in determining Soviet intentions. The implications of the Soviets' acquisition of nuclear weapons were daunting; the United States would have to accelerate and expand its nuclear arsenal if it hoped to maintain a quantitative and qualitative lead over the Soviet Union. The nation would also have to consider building a more powerful thermonuclear weapon.[7] The race was on.

Intense discussions regarding the production of the hydrogen bomb specifically and the broader question of the role of atomic weapons in the nation's military and foreign policy collided with domestic and international developments. In October 1949, one month after the president revealed the Soviets' possession of atomic secrets, communist forces consolidated their control over mainland China, escalating fears of a Moscow-Beijing communist alliance against the Western democracies. And in the concluding months of 1949 and into the new year, the conviction of Alger Hiss for perjury and the discovery of an espionage ring at Los Alamos National Laboratory ignited fears of internal threats to national security.[8]

International tensions and especially the discovery that the Soviet Union possessed nuclear capabilities escalated discussions at the highest levels of the U.S. government about whether to proceed with the production of the hydrogen bomb, a thermonuclear device whose destructive capabilities were projected to be one hundred times greater than those of existing atomic weapons. I. I. Rabi, an experimental physicist and member of the General Advisory Committee of scientists, which provided technical guidance to the AEC, became worried "that the Russian [atomic] achievement brought the prospect of war much closer and therefore prompted the question as to what courses of action should be taken." For Senator Brien McMahon, a Connecticut Democrat who chaired the Joint Congressional Committee on Atomic Energy, nothing less than national survival was at stake. He pressured the president: "If we let Russia get the super first, catastrophe becomes all but certain," McMahon warned, "whereas, if we get it first, there exists a chance of saving ourselves."[9]

High-level discussions among the nation's top scientists, military officials, and congressional leaders focused on the morality of the new "superbomb" as well as its military applications. Led by Edward Teller, Luis Alvarez, and Ernest Lawrence, several nuclear scientists had for years been discussing the possibility and desirability of a fusion bomb. No one questioned the immense power of the super. Detonation of a single hydrogen bomb could destroy roughly one hundred square miles. While fission bombs, like those dropped on Hiroshima and Nagasaki, create temperatures equal to those on the surface of the sun, a fusion bomb, according to Joseph Cirincione, "truly is the equivalent of bringing a small piece of the sun down to earth."[10] State department official George F. Kennan; J. Robert Oppenheimer, scientific director of the Manhattan Project; and other top advisers failed to see how such an apocalyptic device could ever be useful.[11] Further, Harvard University president James B. Conant, a Manhattan Project veteran and an AEC adviser, argued that the hydrogen bomb was morally repugnant and militarily useless. Its only purpose, he argued, was to kill massive numbers of civilians, which amounted to genocide. The bomb would become, in Conant's words, America's Maginot Line, a cheap defense that would give the nation a false sense of security.[12]

Supporters of the thermonuclear bomb made their arguments based on psychological, not military, necessity. Summarizing the psychological argument,

Gaddis writes, "Not having [hydrogen bombs] would induce panic throughout the West if the Soviet Union got them. Having them would produce reassurance and deterrence: whatever advantages Stalin might have obtained from his atomic bomb would be canceled, and the United States would remain ahead in the nuclear arms race."[13] The chief proponent of this argument was General Omar Bradley, chair of the Joint Chiefs of Staff. Bradley argued that the super "should be built even if it had no military purpose. It was justification enough that such a device was possible, and that the Russians might get it."[14] But the decision to move forward with the superbomb would be the president's alone.

In October 1949, the General Advisory Committee, created by the Atomic Energy Act of 1946 and composed of the nation's top scientists, delivered to the AEC a report on the feasibility and utility of the hydrogen bomb. Committee members opposed the development of the superbomb on technical and moral grounds and split on their recommendation to the president, with two members in favor of proceeding with the super program and three opposed. Truman, who had only just learned of the possibility of constructing a thermonuclear weapon, next created a special advisory committee comprised of Secretary of State Dean Acheson, Secretary of Defense Louis Johnson, and David Lilienthal, chair of the AEC, to aid the president in his decision.[15] The special committee itself was so divided that it only held one meeting, in December 1949. The military, however, spoke with a single voice. The following month, the Joint Chiefs of Staff sent a strongly worded recommendation to the secretary of defense, urging creation of the bomb on the grounds that "military considerations" outweighed any moral objections. Calling the superbomb a "decisive" weapon, the military men considered it "necessary to have within the arsenal of the United States a weapon of the greatest capability. . . . Such a weapon would improve our defense in its broadest sense, as a potential offensive weapon, a possible deterrent to war, a potential retaliatory weapon, as well as a defensive weapon against enemy forces." Conversely, the Joint Chiefs believed that "the United States would be in an intolerable position if a possible enemy possessed the bomb and the United States did not." To renounce such a weapon, they argued, would jeopardize "the security of the entire Western Hemisphere."[16]

As Truman contemplated the horrendous decision before him, the atmosphere in Washington "became charged with rancor and fear" following the communist takeover of China and Alger Hiss's perjury conviction. At a press conference on January 27, Truman was asked about his views on the hydrogen bomb. The president replied that he had nothing to say until he had made his decision, his first public acknowledgment that the issue existed and was being debated within the corridors of power.[17] Much to the scientists' dismay, Truman was determined to keep discussions of the new weapon restricted. Consequently, speculation abounded regarding who supported and who opposed the hydrogen bomb. On January 2, 1950, syndicated columnists Joseph and Stewart Alsop laid out the issue of the "super bomb," somberly noting that "dustily and obscurely, the issues of life and death are settled nowadays—dingy committee rooms are the scenes of the debate; harassed officials are the disputants; all the proceedings are highly classified; yet the whole future hangs, perhaps, upon the outcome." The Alsops urged the principals to "bring the present debate out of its native darkness. . . . [T]his must be done, since deeper issues are involved, which have been far too long concealed from the country."[18]

Shut out of the debate, concerned citizens wrote anxious letters to the president. Many sympathized with his "terrible burden" but nevertheless demanded that the discussion and decision for taking such a fateful step be made in the open and not by one man. Some correspondents, like Roy Valencourt of North Manchester, Indiana, anguished over this turn of events, reminding the president that "we American people are ultimately responsible, morally, for the acts of our political officials." Valencourt worried about the consequences of moving forward on the development of the hydrogen bomb, consequences that included provoking the Russians to build their own bomb, "perhaps an even greater number of nervous breakdowns and psycho-neurotic cases as a result of increased psychological insecurity, an increased and intensified antagonism between representatives of the Russian and American governments." Ann Hedges, who identified herself as a "young wife and mother" from Baltimore, likewise saw the question in personal and moral terms, urging the president more aggressively to pursue arms control talks with the Russians. "What will our possession of powerful weapons mean if my family is dead and the world around me all but destroyed?" Columbia University philosophy professor Horace L. Friess stated that "if it should seem necessary to construct this weapon," Congress and the president should resolve "not to use it unless it is used against us. . . . Without some such heroic restraint I believe the moral loss to our cause would more than offset any tactical and diplomatic advantages." Many writers simply told the president that they were praying for him in this difficult time.[19]

It is unclear to what extent the president wrestled with the decision, as he left nothing in writing.[20] On January 31, 1950, Lilienthal, Acheson, and Johnson presented their recommendation that work should proceed on the hydrogen bomb, although Lilienthal continued to express strong reservations. Relying on atomic weapons as the country's chief defense, he argued, was dangerous. Truman asked one question of his advisers: "Can the Russians do it?" When all solemnly nodded, Truman declared, "In that case, we have no choice. We'll go ahead."[21] Later that day, Truman authorized an accelerated program to develop the hydrogen bomb.[22] Almost immediately following this decision, the president, in response to new realities, directed the State Department's Policy Planning Staff to review the nation's security needs. The result was National Security Council Document 68 (NSC-68), a fifty-eight-page memorandum that became a blueprint for American Cold War policy. The authors characterized the Soviet Union as a hostile power "animated by a new fanatical faith" and determined "to impose its absolute authority over the rest of the world." Among other recommendations, NSC-68 proposed meeting the growing Soviet threat with a large arsenal of nuclear weapons.[23]

As the administration was developing policy to confront the new realities of Soviet atomic capabilities, international events dictated an immediate military response to the communist threat. In the early hours of Sunday morning, June 25, 1950, given the green light from Stalin, thousands of North Koreans poured southward over the Thirty-Eighth Parallel into South Korea, a blatant violation of the United Nations–sanctioned boundary and thus a "challenge [to] the entire structure of postwar collective security."[24] Within hours, Truman's administration determined that it would come to the defense of South Korea and would seek United Nations approval and support for that effort. With UN approval, the international community took only days to mobilize against this new threat to international security.[25] The Korean War had begun. Amid these frightening international developments, the AEC undertook a feverish expansion program beginning in October 1950. Key to this expansion was the development of a facility to produce plutonium and tritium.[26] This new plant to create material for the world's first thermonuclear weapon would constitute a key component of the nation's beefed-up arsenal.

With Truman's decision to go forward with the development of the hydrogen bomb, the country began mobilizing in no uncertain terms for a new kind of war, one for which no models existed. This new mobilization demanded new facilities and infrastructure. The AEC was charged with finding a contractor and a site for the new weapons complex.

Established in 1947, the AEC "supplanted the Manhattan Engineering District of the Army Corps of Engineers as administrator of the atomic energy program. The Commission, a five-member body appointed by the president, oversaw a fiefdom of private and government-owned institutions dedicated to all aspects of nuclear development."[27] To build this new plant, the AEC considered a number of corporations, including Union Carbide, Monsanto, Dow Chemical, and American Cyanamid.[28] After much deliberation, the AEC turned to E. I. Du Pont de Nemours Corporation of Delaware. Du Pont had constructed and operated the world's first plutonium production reactors at Hanford, Washington, as part of the Manhattan Project and was a leader in weapons production. Observed one atomic energy expert, "To ask anybody else to build the plant when you could get Du Pont would be like settling for a rookie when you could get Babe Ruth in his prime."[29]

Founded in 1802 on the banks of Brandywine Creek near Wilmington, Delaware, E. I. Du Pont de Nemours and Company is the country's oldest industrial firm and is almost as old as the nation itself. The company worked hard to intertwine its commercial growth with national purpose. Originally a manufacturer of gunpowder, Du Pont received its first government contract from President Thomas Jefferson. From that point on, Du Pont gunpowder was used in every American military conflict and was integral in the expansion and development of the nation. Pioneers used Du Pont powder to clear the wilderness for settlement, build railroads, and raise factories.[30] During World War I, Du Pont supplied 40 percent of all the powder used by the Allies, chalking up more than one billion dollars in sales.[31] Such unseemly profits came under the scrutiny of the Senate Munitions Investigation Committee (more popularly known as the Nye Committee), which investigated the cause of America's involvement in the war. The committee's final report harshly criticized Du Pont's excessive wartime profits, and the company whose success was tied to the nation's own found itself with a new, horrific nickname: "merchant of death." Du Pont worked hard to rid itself of this public relations disaster, downplaying its munitions production and turning in the postwar era to the research and development of consumer and consumer-related products, among them nylon, cellophane, and Freon. By 1940, explosives and gunpowder accounted for only 25 percent of Du Pont's production, far less than the 80 percent that had been the case during World War I.[32]

But World War II drew Du Pont back to its munitions roots and back to government contracts. Du Pont built and maintained the Hanford Engineering Works in Washington, part of the Manhattan Project, and was responsible for creating weapons-grade plutonium that went into the bomb used in the Trinity test and in the Fat Man bomb dropped on Nagasaki. The company accepted the Hanford assignment with trepidation. Crawford H. Greenewalt, who by 1947 had become president of Du Pont, recalled that after deciding to take on the atomic project, "We all . . . had a drink of condolence and commiseration."[33] Eager to avoid the label of war profiteer, Du Pont agreed to participate in the Manhattan Project under two conditions: (1) the company would not make any profits from its association with the atomic project; and (2) any patents resulting from the work accomplished would become the property of the federal government. The government agreed to both conditions, paying Du Pont one dollar a year over costs for the company's contributions.

Following the dropping of the atomic bombs on Japan and the end of the war, however, Du Pont again expressed reluctance to continue at the center of the nation's weapons complex. In 1946, the company turned over the maintenance of the Hanford works to General Electric. In the postwar era, Du Pont invested heavily in research and development, returning to its interwar focus on consumer products and textiles. By 1952, Du Pont offered more than one hundred products in a wide range of industries. The corporation positioned itself as the provider of a veritable cornucopia of products and created a patriotic perception of itself that downplayed its munitions production. President Dwight Eisenhower in particular embraced this perspective in his foreign policy, expanding it to characterize the nation at large in its global struggle with communism. With companies such as Du Pont in the lead, America would provide goods and services superior to those offered by the rest of the world.[34] Still, given their expertise, Du Pont officials could not free themselves entirely of involvement in nuclear matters. In 1947, Greenewalt accepted an appointment as a civilian member of the Atomic Energy Committee of the Military Joint Research and Development Board; in 1948, Donald F. Carpenter, vice president of Du Pont's Remington Arms subsidiary, became chair of the AEC's Military Liaison Committee.[35]

When approached by the AEC about the possibility of constructing the new facility for the hydrogen bomb, Du Pont officials hesitated. Before accepting this assignment, Greenewalt stipulated that "the Company receive from the President of the United States a formal request that included confirmation of the importance of the project." Greenewalt most likely was anticipating not only concerns from the stockholders but also possible negative publicity harkening back to World War I. A direct request from the president of the United

States, Greenewalt wagered, would blunt potential criticism. President Truman complied. On July 25, 1950, roughly one month after the start of the Korean conflict, Truman wrote to Greenewalt that Du Pont "has within its organization technical, scientific, engineering, construction and operating staffs capable of handling a task of this magnitude." Du Pont, the president declared, was "uniquely qualified to undertake this most essential task." Truman impressed on Du Pont the project's status "as one of highest urgency and vitally important to our national security and defense."[36] With the president's request in hand, Greenewalt nonetheless took his time accepting the assignment. He had legal concerns—primarily that by taking on the new atomic project without compensation other than the nominal fee of one dollar, he was exposing the corporation to a possible stockholder lawsuit. He also worried about public relations fallout. Both were addressed by the company's legal department, which assured Greenewalt not only that he was on safe legal ground in accepting the assignment for a one-dollar fee but that such an arrangement could have a positive effect on Du Pont's commercial interests. The company's attorneys further addressed the "merchants of death" stigma, which "the Company is still living down." The materials to be created at the proposed plant "could be the means of inflicting untold death and misery to mankind. To accept fees for participation in such a project would invite renewed public animosity and ill will, which would be reflected in the Company's commercial business." Conversely, the lawyers argued, government service was good for business. "The fact that the Company performed this service to the Nation for only a nominal fee of one dollar can create good will which is bound to be reflected in its commercial business." Indeed, the attorneys noted, an "immeasurable amount of good will . . . resulted and continues to be manifested because of the similar course taken in the Hanford Project."[37] Other factors further induced Du Pont to accept this new assignment. Historian Pap A. Ndiaye points out that by the late 1940s, an economic "page had turned." The face of Cold War America dictated new relations between government and industry. "The federal government had imposed itself as an inescapable partner, primarily in military production, but also in large-scale science projects and economic regulations."[38] Furthermore, Du Pont and other chemical and electrical companies believed that nuclear energy for civilian use would generate huge profits in the future.[39] They wanted to get in on the ground floor.

On October 17, 1950, Du Pont and the AEC executed a contract to cover the design, construction, and operation of the new facilities.[40] In his letter to the corporation's stockholders, Greenewalt reminded the group that the Hanford project was undertaken under a similar fee basis. "While recognizing fully management's obligation to earn a profit on its operations, it is felt that the nature of this undertaking makes it inappropriate to require a fee for the Company's services."[41] Greenewalt moved aggressively to replace the "merchants of death" stigma in the public memory. In his August 1950 statement before the Joint Committee on Atomic Energy, Greenewalt noted that "rightly or wrongly . . . we simply cannot be in a position of making money out of an engine of war that is as horrible as this one is likely to be."[42]

During the summer months of 1950, as UN forces pushed back against the North Koreans in what most U.S. leaders assumed would be a short conflict, AEC and Du Pont officials crisscrossed the country, investigating some 114 potential production sites for "Plant 124."[43] Some communities actively lobbied for the new complex, including Mountain View, Missouri; Harrison, Arkansas; and Beaumont, Texas. The site specifications contained certain criteria. Space was paramount. The original plan called for six nuclear reactors spaced two miles apart, five separation plants spaced one mile apart, and additional manufacturing buildings. The site plans required not only the manufacturing area proper but a 5.5-mile-wide zone outside the critical manufacturing area. Given the dangerous nature of the materials to be produced at the plant as well as the profound security requirements, the report noted that "all inhabitants or personnel not connected with the plant must be evacuated from the total site area." The search for an adequate site for the hydrogen bomb plant mirrored a larger national initiative to move industrial sites away from central cities to more remote locations in the interest of national security.[44]

The site also needed to be within commuting distance of a small city—that is, the edge of the proposed site had to be between 20.5 and 40 miles from the edge of a center of population having at least twenty-five thousand people. The committee likewise considered a potential site's climate, topography, water supply, soil drainage, and prevailing wage rates. Although the committee surveyed more than one hundred sites, detailed evaluations were made of only four sites: the Savannah River site in South Carolina; a Texas location on the Red River, seventy-six air miles northeast of Dallas; a site on the Wabash River in Illinois, twenty air miles southwest of Terre Haute, Indiana; and a Wisconsin site on the south shore of Lake Superior. After careful evaluation, the committee rejected the Texas site because its main water supply was of poor quality for the project. The Illinois site was not sufficiently isolated and was "in a flourishing food-farming area," thus representing "a possible formidable hazard." The Wisconsin site was rejected for military reasons on which the committee chose not to elaborate. The committee concluded that Site 5, in South Carolina, "is acceptable, and it more nearly meets the requirements than do the others."[45]

Numerous factors gave the South Carolina location the edge over its competitors. The committee noted that "Site #5 is favored by a relatively mild climate and excellent soil and drainage conditions." These factors were regarded as essential for meeting strict construction timetables. Site 5 was sufficiently close to population centers but also had room to expand. The report notes that while "all four sites meet the basic requirements for isolation, . . . site #5 is considered as good as, if not better than, the others." It also possessed the lowest cost per acre. Critical to the site was the availability of a large and dependable flow of water of a specified purity, which would be needed to remove the great quantities of heat generated in the reactors and from which heavy water (deuterium oxide) would be extracted.[46] Of course, Site 5 was not perfect. The transportation system between Augusta and the location was considered "inadequate" for the anticipated traffic, although the area was relatively well served by railroads.[47]

Peculiarly southern attributes also played an important role in site selection. Of the handful of sites that made it into the final round of consideration, the South Carolina location was notable for its construction wage rates—the lowest among all possible sites, reflecting the state's historically weak labor movement and hostile antiunion atmosphere. AEC officials responsible for making recommendations regarding the placement of the site likewise noted that most of those living inside the proposed plant boundaries were black tenant farmers. These "colored agricultural workers," noted one official, resided in houses that were of "low value." Removing such residents would be easier than removing residents at alternate sites where property values were higher.[48] Here, government officials exploited the historically vulnerable position of rural blacks trapped in the economic vise that was the South's tenant system. Such residents possessed neither the financial resources nor the political clout to fight their removal from the land.

For South Carolina and the other southern states, the intensification of the Cold War and the expansion of what would later be labeled the military-industrial complex held the potential for economic development. Political leaders and industrial boosters throughout the region hoped to continue the wartime growth that had brought benefits that had eluded the region during the New Deal years. Although the South benefited greatly from New Deal spending, those benefits were not enough to meet the South's need. During World War II, defense contracts and new shipbuilding, aircraft, and munitions plants pumped billions of dollars into the private sector.[49] Defense projects likewise brought unprecedented economic opportunities to southern workers, who saw their annual wages climb by 40 percent.[50] As in so many other states in the region, South Carolina's economy had begun a long-term transition during the 1930s, slowly moving away from a reliance on textiles and agriculture. While New Deal agricultural programs had precipitated the exodus of farm labor from rural areas, the war offered alternative employment opportunities and threatened to drain labor from the countryside.[51] Hoping to capitalize on and expand wartime growth, state leaders aggressively pursued federal projects as part of a long-term growth strategy that would ultimately modernize the region. According to James C. Cobb, "Economic development would even supersede the defense of Jim Crow as, however unevenly, in state after state, the post–World War II era saw the reins of power pass to more dynamic, metropolitan-oriented elites who sought fuller integration of both local and state economies into the national and global economy."[52]

Among this new breed of southern leader was Strom Thurmond. Elected governor of South Carolina in 1946, Thurmond was among the scores of former GIs who returned to the South determined to transform their region and its leadership. "We need a progressive outlook, a progressive program, a progressive leadership," Thurmond declared during his gubernatorial campaign. "We must face the future with confidence and enthusiasm."[53] For Thurmond and like-minded southern leaders, this progressive future depended on private industrial development and federal dollars. A firm believer that the problem of the color line was at heart a case of arrested economic development, Governor Thurmond maintained a firm commitment throughout his administration to the recruitment of new industrial plants and federal projects.[54] The governor's endeavors were complemented by the activities of regional booster programs as well as the efforts of the South Carolina Research, Planning, and Development Board. South Carolina joined other states in what Cobb has called a "regional obsession" with growth and modernization.[55]

The attraction of federal dollars constituted an integral part of South Carolina's overall growth scheme, and the new hydrogen bomb plant was just the latest in a string of federal projects that state lawmakers courted. In 1935, thanks to aggressive lobbying by state leaders, President Franklin Roosevelt approved the Santee Cooper hydroelectric and flood-control project, one of the largest New Deal undertakings. The Clarks Hill Project, a single dam in what eventually would be a series of eleven dams along the Savannah River, was approved by the Flood Control Act of 1944 and was completed ten years later.[56] The resulting public power enterprise was envisioned as critical to the continued development of the Savannah River Valley. State Senator Edgar Brown of Barnwell, nicknamed the Bishop of Barnwell and Mr. Big, was instrumental in securing the Clarks Hill Project and ensuring that it remain a public power enterprise. Brown considered the project essential to regional development. When approached by the AEC about Barnwell County as a possible location for the hydrogen bomb plant, Brown "linked the completing of the federal dam project" to the new plant. The South Carolina Research, Planning, and Development Board supplemented Brown's efforts by marshaling pertinent data on Aiken and Barnwell Counties in promotional brochures, one of which was already in the possession of Du Pont officials when they began searching for the site for the new weapons plant. South Carolina development officials had sent the document several years earlier in an effort to lure Du Pont's new Orlon plant.[57] Never in their wildest dreams had they imagined that a brochure designed to lure traditional low-wage industry would help secure for them a place in the nation's expanding Cold War arsenal. The completion of the Clarks Hill Dam and its ability to provide hydroelectric power to the region ultimately made South Carolina an attractive location for the nuclear weapons plant. According to one historian of the site, "The presence of a smaller fish had enticed a larger fish into the pond."[58]

While the pursuit of federal dollars encouraged southern state leaders to adopt a more expansive and benign definition of *federal intervention*, so too did the economic salvation promised by the arrival of federal projects blur other traditional political boundaries. Although winning projects for South Carolina held the greatest political benefit for the state's elected officials, geographic realities such as flood control often dictated that states work together to secure federal aid. Thus, Brown joined his efforts to those of Lester Moody, secretary of the Chamber of Commerce of Augusta, Georgia, to complete the Clarks Hill Project. Through similar combined efforts, the area of South Carolina and Georgia surrounding the Savannah River basin developed a regional identity, grounded in geography but ultimately crafted from federal dollars, and eventually came to be called the Central Savannah River Area.[59]

The Cold War accelerated and intensified the militarization of the southern economy. Private industry competed for defense projects, and states aggressively pursued funds for infrastructure improvement. Although Southern California emerged as the largest beneficiary in terms of total defense dollars received, the South surpassed the national average in terms of dependence on the defense establishment for both employment and income.[60] Furthermore, argues sociologist Gregory Hooks, because postwar industrial development in the South still trailed that of the rest of the nation, "federal investments and activity have had a relatively greater influence over the economic development of southern counties" than in other regions.[61] By the early 1970s, the southern states were providing the Pentagon with 52 percent of its ships, 46 percent of its airframes, 42 percent of its petroleum products, and 27 percent of its ammunition. From Tenneco's Newport News shipbuilding plant in Hampton Roads, Virginia, to General Dynamics and LTV Corporation in Texas, the military and the federal government created a new, high-tech industrial workforce whose cultural tastes, spending habits, and political allegiances changed the face of the South.[62]

State leaders facilitated the militarizing of South Carolina's economy. As the Cold War intensified, politicians stood poised to take economic advantage and provided a critical human link between state developments and world events. At the vortex of South Carolina's early Cold War–era politics stood James F. Byrnes. A former secretary of state with a long and distinguished career in public service, Byrnes was elected South Carolina's governor in 1950, and he embodied the state's new role in world affairs and the national security establishment.[63]

Other South Carolina leaders similarly built their careers on the emerging Cold War. Congressman James P. Richards served for years on the House Foreign Affairs Committee, eventually becoming chair in 1951. As a member of the committee, he worked closely with secretary of state Dean Acheson on a $150 million aid package to South Korea. Even after the Republicans captured the House in 1951 and Richards lost his leadership post, he remained a valuable senior member, developing a strong relationship with the new secretary of state, John Foster Dulles.[64]

No single member of Congress did more to cement the relationship between his district's growth and the country's Cold War military needs than did Representative Mendel Rivers of Charleston. Elected to Congress in 1940, Rivers moved quickly to secure projects—particularly naval—for his district. As member of the House Merchant Marine and Fisheries Committee, he played a part in establishing a new Coast Guard district with headquarters in Charleston in 1941. He parlayed his service on the Public Buildings and Grounds Committee into a twelve-billion-dollar navy hospital in Beaufort. Within a few months, Rivers received a plum assignment on the Naval Affairs Committee and became a protégé of the committee's powerful chair, Georgia's Carl Vinson. During the war, Rivers worked to turn Charleston Naval Station into a first-class defense site. Rivers ensured that his district experienced smaller reductions after the war than did other regions. He continued to cultivate his relationship with high-ranking navy officers, and in 1956, the Charleston Naval Shipyard received a sizable contract to construct several nuclear submarines and modernize other naval vessels.[65] The new hydrogen bomb plant contributed to a state economic profile that was increasingly reliant on defense expenditures to bring South Carolina into the modern era.

John Shaw Billings remembered the morning of Tuesday, November 28, 1950, as unseasonably cold in South Carolina. Billings, the great-grandson of former South Carolina governor and U.S. senator James Henry Hammond and an editor of *Time* and *Life* magazines, had purchased the Hammond homestead, Redcliffe, in Aiken County in 1935. The once sizable Hammond estate had been reduced over the years to 373 acres and a house in desperate need of repair. Despite the late-fall cold snap, the day began like any other. Billings and his dog, Lucky, took their usual morning drive through the woods in Billings's jeep. Lucky was aptly named. Billings noted in his diary that over the years, Lucky had bitten both him and his wife several times, seriously enough to break the skin. Yet for reasons known only to dog lovers, they refused to get rid of him. That morning, Billings was suffering from yet another nip from his pet. The finger grew more painful; fearing an infection, Billings drove to see his doctor. The doctor saw no sign of infection and recommended Epsom salts. Billings wrote, "Greatly relieved in my mind, I drove back to Redcliffe by 1:15 with my good news." He was met by his cousin, Harry Hammond, who had "even bigger news: The Atomic Energy Commission is taking over 250,000 acres from Jackson to Ellenton to Snelling and Dunbarton to construct a series of great plants at which materials for the HYDROGEN BOMB will be manufactured." Billings's first concern was safety. "Oh God," he wrote, "that puts Redcliffe dangerously close to a prime military target for Russian bombing!" On further reflection, his thoughts became more melancholy. He worried that "this vast military

Figure 1. Redcliffe, 1941. Photograph courtesy of South Caroliniana Library, University of South Carolina, Columbia.

industrialization will utterly ruin the quiet rural charm of Redcliffe—& the surrounding area." Cousin Harry, however, "was wildly excited at the prospects of making money out of the enterprise."[66]

The combination of fear, sense of loss, and the potential for profit exhibited by Hammond and Billings captured the range of reactions throughout the region as residents grappled with the news that their communities were to become the latest outposts on the nuclear frontier. The announcement about the plant came amid Chinese involvement in Korea and the prospect of a war whose boundaries of time and space were ever expanding. Billings noted on that fateful day that "the Chinese Reds, in overwhelming numbers, are beating the hell out of us in Korea and driving us back in what may be a major military disaster. I am deeply worried lest we . . . slip into World War III with China united with Russia, our no. 1 antagonist. A dark day for the U.S."[67] International events and local consequences collided with devastating ferocity.

At midday, the Cold War came home to South Carolina. The official announcement of the plant was released at noon on November 28, 1950. An hour

Figure 2. John Shaw Billings on the balcony of Redcliffe, 1941. Beginning with the plant announcement in late 1950 and continuing throughout the remainder of his life, Billings chronicled the impact of the creation of the Savannah River Plant on his property and the surrounding communities. Photograph courtesy of South Caroliniana Library, University of South Carolina, Columbia.

earlier, twelve teams of AEC and Du Pont officials blanketed both Georgia and South Carolina, meeting with state and city leaders.[68] Local residents had for some time noticed the presence of federal officials and survey crews in the area, but no one knew the nature of their business. E. C. Thomas, on jury duty when the announcement was made, remembered that "the judge stopped court and made a big announcement [about the coming of the plant]. Everyone cheered because the judge flowered it up, talking about what a boon it was going to be for Aiken County."[69] Employees of the Leigh Banana Crate Company, aware that an important community announcement was imminent, spent their lunch breaks tuned in to their car radios.[70] Samuel Swint, president of the Graniteville Company, the region's second-oldest textile operation, wrote a confidential memorandum in which he recorded his thoughts about the potential disruption caused by the new AEC project. He worried about projected shortages of construction materials and expressed concern about "General MacArthur's recently announced 'new war' with China. . . . It looks as if we are in for troublesome times."[71]

In the days following the announcement, managers of what was being called the Savannah River Plant appeared on local radio programs, at farmers' meetings, and at Rotary Clubs to address citizens' concerns. The Aiken newspaper commented that "this community's life would have to be altered to get in line with this tremendous undertaking by the government of our country." But what exactly would that entail? The *Aiken Standard and Review* assured its readers that they had no reason for fear, that the arrival of the plant would not expose nearby residents to radiation, that it would not turn the region into a boomtown; the area would experience only gradual growth, boosters claimed, and property values would not be negatively affected.[72] State representative John A. May assured his constituents that every effort would be made "to prevent a 'shantytown' like that at Oak Ridge [Tennessee]. We don't want any hoodlums or honkytonks or labor racketeers."[73] Area residents initially expressed cautious optimism about the possibilities for growth, prosperity, and employment. For residents of Horse Creek Valley, home to numerous textile mills and the accompanying villages, the arrival of the plant seemed to herald economic salvation and began in some respects to break down parochialism. "As far as I was concerned," recalled Graniteville resident Ronnie Bryant, who was seventeen when the nuclear plant arrived, "it looked like there was no future [in textiles]. All the good jobs were taken, or there were people in line for the good jobs, so it seemed that you had to go somewhere else to find opportunity." For Bryant and others entering adulthood in the early 1950s, this new Cold War enterprise promised new opportunity.[74]

Residents seemed to take a relatively calm view regarding the potential hazards of having a hydrogen bomb plant in the region. Perhaps many agreed with Mrs. Thomas Rutledge, a real estate agent who commented that "if Aiken isn't blown up, it will certainly grow."[75] To familiarize themselves with the hydrogen bomb and nuclear weapons in general, residents were urged to travel to the downtown McCrory's five-and-dime where they could view an exhibit, *Can the H-Bomb Destroy the World?*[76] Although the plant's economic promise encouraged some valley residents to look beyond the mill, in terms of concerns for their safety, the area's insular nature seemed to persist. Graniteville Company employee Lenwood Melton recalled that "to us down here in Graniteville, we felt like . . . that if [the plant] blew up, it wouldn't affect us in the Valley because we were fifteen miles away."[77] That distance, which seemed so vast to Melton and other textile workers, would ultimately prove much smaller. Construction within the three hundred thousand acres of Site 5 would soon begin to transform everything.

The 1949 Cotton Festival had been routine. But within a year and half, life in this region of South Carolina had changed dramatically. By early 1951, thirteen miles from the festival site in the town of Aiken, men and materials from across the nation were streaming into the area to begin the process of transforming farmland and rural hamlets into a sprawling facility to create materials for a bomb whose destructive capacity few could fathom. The entire region's attention was riveted on the enormous project and what it meant for South Carolina's role in the expanding Cold War. In May, tucked away amid headlines about the fighting in Korea, military contracts, and the AEC's work was a small story announcing that because of a shortage of labor and materials, the 1951 Cotton Festival was canceled.[78]

Never again would life be routine.

CHAPTER TWO

A Varied Landscape
Geography and Culture in the Savannah River Valley

Geography and environment played a critical role in bringing the new atomic weapons plant to western South Carolina. The temperature and purity of the Savannah River and the superior drainage qualities of the region's sandy soil had rendered the area closer to ideal than any other location for this new project, securing South Carolina a place on the far reaches of the expanding nuclear frontier. Yet the Cold War plant was not the first venture to meld the region's particular natural characteristics with the latest applications of science and technology. The history of western South Carolina is in part a story of the interplay of individuals, landscape, and innovation. In the antebellum era, the Edgefield and Barnwell Districts (as the area was then divided and designated) were home to early practitioners of scientific farming, boasted one of the nation's first railroad lines, and possessed the South's first textile mills and early advocates of industrial diversification. In addition, in the postbellum era and early twentieth century, the town of Aiken in particular became first a favored destination for consumptives and other sufferers of a host of respiratory illnesses and later a magnet for owners and trainers of champion racehorses. One would be hard-pressed to argue convincingly that the region offered picturesque scenery. Nor did it reveal immediate or obvious benefits for those looking to invest. But for a wide range of people with dissimilar interests, the Savannah River Valley possessed particular and peculiar attributes that promised and encouraged innovation.

Coinciding with and often undergirding the region's eager reception and adoption of technology and scientific advances was a system of racial hierarchy and control that was oppressive and frequently violent. Antebellum cotton farming in western South Carolina benefited not only from the impact of scientific farming methods but also from the labor of vast numbers of enslaved

Africans. By the early nineteenth century, the region had a majority-black population. With emancipation and the end of the Civil War, this black majority demanded the rights and privileges of citizenship. Heightened white anxiety regarding blacks' newfound freedom frequently exploded into bloody confrontations. During Reconstruction, Aiken County was the site of two of South Carolina's most violent race riots. Neighboring Edgefield County spawned political leaders Benjamin Tillman and Coleman Blease, who became synonymous across the region and nation with virulent white supremacy. The numerous textile mills that dotted Aiken County's Horse Creek Valley were innovative industrial enterprises designed to uplift the region's poor whites, and these textile workers jealously guarded their status in the New South's racial hierarchy, even if that status was compromised by exploitive wages and oppressive working conditions. Mill villages, racially and geographically insular, became notorious among the region's blacks and higher-status whites as pockets of frightful racism and casual violence that were best avoided. Faced with limited economic opportunity and a continuing undercurrent of violence, blacks steadily left the area into the twentieth century. Such social tensions continuously complicated the development of a region that hosted a varied and fruitful natural landscape.

The Atomic Energy Commission (AEC) and Du Pont chose South Carolina as the location for the new nuclear facility because they were attracted, like earlier entrepreneurs, by the particular qualities of the environment. The soil, the climate, the purity of the Savannah River—all had a hand in convincing the architects of America's latest war to bring their enterprise to the state. But as the atomic age dawned in South Carolina, questions arose about what shape progress would take: Would this latest scientific venture—overseen by the federal government and operated by a northern corporation—rely on and further the means of white supremacy or undermine it entirely?

Described by one riverboat captain as both "the prettiest river in the world" and "the meanest to navigate," the Savannah River forms the western border of South Carolina. It is a massive river with tributaries that drain more than ten thousand square miles.[1] But the river was not always the region's dominant feature and was not the force that most defined and shaped the particular characteristics that earned the area so much attention in recent history. Approximately fifty-five million years ago, after the glacier belt receded, a vast inland sea covered portions of South Carolina, with the peaks of the Appalachians and the Cumberland Mountains poking through as islands. Over time, the land rose from the sea.[2] At the halfway point along the Savannah River's journey from its beginning at what is now Hartwell Lake and where it meets the Atlantic Ocean, is the region appropriately named the Midlands, once the site of the shoreline of the prehistoric sea. Also known as the sandhills because the sandy material extends down more than six feet, this narrow, discontinuous band of hills stretches from northeast to southwest.[3] The landscape is distinctive, marked by sand dunes and home to the longleaf pine and the turkey oak.[4]

Overlapping the sandhills and running northeast to southwest is the fall line, which marks a significant drop in elevation and spawned numerous fast-running rivers and large streams.[5] While sandy soils initially made this region unpromising for agricultural pursuits, it possessed a long growing season and was reasonably well watered; furthermore, the numerous rivers and streams provided transportation, and engineering know-how enabled the abundant swampland to be drained and transformed into productive farmland.[6]

Algonquian speakers, primarily Savannahs and Westoes, populated the region when Spanish explorer Hernando de Soto and his entourage crossed the Savannah River, probably near Silver Bluff in present-day Aiken County. After de Soto, successive waves of European adventurers, traders, and settlers swept over the sandhills. Savannah Town, an Indian trading post on the fall line, was founded in the late seventeenth century. European colonists constructed Fort Moore at Savannah Town in 1715, following the Yamasee War. In the mid-1730s, George Galphin, an Irish trader, came to Silver Bluff and established a highly profitable trading empire. He acquired vast acreage from the Crown and maintained generally good relations with area Indians. Early trade in South Carolina focused primarily on deerskins.

European settlements began to crop up in what was called the backcountry in the 1730s. In 1737, a planned township, New Windsor, was established some seven miles north of Fort Moore. Populated by Swiss immigrants, New Windsor was one of several settlements created to attract European settlers to the South Carolina backcountry.[7] Greater numbers of migrants from Pennsylvania, Virginia, and South Carolina's coastal regions moved into the region in the 1750s and 1760s, sometimes with chaotic results. Small bands of outlaws roamed the area during the 1760s, and in 1767 residents organized vigilante groups to "regulate" the outlaws. The vigilantes, however, were equally guilty of excesses. During the American Revolution, the backcountry erupted in civil war, with loyalists and rebels committing heinous acts against each other in a bloody guerrilla war.

With the cessation of hostilities with the British, migration of Europeans and their African slaves into the old backcountry increased in the 1790s. Expanding settlements in the region necessitated new political boundaries and divisions. In 1800, the state legislature created the districts of Edgefield and Barnwell, and settlers there increasingly turned to agriculture. The first staple crop to be cultivated in the region was tobacco, which was soon eclipsed by the production of short-staple cotton. The success of cotton cultivation was quickly followed by an influx of African slaves, who outnumbered white settlers by the first decade of the nineteenth century.[8] In 1801, the entire state produced twenty million pounds of cotton, but by 1830, the backcountry districts of Abbeville, Edgefield, Fairfield, and Laurens accounted for almost half of the statewide total crop of sixty million pounds.[9]

Perched atop the region's planter elite was James Henry Hammond. Born in Newberry District in 1807, Hammond married Catherine Fitzsimons, a wealthy daughter of the lowcountry, in 1831.[10] Her dowry included a large plantation, Silver Bluff, in Barnwell District. The property was 10,800 acres, only 10 percent of which was cultivated. About half the acreage was rich swampland, while the rest consisted of clay-soiled wooded plateaus. Hammond devoted himself to overseeing his agricultural empire and before long was the area's wealthiest planter and largest slaveholder.[11] According to historian Carol Bleser, Hammond's landholdings were so vast that he "could ride all day on horseback without seeing another man's land."[12]

Elected to the U.S. House of Representatives, to the governor's chair, and to the U.S. Senate, Hammond was best known as a tireless and outspoken proslavery apologist. But Hammond was also, according to biographer Drew Gilpin Faust, an "agricultural entrepreneur," a founder of the state's agricultural society and "vocal advocate of economic diversification and scientific farming." Hammond succeeded not only by putting more land into cultivation but also by improving the productivity through the application of principles promoted by advocates of scientific farming. When he took over the plantation at Silver Bluff, the average net income was paltry. Much of his land, like the rest of the region, was sandy and sterile, while the remaining acres were characterized by "black mucky loam." Hammond began experimenting with marl, "a kind of clay rich in calcium carbonate that is used even today on acidic soils to increase their friability and their receptivity to the enriching effects of animal manures."

Though marling was almost unknown in South Carolina at this time, it proved an excellent supplement for Hammond's sandy soils, and his efforts were richly rewarded: his cotton productivity increased by 50 percent within the first year of his experiment.[13]

Hammond continued to experiment with scientific principles. In the late 1840s, Hammond established another plantation, Cowden, covering more than twenty-seven hundred acres in the Savannah River swamps below Silver Bluff. Cowden held significant promise but required a fairly extensive engineering project to clear and drain it. Hammond installed a ditch-and-drain system that ultimately allowed him to reclaim seven hundred acres of swamp for cultivation. The financial rewards were well worth the effort, as Cowden's yields proved extraordinary.[14] Again and again, Hammond proved to be a formidable and progressive agricultural thinker, learning the value of the land and adapting his husbandry to its features. This ever-expanding mind-set, however, did not translate to his understanding of or dependence on forced labor.

None of the scientific advances made on the Hammond properties would have been possible without the backbreaking labor of hundreds of slaves. Just as he sat atop the planter world in a financial sense, so too did Hammond provide a model of white manhood for others to emulate. Dedicated to the total mastery of all in his world, Hammond practiced a patriarchal dominance over his more than three hundred slaves in which paternalistic practices were undergirded by brute force.[15] Whereas Hammond employed an innovative approach to agriculture, his approach to slaves was as old and exploitative as humankind.

Although agriculture dominated the region, the cultivation of cotton was not the residents' only economic pursuit. The region also supported a number of sawmills and gristmills. All along the fall line lay beds of kaolin (fine white clay), which was used in the manufacture of china. Large quantities were shipped to the Wedgewood Potteries in England. Eventually, local potters exploited this resource, and by the early 1860s, Horse Creek Valley boasted at least five pottery works.[16] The region also developed a commercial center, Hamburg, where planters and farmers hauled their cotton. Located on the Savannah River opposite Augusta, Hamburg was laid out by entrepreneur Henry Shultz in 1821. An ambitious German immigrant, Shultz created Hamburg as a challenge to the "aristocrats of Augusta," whom he felt had treated him poorly. He sought to develop an interior market and to draw trade away from Augusta. By 1826, Hamburg was thriving, boasting some twelve hundred residents and sixty businesses.[17]

Hamburg's growth and the expansion and prosperity of Edgefield and Barnwell Districts were furthered by the coming of the railroad. Incorporated in 1827, the South Carolina Canal and Railroad Company connected Hamburg with Charleston. The total cost of construction was more than one million dollars.[18] At the time of its completion in 1833, this 136-mile railway was "the longest railroad under single management in the world."[19] As historian Tom Downey contends, "Nothing provided a more tangible sign of modernity. By combining power, speed, innovation, and precision, the railroad quickly became the physical definition of 'progress' in Edgefield and Barnwell."[20]

Residents of small settlements along the railroad's proposed route anxiously awaited news about where depots would be established. Among those residents were the owners of land on the present site of the town of Aiken, seventeen miles from Hamburg, who understood that a depot would bring growth and profitable trade and consequently offered the railroad company property on which to lay out a town.[21] According to local legend, the location of the depot and subsequent town grew from a romance between railroad surveyor Alfred Dexter and Sara Williams, daughter of area planter William Williams.[22] Trained as a civil engineer, Dexter was authorized to lay out the town.[23] Williams apparently wanted the railroad to run through his property and used his fetching daughter as bait: "No railroad for me, young man, no girl for you," Williams is alleged to have insisted. Bargain or no, the young couple wed, and the railroad passed through Williams's property.[24]

With the establishment of the depot, the settlement around it grew. The town was incorporated in 1835 and was named for William Aiken Sr., a prosperous Charleston cotton merchant and president of the South Carolina Canal and Railroad Company.[25] Before long, the town boasted a few stores and warehouses, along with a branch of the bank of the state. One early chronicler of the history of Aiken wrote that "rough, sunburnt farmers, dressed in gray homespun, could be remarked along the sidewalks or at the doors and windows of the shops, some accompanied by their wives and daughters, and all eager to secure, in exchange for the provisions or game they had brought in, some precious luxury of civilization." As a trading post, Aiken attracted its share of unsavory characters, meeting "with kindred spirits in the low groggeries and barrooms." Fistfights and bloodier altercations involving bowie knives and rifles were not uncommon.[26]

With the commercial expansion and prosperity of nearby Hamburg furthered by the coming of the railroad, Aiken was destined to remain at best a secondary depot and paltry trading post. The struggling town's fortunes changed considerably when invalids and others suffering from a variety of respiratory illness began raving about the "sanitary nature" of the region's climate and spreading stories of extraordinary cures experienced by the "hopelessly ill." Particularly salutary to invalids was Aiken's "dry tonic air." Following on the heels of the infirm were large numbers of planters and merchants from Charleston, hoping to escape the heat and mosquitoes of the lowcountry and leading Aiken to become known as "a ward of Charleston," according to local author Wilkins L. Byrd.[27] The value of the fall line—a sharp enough change in elevation, it was believed, to reduce mosquito populations but mild enough to keep the rolling landscape open to wide variety of manipulation—cannot be overstated.

One journalist noted that Aiken sported two tourist seasons: "The one from November to June, for Northern consumptives; the other from June to November, for Southerners from the lowland parishes."[28] Brochures promoting Aiken as a health resort played up the region's relative dryness. Also promoted were the area's prodigious pine trees. Boasted one brochure, "It is to the soothing and purifying effect exerted upon the mucous membrane of the respiratory passages by the exhalations from this tree, that the climate of Aiken owes much of its well-deserved reputation as a Health resort for persons suffering from all forms of disease affecting the respiratory tract." Resort promoters raved about Aiken's mild winter climate and "the preponderance of bright sunny days, which enable the invalid to pass much of his time in the open air; the protection against the wind afforded by the dense growth of forest trees; and last, but by no means least, the remarkable dryness of the air . . . depending upon the peculiar character of the soil and the distance from any large body of water."[29]

Landscape likewise was key to bringing industry to the region. The energy potential of the region's fast-running streams (as a consequence of the fall line's transition in elevation) soon caught the attention of industrial developer William Gregg. The South's first cotton factory, Vaucluse, was built by European immigrant and wealthy Edgefield planter Christian Breithaupt in the late 1820s at the source of Horse Creek, a stream that cut through the valley in southern Edgefield County. Vaucluse limped along through the 1830s. In 1837, the factory was purchased by Gregg, who reversed Vaucluse's declining fortunes in just eight months. Gregg eventually sold the factory at a profit and moved to Charleston, where he grew wealthy as a partner in a jewelry dealership and "emerged as the South's leading advocate of industrial development in the antebellum era." He returned to Horse Creek Valley in 1843 and joined with his brother-in-law to buy back Vaucluse plus an additional eleven thousand acres along Horse Creek and neighboring streams.[30]

Gregg recognized industry's revolutionary potential for the region. He criticized the former owners of Vaucluse for using slave labor and for neglecting the employment needs of poor whites. His management philosophy was simple but extraordinary in this context. Refashioning the illiterate and landless into textile workers and bringing them into "daily contact with the rich and intelligent" could mean their economic and moral salvation. It also made good business sense. In December 1845, Gregg and a small group of investors received a corporate charter from the State of South Carolina for the Graniteville Manufacturing Company, "for the purpose of Manufacturing, dying, printing and finishing all goods of which Cotton or other fibrous articles may form a part."[31]

Gregg envisioned Graniteville not only as an industrial enterprise but also as a comprehensive social, cultural, and economic entity. At the center of this enterprise was the factory, a massive 350-foot-long granite structure that dominated the surrounding landscape. Gregg oversaw the construction of an elaborate and effective power system that harnessed the Horse Creek to generate power to run a set of turbines. Full production was under way by 1849, when the Graniteville Company produced thousands of yards of cotton shirting, sheeting, and yarn per day. Tending the spindles and looms for twelve hours each day were more than three hundred operatives, most of them young women and teenagers and many of them housed in the tidy, newly constructed village surrounding the plant. Even when not laboring in Gregg's factory, employees remained under his control. Workers who failed to meet Gregg's definition of high moral character were summarily dismissed. Enormously successful as both an economic enterprise and a social institution, the Graniteville Company and village became the model for the mill-building explosion later in the century.[32]

By the eve of the Civil War, western South Carolina supported thriving plantation and industrial sectors as well as a burgeoning tourist industry, with the success of all dependent in part on modern advances in science and technology in direct conjunction with the unique geographical features of the area. Four years of war interrupted but did not permanently thwart this development trajectory. South Carolina's role in the outbreak of the Civil War earned it the wrath of Union forces, and the state consequently incurred grave damage. Aiken and the surrounding region, however, suffered relatively little. One military

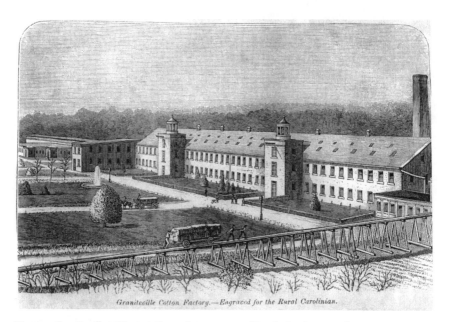

Figure 3. Graniteville Mill, 1858. Engraving courtesy of South Caroliniana Library, University of South Carolina, Columbia.

engagement—a skirmish later known as the Battle of Aiken—occurred between Union and Confederate cavalry on February 11, 1865, as General William Tecumseh Sherman's army marched through on its way to the sea. When Sherman reached Blackville, he set his sights on the nearby Graniteville cotton mill. Sherman dispatched General Hugh Judson Kilpatrick to destroy the factory.[33] Kilpatrick, however, was intercepted by General Joe Weaver's rebel cavalry and forced to retreat. While of little larger significance, the skirmish—one of the last southern victories of the war—saved the town of Aiken and the Graniteville mill from Union depredations.[34]

Although western South Carolina languished as a military backwater during the Civil War, the violent response of local whites to the challenges of Reconstruction made the region infamous. Throughout the era, disgruntled whites and newly freed slaves confronted each other in bloody battles as both groups sought to shape the region's future. Freedmen, who constituted a voting majority in the western counties and in the state as a whole, were determined to exercise their newly won rights and liberties, while whites were equally determined to reestablish the racial hierarchy destabilized by Emancipation and the war. It was a zero-sum game. As the state's leading historian has noted, "White soldiers may have taken off their uniforms in 1865, but they did not stop fighting for the right to control their own affairs and restore order and harmony to their community." The result was some of the era's most destructive racial violence.[35]

Reconstruction brought population shifts and new political divisions. In 1871, the state legislature created the county of Aiken out of portions of Barnwell, Edgefield, Lexington, and Orangeburg Counties. Aiken County was the state's first to be represented in the South Carolina Senate by an African American legislator. No longer tied to farms and plantations, scores of freed slaves from the plantation areas gravitated to the river town of Hamburg, while white residents fled. Consequently, postbellum Hamburg's large black population made the town a Republican stronghold. By the Reconstruction era, what had formerly been a rising mercantile center with a bright future had suffered a series of calamities both natural and man-made that threatened its survival. Ruinous floods drenched the town in the 1840s and 1850s. River traffic that had previously stopped at Hamburg flowed into Augusta after the construction of the Augusta Canal in the late 1840s. The biggest blow came when the South Carolina Canal and Railroad extended its line across the Savannah River into Augusta, taking with it most of the interior cotton trade. With the decline of the cotton trade, many merchants abandoned the town.[36]

The state's Republican government, which held power from 1868 to 1876, was a thorn in the side of militant white Democrats determined to reclaim political power. Blacks constituted 60 percent of the voting population, and black and white Republicans held most state and local offices.[37] This majority went further than any other legislature at the time in establishing laws designed to improve the condition of the former slaves.[38] These measures included new civil and criminal protections that allowed freedpeople to begin using the courts and the law.[39] Temporarily out of power, white Democrats turned to extralegal means to pursue their agenda, with the Ku Klux Klan becoming the major instrument of terror. Klan forces assassinated three Republican legislators in 1868. The governor, white Republican Robert Scott, responded to Klan depredations by creating a volunteer militia, which was virtually all black. Violence again exploded in 1870 and never really abated until 1877. Following the election of Ulysses S. Grant in 1868 and the passage of the Ku Klux Act, federal officials cracked down on violence in the state. Federal officers placed nine upcountry counties under martial law. Officials arrested hundreds of alleged perpetrators but secured few convictions.[40]

The sight of armed black militiamen enforcing their rights of citizenship particularly enraged South Carolina whites. The implied use of violence and the rights and privileges associated with military service had forever been a white male prerogative, and whites were determined to keep it that way. In 1872, whites began organizing rifle, gun, and saber clubs following the declaration by wealthy planter and former Confederate general Wade Hampton III that the time had come for whites to dedicate themselves to the redemption of the state.[41] Tensions culminated during the election campaign of 1876, with Hampton running as the Democratic candidate for governor. More than fifteen thousand of his enthusiastic supporters organized themselves into paramilitary units, donned red shirts, and toured the state with Hampton and other Democratic candidates, intimidating Republican leaders, candidates, and especially black voters.[42]

The campaign of 1876 became a racialized confrontation between mostly black Republican militiamen and white members of Democratic rifle clubs for political control of the state. At heart, notes historian Stephen Kantrowitz, many of these confrontations were "conflict[s] over the right of black men to act as citizens and soldiers."[43] The most deadly clashes occurred in Aiken County. On July 4, a black militia company paraded on a main avenue in Hamburg. Two young white men from wealthy local families attempted to drive a buggy through the militia's ranks. The black soldiers fixed their bayonets, and the white men drew their pistols. After a few tense moments, cooler heads prevailed, and the soldiers allowed the buggy to pass. But the conflict did not end there. The white men filed charges against the military commander, who filed countercharges. On July 8, the day of the hearing, armed whites, now calling themselves Red Shirts, descended on Hamburg and nearby Augusta. Their ranks included a young Ben Tillman. Fearing for their lives, the militia commander and his soldiers took refuge in their drill room above a Hamburg store. The white mob laid siege to the store. Militiamen were shot as they attempted to escape, and about thirty were captured. Five of the captives were murdered in cold blood, shot through the head. When the dust had settled, seven militiamen lay dead. No Red Shirts were ever punished for the murders.[44]

The worst of the "redemption" violence came two months later, in the tiny town of Ellenton in Aiken County. Rumors spread throughout Aiken and Barnwell Counties that African Americans had assaulted an elderly white woman. According to historian Mark M. Smith, the origins of the riot were political. Tensions had been rising in Ellenton prior to the outbreak of actual violence. Local officials there and throughout Aiken County were particularly concerned with the proliferation of rifle clubs. Officials issued a warrant for the arrest of the alleged rapists. In response, the local black militia gathered to protect the accused. With local blacks quickly arming themselves, numerous white gun clubs and rifle clubs mobilized around the area. From September 16 through September 19, white gun club members rampaged through the area around El-lenton, "ostensibly searching for the attackers of the elderly woman." Hundreds of armed whites invaded black homes, churches, and political meetings. No one was safe from the mob. By the time the U.S. Army intervened, at least two whites lay dead, with three wounded; estimates of the black death toll ranged from twenty-five to more than a hundred. African American state legislator Simon Coker was shot in the head while on his knees, praying for mercy.[45]

Massive voter fraud and intimidation marred the November election. The contest ultimately ended in a stalemate, with both Republicans and Democrats claiming the right to the statehouse. Even after the election, voters could switch their allegiance, and Democrats pressured landless Republicans to switch their votes by urging Democratic landowners to evict any sharecroppers or tenants who had voted Republican. Faced with the option of "Hampton or starvation," scores of landless blacks withdrew their support from the Republicans, and the Democrats emerged victorious.[46]

The future for the region's African Americans appeared grim. Once a Re-publican stronghold, the town of Hamburg literally disappeared. Its charter was repealed by the General Assembly after the Democrats regained power, and the town withered away.[47] With their political and civil rights violently ripped away, Aiken's African American community quietly struggled to regain some equilibrium. For the next several decades, mired in fear and hemmed in by declining economic opportunity, the black population slowly but steadily declined, as did the region's agricultural fortunes.

An area recently infamous for bloody racial confrontations seemed an un-likely tourist destination. Yet by the turn of the century, Aiken had reinvented itself as a sporting paradise. Wealthy racehorse owners and vigorous outdoor enthusiasts from the North replaced pale consumptives as the chief tourists to Aiken, which began billing itself as the "Sports Center of the South." According to Irish novelist Edith Anna Somerville, "With its perfect winter and spring climate, its gardens and woods, [Aiken] is an ideal pleasure place, but preemi-nently it is a place devoted to the worship of the Horse. . . . Hunting, Racing, Polo, Coaching, the cults are many, but all do homage at the same shrine." Residents and visitors pursued other sports, such as golf and tennis, but these,

Figure 4. Louise Hitchcock engaged in her
favorite pastime, 1910s. Louise and Thomas
Hitchcock were at the center of Aiken's
sporting life. Photograph courtesy of the
Aiken County Historical Museum, Aiken,
South Carolina.

Somerville notes dismissively, were "false gods." The horse, she noted "is (and very properly) the tutelary deity of Aiken."[48] Louise Eustis "Lulie" Hitchcock and Thomas Hitchcock were at the core of Aiken's sporting life and accompanying social scene. Louise Hitchcock had come south from Long Island, New York, in the 1870s after she discovered that Aiken's temperate climate and sandy soil were ideal for raising and training thoroughbreds. She and her husband owned a stable of racehorses and brought their equine passion to South Carolina. "To speak of Aiken and not to mention Mrs. Thomas Hitchcock, would be like playing 'Hamlet' without the Prince of Denmark," Somerville observed.[49] Lulie Hitchcock soon convinced many of her wealthy New York friends to make Aiken their winter home. These northern visitors collectively became known as the "Winter Colonists." They built sprawling mansions along the beautifully landscaped 150-foot-wide boulevards and bestowed these "cottages" with such names as Rosehill, Whitehall, and Joye Cottage.[50] Dividing the boulevards were lovely parks, lush with towering magnolias and filled with the riotous color of that magnificent southern trifecta of dogwoods, camellias, and azaleas. The city proudly adopted the slogan City of Parkways. Most of these broad avenues were still unpaved in 1950, not because of lack of public funds or progressive infrastructure but simply out of consideration for the sensitivity of horses' hooves.[51] When not extolling its parkways, the city promoted its budding reputation as a sports and leisure destination. Colorful brochures

Figure 5. Banksia, named after the Banksia rose, is typical of the "cottages" of Aiken's Winter Colonists. Sections of this 17,500-square-foot house date back to 1841. It was purchased in 1931 by Richard Howe of New York, an avid horseman and former vice president of International Harvester whose wife was a member of the Deering family. In the early 1950s, Banksia was used as a boardinghouse for construction workers building the Savannah River Plant. Photograph courtesy of the Aiken County Historical Museum, Aiken, South Carolina.

and promotion pieces heralded the region's luxurious accommodations and upper-class recreation. Polo players began arriving in Aiken shortly after the first recorded game in 1882; for the next half century, Aiken was known as the Newport of South Carolina, attracting polo players from throughout the "civilized world." The city's entertainment options reflected the desires of its well-heeled winter residents. By the early 1940s, Aiken boasted seventeen polo fields but only two movie theaters.[52] The town's baseball team (which played in the Tri-County League) was the Tourists.[53] The town's pre-1950s promotional materials likened Aiken's sporting culture to that of European nobility. Aiken's wealthy could enjoy flat racing ("the sport of kings"), drag hunts ("colorful replicas of the old type of fox hunting, accompanied by all the thrills and ceremonies so well known in England and other European countries"), steeplechases, and horse shows. Visitors to the area could go horseback riding along the hundreds of miles of bridle paths in the eight-thousand-acre Hitchcock Woods, hunt in the many nearby fields, or fish in one of the county's nearly one thousand ponds and lakes. The region was home to numerous fine turn-of-the-century-era hotels that had been host to such luminaries as Winston Churchill, John Jacob Astor, the wife of actor John Barrymore, and an assortment of dukes, duchesses, barons, countesses, and ambassadors.[54]

Although the number and prominence of the Winter Colonists declined during the 1930s and 1940s, they still played an important role in Aiken's economy, identity, and mystique. Aiken resident Nancy A. Wilds recalled, "I was impressed by the fact that nobody [among the Winter Colonists] worked; and yet they were just as busy and just as scheduled as people who worked. And as I observed their daily schedule, I realized they hadn't changed very much from Jane Austen's *Pride and Prejudice* or Edith Wharton's *The Age of Innocence*.... Their daily schedule was based on very serious play." The region's permanent residents also found economic sustenance in the Winter Colony. Wade Brodie recalled that during the Great Depression, his father, who was "a great shot," made money selling quail to Winter Colony folk. He made between seventy-five cents to one dollar per bird, more than he could have earned doing farmwork. Mary Dyches Kenney and her family rented their house to Winter Colony visitors during the "season," which ran from October to April, because, her mother said, "that's the way we paid for the house." Some residents went to great lengths to cater to the Winter Colony. Rosemond McDuffie recalls how, one fall, Lillius Gilchrist Grace, wife of W. R. Grace, the founder of the chemical giant that bore his name, was due to arrive in Aiken, but her pansies had not yet bloomed. Not wanting her to be disappointed, McDuffie's father and his gardener dug up all of the pansies in the McDuffie yard and replanted them on Grace's property.[55]

Just beyond the stately mansions and stretching into the county, however, were a very different Aiken and a very different South mired in poverty and fear. Well into the twentieth century, the region continued to suffer the chilling aftereffects of Reconstruction-era violence. The majority of houses in Aiken County were regarded as "dilapidated," and a good many residences within the city proper still possessed open pit toilets as late as 1950. Aiken County residents also ranked near the bottom in educational achievement, with the state's second-lowest rate of high school graduation. Assessing the conditions at midcentury, Clarence Mitchell of the National Association for the Advancement of Colored People (NAACP) described this region of South Carolina in the early 1950s as a "fearful place. There are Jim-Crow waiting rooms in stations, hundreds of shacks and run-down houses in what are referred to as Negro areas, dilapidated schools staffed by poorly paid teachers, and active Ku Klux Klan groups which seek to intimidate colored and white people." But Mitchell also noted that Aiken had patchwork housing patterns, with white and black homes interspersed, and had black businesses that served white customers.[56] Janie Key, the daughter of an African American Baptist preacher in rural Aiken County, recalled that her family had little contact with whites, with encounters limited to business transactions. However, the Keys' closest neighbors were white, and she recalled that the two families "were neighborly." In a region where the majority of African Americans made their living in the fields, working for the Winter Colony residents constituted a step up. Winter Colonists employed local blacks as gardeners, butlers, maids, bartenders, and stable hands. Those working for the Winter Colonists joined with local black educators and entrepreneurs to create an organization known as the Royal Aikenites, and its members were the community's social elite. Membership was by invitation only. James Gallman, later the leader of the local NAACP and the son of a man who worked for one of the northern families, noted that while Aiken was hardly a bastion of equality, the presence of the Winter Colony mitigated some of the harsher aspects of racial discrimination.[57]

The mill villages, however, were places to avoid, especially after dark. Key remembered that her family never traveled through Graniteville at night. In 1925, the county again became the object of national attention when the sheriff, Henry Hampton Howard, was shot and killed during a raid of the home of the Lowmans, a local black family. Howard was searching for illegal liquor, which was never found. Three members of the Lowman family were convicted of the murder and were lynched. Racial discrimination and terror kept a tight grip on the region. Cole Blease, a protégé of Tillman's, drew considerable political support from the mill villages of Horse Creek Valley, where a third of Aiken County's electorate resided. By 1940, the black population rested at around 42 percent for the county.[58]

The textile industry in the Horse Creek Valley had expanded in the late nineteenth century, although it was dwarfed by the upstate mill-building boom. Nevertheless, textiles constituted a critical component of western South Carolina's economy, and small, cloistered, segregated textile villages such as Warrenville, Langley, Bath, and Clearwater joined Graniteville in the valley. By the 1920s, the region still supported an active Klan, with key members also serving in the county's law enforcement establishment, and remained a stronghold of white supremacy. Aiken County was indeed an unusual place. Writes one historian, "By the middle of the 1920s . . . one could read in the [local paper] about a party at the Vanderbilt home, a Friday afternoon Klan rally, evangelical revivals, the reminiscences of an aged Confederate veteran, gunplay on noonday streets, a labor strike, [and] all manner of whippings and homicides."[59]

Industry in the region weathered lean years in the 1920s and 1930s but rebounded with government orders during World War II. The valley's textile mills continued to hum in the immediate postwar era, but returning veterans remained wary about whether they would have a place in the postwar economy. Depression and war sent western South Carolina, like so many parts of the South, lurching toward transition. During the 1940s, sparked by a declining agricultural economy and economic opportunity elsewhere, the tricounty region out of which the Savannah River Plant would be carved was undergoing economic and demographic changes. The cotton economy was in decline. The rural areas of Aiken County had lost population, with sharecroppers in particular leaving in droves. Scores of vacant farmhouses bore testimony to the exodus. Across the South, four million migrants—a quarter of the region's rural population—left the South during the war years. Many of the remaining farmers began the slow process of diversification.

As the Cold War loomed over South Carolina, Aiken existed, as South Carolina writer Pat Conroy would later observe, as "a town of categories"—one either belonged to the Winter Colony, Old Aiken, or the valley. Old Aiken—the longtime residents of the town who could trace their ancestors back several generations—found its economic salvation in the Winter Colony. Old Aiken included the year-round merchants and professionals who made their living off of the northern visitors. With the arrival of the Winter Colonists, Conroy observed, Aiken developed a "social schizophrenia: The Old Aikenite seems inferior to the Winter Colony, but, by God, he feels superior to every other bastard that comes to town."[60] At the bottom of the social ladder in Aiken County were the mill folks from the valley, a region Conroy called "the nasty little secret of Aiken County."[61] Only a few miles separated the valley from the city, but mill village residents lived in an entirely different social and economic world from city inhabitants. William Gregg built his home on Kalmia Hill, overlooking the valley; Aiken residents would adopt the same perspective. Although Aiken's merchants considered themselves a class apart from the mill workers and farmers, they nevertheless welcomed mill dollars. Few mill workers from the valley, however, could afford the prices at Aiken's small, locally owned shops.[62] Esther Melton, born and raised in Graniteville, recalled that in 1946, it cost her two months' salary to purchase a dress from Julia's, a pricey dress shop in downtown Aiken. Melton and her family and friends preferred the larger, more affordable chain department stores, such as J. B. White, Belk, and J. C. Penney, located in Augusta, some ten miles away.[63] Some valley shoppers may have also appreciated the greater degree of anonymity provided by the larger city; still others perhaps wanted to avoid the simple geographic reality of always having to go "up" to Aiken. A robust taxicab system made the trip to Augusta feasible and affordable. The trip over the Savannah River to Augusta might have been longer in terms of miles, but it was not as distant socially as the journey up to Aiken.

Radiating out from the town and valley, the region's many white and black residents in hamlets in the countryside remained wedded by tradition or economic means to farming practices that had not changed since the end of the Civil War. Nevertheless, Conroy's portrait is essentially accurate. Aiken County featured interlocking populations in a relatively strict racial and social hierarchy, many of them drawn to the region by the promise of some notion of progress made possible by a collection of geographical oddities.

Collectively, the greater Aiken County community held its breath in anticipation of the arrival of a Cold War project that melded the region's particular environmental attributes with the latest scientific and technological advances. Although few locals could comprehend the scientific feats to be undertaken at the new Savannah River Plant, most understood that some measure of economic and social change would accompany the new enterprise. What shape would change take, and how extensive would it be? Would the plant reconfigure the region's unique social categories? More critically, perhaps, would the plant undermine the region's rigid racial hierarchy by providing economic opportunity to African Americans, severing forever the stranglehold in which the agricultural economy and a history of racial violence held them fast? The magnitude of the enterprise, undergirded by furious Cold War pressures, held the potential for swift and dramatic social and economic change that could render the region unrecognizable.

CHAPTER THREE

"A Land Doomed and Damned"
The Costs of Militarization

Everyone knew there were strangers in their midst. In the late summer of 1950, residents of Ellenton, South Carolina, population 739, had spotted men surveying the land, boring into the earth, taking soil samples here and there. "What was their business?" locals asked themselves. Ellenton schoolteacher Louise Cassels later recalled that "speculations flew over the community like migrant birds." Residents were hopeful in anticipation of new industry that, she remarked, would bring "the progress the people longed for." Some heard reports that a glue factory was going to be built; others claimed it would be an aluminum plant; still others figured that the men were prospecting for oil or kaolin.[1] Jack Harden, son of the town depot agent, told a friend, "My daddy is getting some strange type of telegrams he doesn't understand. . . . They are gonna make tanks or some kind of bullets or some kind of ammunition, he thinks from what these telegrams say." Young Harden did not know where this new plant was going to be located, perhaps "in the Pineywoods, back behind the Blue Goose [café] somewhere."[2] John Shaw Billings noted that "nobody knows anything [about the plant]—but everybody has loud ideas."[3]

The official announcement of the creation of the plant on November 28, 1950, settled some of these questions but posed a much more provocative and unsettling one: How would this new plant affect the residents? Theories abounded. For more than a week, rumors raged. Even as well-connected an individual as Billings remained in the dark regarding the plant's exact location and geographical boundaries. "Nobody knows for sure," he wrote in his diary in early December.[4] Reporter William D. Workman echoed this uncertainty. Noting that the residents of the region "have been passed by for the most part in the state's industrial progress . . . they are now to be up-rooted from their own soil and transplanted to some other place, and all they can see right now is the dark cloud of the atomic age."[5]

Just over a week later, on December 6, 1950, some five hundred individuals and families whose homes fell inside the sprawling boundaries of the country's latest Cold War project crowded into the Ellenton school auditorium—whites seated in the middle, blacks lining the room's periphery—to learn their fate. The auditorium could not hold them all, and the crowd spilled outside, leaving anxious landowners straining to hear the news. An inhospitable winter drizzle and a squalling baby only compounded their discomfort.[6] Workman, covering the story for several South Carolina newspapers, noted that the crowd was not in the mood for bad news from federal officials, and he overheard "mumbling about another Ellenton riot."[7] Men in double-breasted suits, officials from Du Pont and the Atomic Energy Commission (AEC), told the residents that they were going to have to evacuate—not just temporarily, but forever. "We came here," Curtis A. Nelson, manager of the new operations office, stated, "not just to build a war plant but to make things that can be used for peace. We plan to be with you a long time. And to be good citizens of South Carolina."[8]

To make way for these new citizens and their Cold War mission, some fifteen hundred families—approximately eight thousand individuals—many of whom had lived on their land for generations, were going to have to move. What they had hoped would bring economic opportunity had instead brought devastation. "We wanted an industry," Judge P. H. Buckingham, Ellenton's magistrate, told a reporter from the *New Yorker*, "but instead we all got drafted—men, women and children."[9] Slated for removal were six small towns and villages: Ellenton, Dunbarton, Hawthorne, Leigh, Meyers Mill, and Robbins.[10] Lester C. Moody, secretary of the Augusta, Georgia, Chamber of Commerce and a key regional development booster, speculated that the arrival of the Savannah River Plant would "mean empire-building to us. Augusta is going to grow and grow and be prosperous. Of course the folks around Ellenton are being inconvenienced, but you can't have progress with sentiment." Pausing, Moody concluded, "The hand that shuns the thorn can't have the rose."[11] He did not make clear whose hands got flowers and whose got thorns. Billings called the removal of fifteen hundred families "a deep personal tragedy," noting that "only the fluke of ten miles saved Redcliffe from such condemnation and obliteration. The war creeps in upon private lives at every turn."[12]

Anxious residents greeted the news of their impending removal with grim acceptance, comforted only by the fact that theirs was a sacrifice for the greater good of American postwar security. Still, bad feelings festered. In testimony before the House Banking and Currency Committee in February 1951, just a few months after the plant's announcement, Congressman John J. Riley of

South Carolina's Second District, which included Aiken County, compared the experiences of the residents within the plant area to "the consternation created when General Sherman made his march to the sea in 1864." Declared Riley, "The people there are casualties of the Defense effort. They must accept what is being done to them as their patriotic contribution to the Defense effort of this country."[13] Ellenton resident Stanley Eubanks echoed Riley's sentiments: "We're sad. We're heartbroken, I guess you could say. But we're not bitter. Our country has asked us to move, and we are going to move. But sometimes we wonder—why did it have to be *Ellenton*?"[14]

The acceleration of the arms race, the militarization of the southern economy, and the accompanying modernization of the region came with huge costs. The creation of the Savannah River Plant accelerated the rural transformation already under way by wiping out a great swath of countryside and several small rural communities in one fell swoop, and by dramatically transforming the existing communities outside the plant's borders. One-third of the 315 square miles acquired for the construction of the plant was cropland or pastures. The majority of the farming tracts were small and grew peanuts, corn, and cotton. The larger tracts were operated by sharecroppers or tenants, the majority of them African American.[15] The process of carving out land for the new Cold War project and the subsequent dislocation of the region's residents reveals competing definitions of land, space, and community espoused by the area's long-term residents and the architects of America's new war. The rapid nature of the militarization of the southern economy left many of modernization's losers in its wake, struggling with the cultural loss that often accompanies progress.

Situated approximately two miles from the Savannah River and about twenty-five miles southeast of Augusta, Georgia, Ellenton was the largest community eliminated to make way for the new plant. The small town got its name from James Robert Dunbar Jr. In 1870, Dunbar ceded some property near the Savannah River to the Port Royal–Augusta Railroad, which later became the Charleston and Western Carolina Railroad. The superintendent of railroad construction, who boarded at the Dunbar home, was charmed by Dunbar's nine-year-old daughter, Ellen, and named the depot after her. As a settlement grew up around the junction, Dunbar ceded additional property for streets, and the tiny hamlet became known as Ellen's Town and later Ellenton.[16] The small town's subsequent eighty-year history was modest but never static.

National attention first came to Ellenton with the 1876 riots. The spotlight quite literally returned in 1929 when Ellenton got electricity and became "the only town in the nation that burned its street lights day and night."[17] Despite the relatively poor, sandy soil, the small farming community of Ellenton expanded during the late nineteenth and into the twentieth century. By 1949, 135 families (102 white and 33 black) owned property within the town limits.[18] Landowner-ship was dominated by a few families—the Bushes, the Cassels, the Brinkleys, and the Dunbars—who collectively controlled thousands of acres. Working many of these acres were the landless, tenants and sharecroppers who did not own land but were nevertheless wedded to it, to the community, and to the agrarian way of life.

The region's major cash crop was cotton, but, unlike their Piedmont coun-terparts, farmers in and around Ellenton were relatively diversified. They also grew corn, peanuts, watermelons, cantaloupes, sugarcane, wheat, oats, rye, millet, and rice, either for the market or for personal consumption.[19] Resi-dents grew or raised much of what they needed. Ellenton resident Annie Polk Linder recalled that the only goods her mother ever bought were sugar, coffee, and rice.[20] Many farmers also kept livestock, to which they fed their wheat, corn, and oats. "My daddy always kept a cow, horses, chickens, hogs, and all those things," Bennie Bowers remembered. "Most everyone had livestock."[21] Even town folk maintained vegetable gardens and livestock for their families' consumption.[22]

As was typical in agrarian communities, services in Ellenton were some-times worked out through barter. "You see," resident Carl Brinkley pointed out, "You didn't pay to have [your corn] ground. You'd carry so much corn, say a bushel of corn. Well [the miller] took out his toll at the end. When he ground it out, he kept so much and gave you back yours. . . . You didn't pay. Nobody paid for anything. We just interchanged among ourselves."[23] Although Brinkley's recollection about the absence of cash payment was exaggerated, rural ways of exchange were deeply woven throughout the community. Stephen Harley recalled that Paul Culbreath, one of the town's two doctors, charged "fifteen dollars and a country ham" to remove Harley's adenoids.[24] The town's other doctor, Fred C. Brinkley, also owned one of the town's gristmills.[25]

Most of the region's farms had yet to modernize by 1950. Although pesti-cides had begun to be used in farming with greater frequency, farmers along the Savannah still used traditional labor-intensive methods to combat pests. Farmers still waged an exhausting struggle against the boll weevil with nothing more than molasses, poison, and a mop. Nixon Tutt recalled, "We had a poison we would put in molasses, and you would take your mop, and go along and hit each piece of cotton on the top, and that boll weevil would get in that and he'd just be dragging on the top up there and just the least bit get on him and it would kill him."[26]

Many Ellenton residents combined farming with wage labor at the Leigh Banana Crate Company, the town's only industry.[27] Located on the edge of Barnwell County, Leigh Banana Crate crafted containers for transporting fruits and vegetables.[28] Founded in 1905 by Charles Q. C. Leigh, a produce merchant in Paducah, Kentucky, the company moved to its new location just three miles from Ellenton in 1926 "because there was a good supply of hardwoods, especially cypress and sweet gum, in the swamps around Ellenton."[29] It was an enormous enterprise, with its own logging crew and train system. In the 1940s, the plant employed around 350 people during the spring peak season.[30] Those residents not employed by Leigh Banana Crate found work in the area's many grist- and sawmills.

As the twentieth century dawned, town life in Ellenton was on the rise. As one historian notes, although "the farmers established a solid economic foundation for Ellenton to develop upon . . . it was the local merchants who stimulated and maintained a steady growth in the financial and social status of Ellenton."[31] Ellenton eventually became a trading and commercial center for the surrounding agricultural region, linking the rural hinterland to the outside world.[32] By 1950, Ellenton boasted fifty-six merchants, including several barbershops, a few auto-repair shops, a movie theater, a drugstore, a dry cleaner, a Chevrolet dealership, a post office, several restaurants, and a hotel. On the eve of its destruction, the town had just completed a new thirty-thousand-dollar school.[33] Residential and business areas were interspersed in a patchwork fashion that one resident believed "marred its overall beauty. It reminded one of a ragged person with well-formed features and a fine physique."[34]

Sitting atop Ellenton's merchant class was the Cassels family. Family lore maintains that patriarch Horace Michael Cassels arrived in Ellenton in 1881 at the age of seventeen with only a dollar in his pocket and a puppy in his arms. Cassels found work in one of the local sawmills; within a few years, he had saved enough of his wages to buy a farm and build a home. He married Gazelle Bailey in 1888, and together they had seven children, six of whom survived childhood: Wallace Bailey, William Porter, Horace Michael Jr., Mamie, Augusta Louise, and Sumpter Marion.[35] Cassels expanded his landholdings and developed many commercial enterprises in and around Ellenton, including the

Western Carolina Oil and Power Company, which furnished electricity to the town and the surrounding area. When he died in 1931, Cassels's commercial assets included a wholesale grocery business, a seed and feed business, a bank, a funeral parlor, a dairy, and a canning factory. He also owned several farms totaling more than twelve thousand acres.[36]

After his death, many of his business operations were taken over by his sons, Horace Michael "Mike" Cassels Jr. and Wallace Cassels, and son-in-law, Arthur Foreman, husband of Mamie Cassels. Rather than split their holdings among the siblings, the family members incorporated into the Cassels Company.[37] Mike Cassels became the public face of the Cassels family and one of Ellenton's leading citizens. He oversaw the family's wholesale and retail businesses and served as the town's mayor for twenty years.[38] Mike Cassels was best known as the owner and operator of the Long Store, a general store so named because it was 210 feet long. His nephew, Fielding Foreman, recalled that the store sold everything "from silk dresses to horse collars." Like other general stores in other small towns, the Long Store became a community gathering place where locals could share information, seek assistance or advice from "Mr. Mike," or just shoot the breeze.[39] In his role as Ellenton's magistrate, Mike Cassels, his son recalled, "held court every Monday night from a wooden bench in front of the Long Store. Large crowds attended these sessions, which usually provided the town with abundant conversational material for the coming week." The assembled townspeople often served as an informal jury: "If there was doubt in my father's mind about the guilt or innocence of the accused, or there seemed to be extenuating circumstances, he would call upon the assembled crowd for an expression of sentiment."[40]

Augusta Louise Cassels, sister of Wallace and Mike, was born in Ellenton in 1899. She attended Shorter College in Rome, Georgia, where she received a degree in music. An accomplished musician, Louise returned to Ellenton, where she lived in the family home with her sister and brother-in-law, Mamie and Arthur Foreman. She taught music and art at Ellenton Grammar School and played piano and organ at the Ellenton Baptist Church.[41] An astute observer, Louise Cassels became Ellenton's chronicler, penning a memoir during the years of Ellenton's removal. With clarity and honesty, Cassels's book, *The Unexpected Exodus*, provides a unique look at the local and personal impact of the expanding and menacing Cold War. Throughout her brief tale, Cassels's emotions run the gamut from proud and patriotic to resentful and melancholic. She captures the distress of her neighbors, who tried to comprehend the fate

Figure 6. The Ellenton depot, 1951. Photograph courtesy of the Savannah River Site, U.S. Department of Energy.

Figure 7. Ellenton businesses: Jean's Place café, the theater, and a store, ca. 1951. Photograph courtesy of the Savannah River Archaeological Research Program, South Carolina Institute of Archaeology and Anthropology, University of South Carolina, Columbia.

Figure 8. Cassels's Long Store, Ellenton, ca. 1951. Photograph courtesy of the Savannah River Site, U.S. Department of Energy.

that had befallen them and the great sacrifice they were being asked to make. Cassels's story offers poignant testimony to the power of place and the destruction of a rural community in the wake of the militarization of the South.[42]

At the moment of the arrival of the AEC and Du Pont, then, Ellenton was a small town on the rise. But the growth of a rural community and the requirements dictated by the new Cold War enterprise came from completely different perspectives, promoting entirely antithetical interpretations and understandings of rural landscape and space, one traditional and one modern. The modern notions of landscape ultimately would transform the traditional. Site planners for the AEC as well as journalists writing about the destruction of Ellenton and the other small communities observed incorrectly that the residents lived in "rural isolation." On the contrary, they were rather well connected to larger urban areas. Although most residents shopped for food and sundries in Ellenton, they regularly traveled to Augusta for clothing and shoes. The region was well served by the railroad. The Charleston and Western Carolina and the Atlantic Coastline trains came through Ellenton three times a day. Those who preferred the bus could catch the Greyhound at the Blue Goose restaurant.[43] The AEC's use of the term "sufficiently isolated" to describe the proposed area of the new plant points to a stark contrast in the understanding of rural space. To the residents, the land was alive and productive. Land that was not cultivated could be used for recreation. They hunted in the woods; fished in the rivers and streams; swam in the many lakes, ponds, and creeks; or simply enjoyed the beauty of the landscape. Louise Cassels referred to Ellenton as "a hunter's town," illustrating the intertwining of town and country life. The AEC and Du Pont, conversely, regarded this space as nearly "empty" and easily cleared. Great swaths of land were to be used as a buffer between human populations in the region and the plant operations. In Du Pont's hands, this would be a controllable landscape, a dividing line.[44] This and other realities of the Cold War would come swift and hard. Not only were residents being pushed from their homes, but they also witnessed the painful reality that those in charge of the design and construction of the plant saw little or no intrinsic beauty or value to the landscape that local denizens had loved so dearly. For many, the whole enterprise felt like a vicious insult.

Also slated for removal were the crossroads communities of Dunbarton and Meyers Mill. The Dunbarton community, named for the Dunbar family and home to three hundred individuals, grew up around the railroad depot in the early nineteenth century. Meyers Mill was a small community of primarily African Americans who settled in the region in the late nineteenth century. These hamlets, though small, were part of an extensive series of rural communities bound together by familial ties and connected to the larger commercial world through Ellenton and Augusta. To view them as isolated denied the essential fabric of life in the region and, for that matter, the rural South at large.[45]

Upset by the announcement that they would have to relocate, Ellenton's residents sought consolation and counsel in familiar places. Observed one reporter, "In the first few days after the news got around, most of Ellenton's men of consequence, those who have access to Mister Mike Cassels, pushed on, deep into the store. . . . At the farthest reach and recess in the rear is Mister Mike's 'bull pen,' a tiny, dark office. . . . From these meetings came the earliest notes of Ellenton's bewilderment and dismay. Everybody soon discovered . . . that Mister Mike didn't know what to do, and if *he* didn't know, then there just wasn't any hope that anybody else in Ellenton could figure the thing out."[46] Without any answers, Cassels himself was anxious at the prospect of pulling up roots. "Makes you kind of jittery," he told a reporter for *Time* magazine. "We've got to decide where to go. . . . It's like having a death in the family, going to the funeral, then returning home and realizing the emptiness of the house."[47] Cassels moved quickly. Within a few months, he and several other prominent Ellentonians had acquired property just outside the plant boundary along Highway 19, also known as Whiskey Road, the main artery into Aiken.

The announcement of the creation of the plant and the destruction of Ellenton and the surrounding communities prompted a flock of sightseers to the doomed rural outpost, like rubberneckers at a car wreck. Here, though, the wreck had not yet happened. William Stephen Harley recalled that "the very first Sunday after the news broke, you could see a tag from just about every state in the Union coming down here to look. You couldn't walk across the street 'cause there was so much traffic. It was bumper to bumper both ways, just with people looking." An irritated Louise Cassels observed the "curiosity seekers [who] had come to scrutinize the little town destined to die." They gave the town its first traffic jam.[48] Journalists, too, flocked to the region to record the final days of the doomed city, much to the annoyance of the residents. "Like a communicable, sporadic disease," Cassels caustically observed, "they appeared almost anywhere at any time." Photographer Ike Vern and reporter Booton Herndon of *The Reporter* were beaten up on the front lawn of the Ellenton Baptist Church by members of the congregation, who claimed that the magazine representatives had referred to them as "Sharecropper Baptists." According to one church member, Vern and Herndon "were attempting to get us to pose for *Tobacco Road* type pictures."[49]

Nerves were on edge. Louise Cassels recalled the flood of emotions she experienced in the days after the announcement. To resume some sense of comfort and routine, she went to her church to practice the organ for an upcoming service. "The serene atmosphere of the sanctuary and the inspiring music served as a therapy. I could sense my built-up tension of the past week vanishing like a bird disappearing into the sky. I was normal again." But as she departed the church she was stopped by the sound of animated chitchat: "I stopped dead; the scene offended my sensitive nature. A gay middle-aged couple, bubbling over with repartee, were taking pictures of our doomed church. I felt hot blood rush to my face. Then anger seized me. Trembling violently, I braced myself against the closed door." With tears in her eyes, she asked them, "How can you feel so indifferent and happy over our calamity?" The flustered couple beat a hasty retreat.[50]

John Shaw Billings and his wife, Frederica, were among those who traveled to Ellenton to glimpse what was about to be destroyed. Billings later recorded his mixed emotions: "The flat scrubby wasteland lay under a grey sky. It was ugly landscape—yes. It was ideal for plants of death—yes. But I loved it all and

I hated to see it lose its look and character to an unknown unseen force." They drove on through the condemned communities. He later wrote in his diary, "The little towns were nothing—but what some people called home. A land doomed and damned—and withdrawn from civilization."[51]

The dismantling of Ellenton and other communities was not a foregone conclusion among the chief decision makers. Even as AEC and Du Pont officials were planning to inform the residents of their fate, the complete absorption of Ellenton and Dunbarton and the removal of their populations was still under discussion, with several within the AEC questioning the decision. In a letter to the AEC, R. M. Evans, assistant general manager of Du Pont's explosives department, complained that "unwarranted importance [has been] given to protecting the several small towns in the area." To allow Ellenton and Dunbarton to remain, he argued, "present[s] the most serious problems. To permit them to remain as uncontrolled communities would . . . create an almost intolerable situation. As islands of uncontrolled population they would present serious security and safety problems. It is inconceivable that they could retain their present character in the changing environment and, deprived of their surrounding agricultural areas, it is unlikely that they would retain their present means of livelihood." In addition, Evans noted, "we would expect them to become increasingly unattractive places of residence to many of the present inhabitants." The inclusion of Ellenton and Dunbarton within the plant's boundaries and the removal of the inhabitants, in his opinion, "should be attacked positively at the outset when public-mindedness can be expected to be highest. Temporizing with the problem can be expected to aggravate it." He argued that it was better to err on the side of overacquisition of land than to underestimate it.[52] Still, M. W. Boyer and two other members of the AEC asked Du Pont to "review in detail" the necessity of acquiring Ellenton. Boyer asked whether it was feasible to allow Ellenton to remain intact while "securing zoning restrictions which would discourage or prohibit the growth along undesirable lines of Ellenton and other nearby towns."[53] Boyer's arguments were dismissed as impractical from a cost and safety standpoint. The required spacing of the reactors and the location of water sources required the inclusion of Ellenton. The project went forward as planned.[54] It was a matter of efficiency.

Residents did not have the luxury of time to ponder their next move. With the specter of Soviet nuclear capabilities looming and with the Chinese involvement in the Korean conflict threatening to bring on a larger Asian land war, the government seizure of land proceeded at a rapid pace. Moreover, as Evans had asserted, the takeover also depended on a spirit of patriotic sacrifice among local citizens. Time was considered short on both fronts. The job of assessing and acquiring the property was handled by the Land Acquisition Division of the Army Corps of Engineers (COE). COE personnel arrived in western South Carolina on November 29, the day after the plant announcement, and within two weeks, their office was fully operational.[55] The COE divided the massive plant site into six priority areas; the first evacuations were scheduled for March 1, 1951, with the region cleared of its resident population by June 1, 1952.[56] Property appraisals for the high-priority areas began in December 1950, and the first real estate purchases were made in January 1951. Real estate property appraisals in Ellenton started in mid-August 1951.[57]

To answer questions and squelch rumors regarding the land-acquisition and relocation process, the COE distributed regular information bulletins addressed to "Mr. Landowner." Two weeks after the announcement of the plant, affected residents received a bulletin explaining the process. First the government would appraise the property; if the homeowner agreed that the price was fair, he or she would be asked to sign an option contract. If the government and owner failed to reach an agreement, the matter would be turned over to the federal court in a condemnation proceeding. Residents would not be compensated for the cost of moving off their property.[58]

Within weeks in some cases, months in others, residents of the condemned regions had to decide whether to accept the government's offer; they also had to locate new housing in a very tight market. Louise Cassels and her sister, Mamie, stayed in Ellenton beyond the "final" evacuation date of March 1, 1952. Their new home in Aiken was not yet ready, nor had they received reimbursement from the government for their Ellenton house. In her memoir, Cassels bitterly recalls the frequent visits of the "Government man, Mr. Bell," who routinely inquired when they would be moving. One evening, Bell arrived when Cassels was making supper, and she answered the door holding a knife. As he had for weeks, he asked again when they would be moving, and eyeing the knife, he blurted out, "You know, this property belong[s] to the Government." Cassels reaction was visceral: "Was he saying the house I was born in and had lived in all my life wasn't mine? For a moment I stared beyond him into the darkness. I shivered inwardly at the thought; then dizziness overwhelmed me. I steadied myself by grasping the open door with my free hand. . . . I am a stranger in my own home, I thought." Bell retreated, but the following day, the Cassels sisters found a large banner stretched across the railing of their front porch. It read, "This is government property."[59]

Conflicts almost immediately arose between other soon-to-be-displaced residents and government appraisers. The increasingly defensive nature of the information bulletins indicates the residents' mounting displeasure and suspicions regarding the appraisal process. The COE took pains to explain that the land-acquisition policy had withstood legal challenges and "the test of time." It explained what was meant by "fair market value," a meaning quite at odds with that possessed by the landowners themselves. Aware that displaced residents viewed the Corps as a federal interloper, one bulletin pointed out, "Most of the men handling this appraisal work are long time residents of this part of South Carolina. Most of them have many years of experience in this work, are familiar with local conditions, and invariably are inclined to bend over backward to be fair with all the landowners."[60] This assertion was accurate. Of the nineteen local men hired, the majority were from Aiken County, and five were from Ellenton.[61]

Landowners nevertheless questioned the process. An aide to Senator Burnet Maybank reported that residents complained of "a difference of fifty percent in [the appraisal of] adjacent farms." He noted that many residents "are not going to accept the offers." Such discrepancies, he surmised, were the result not of "an effort to defraud but" of incompetence.[62] But some citizens suspected a very definite effort to defraud them of the rightful value of their property. Louis Cassels, son of Mike Cassels and nephew of Louise, who became a senior editor for United Press International, reported as much in his 1974 book, *Coontail Lagoon*. In 1970, Cassels sought out a retired government official who had played a "key role" in the land appropriations. According to Cassels, the official confessed, "I always was and still am deeply ashamed of the prices we paid those folks. We knew we were robbing them, but we had explicit orders from Washington to reduce settlement offers drastically."[63]

Residents also had to make quick decisions with regard to the resources on their property, such as pecans, fruit, crops, livestock, and timber. Landowners could ask that the value of the timber be included in the appraisal, but the offer from the government deducted the cost of transportation of that timber from the final amount. A better option would be for residents to contract with a local outfit to cruise and cut the timber. But quality timbermen were in short supply, with more work than they could handle.[64] Government representatives' desire for haste clashed repeatedly with residents' need for more time and proved to be a constant strain on the displaced communities. Sometimes, the tensions produced absurd conflicts. Two weeks prior to the plant's announcement, Arthur Foreman had purchased a herd of cows for his Ellenton dairy.

Unfortunately, his dairy and pasture were situated on property the government demanded immediately. As Foreman searched desperately for a buyer for his bovines, government workers began tearing down the pasture fences, oblivious to or completely dismissive of the inevitable, chaotic result. Cows roamed everywhere, taking up residence on the railroad track leading to the construction site, an apt symbol for the uneasy tension between the traditional rural world and the modern world. Similar conflicts played out continuously across the region.[65]

In total, the COE acquired more than seventeen hundred separate tracts, nearly half as a result of condemnation.[66] Those with limited financial means often took what the government offered and tried to begin life anew. Those with resources could hope for a favorable settlement or a positive jury verdict. Justice, such as it was, was not often swift, and it sometimes took years to settle a dispute, with a large chunk of the settlement going to attorneys' fees. Strom Thurmond, a former South Carolina governor and at the time a partner in an Aiken law firm, Thurmond, Lybrand, and Simons, represented many of the homeowners, as did Aiken attorney Henry Busbee. Thurmond's firm and another local firm received more than a third of the settlement in fees.[67] Thurmond represented the members of the Cassels family in their disputes over government appraisals. Louis Cassels later wrote that Thurmond's "fees from my family alone were sufficient to finance his successful campaign for election to the U.S. Senate [in 1954], a circumstance that has always made me feel a vague personal responsibility for his subsequent political career."[68]

The land condemnation disputes mark an interesting time in Thurmond's already high-profile career. Elected governor in 1946, Thurmond entered the office with a reputation as a modernizer, hoping to lure industry and government contracts to the state. By early 1948, he had developed a positive reputation nationwide as a new breed of southern governor. But while he looked to federal spending as a method by which the South could modernize, he drew the line at federal intervention in race relations. In early 1948, Thurmond took the lead in a revolt among Deep South Democrats furious over President Harry Truman's civil rights proposals. Later that year, Thurmond ran as the presidential candidate of the States' Rights Democratic Party, winning the electoral votes of South Carolina, Mississippi, Alabama, and Louisiana but finishing a distant third. Two years later, he ran unsuccessfully for the U.S. Senate, losing to incumbent Olin D. Johnston, a strong New Deal Democrat.[69]

After leaving the governor's mansion, Thurmond and his wife, Jean, moved

Figure 9. Strom Thurmond in his law office, Aiken, South Carolina, early 1950s. Photograph courtesy of Special Collections, Clemson University Libraries, Clemson, South Carolina.

to Aiken, where Thurmond took up the practice of law. Although he had re-turned to private life, Thurmond remained very much a public figure. His comings and goings made front-page news, and he continued to be active in civic affairs. The arrival of what locals called the Bomb Plant provided Thur-mond a lucrative opportunity with a large political payoff. By winning returns for landowners that were well above the initial government offers and that reflected local notions of the land's true value, Thurmond strengthened his image as a defender of vulnerable localities against federal encroachment.

Testimony of land appraisers, property owners, and other witnesses given during a number of jury trials in which the owner and government disputed the value of a particular piece of property reveals conflicts between traditional and modern notions of how the value of land and property could be judged. The creation of the atomic bomb and the escalating Cold War had placed sci-entists and technical experts at the forefront of American popular culture, and scientific knowledge and expertise held an exalted position over more tradi-tional forms of knowledge. In October 1951, the court heard the case of Sleepy Hollow Farms, a 703-acre tract owned by Albert A. Weathersbee and Frank

Weathersbee Jr. The Weathersbees, represented by Thurmond, Lybrand, and Simons, had been offered $37,931 for their property.[70] To dispute the government's assessment, the Weathersbees hired C. M. Turner of Barnwell, South Carolina, to appraise the property. Attorney Dorcey Lybrand pointed out that Turner possessed historical as opposed to technical know-how regarding local real estate. Although Turner lived in Barnwell and had done so for ten years, he maintained that Ellenton was his home. "I was born and reared in the vicinity of Ellenton—the post office, church and school in Ellenton. Since I have been working around I have had different [homes], but Ellenton was always my [primary] residence. My church membership, Masonic Lodge and agriculture club, I have always maintained is in Ellenton—and still is."[71] Lybrand also asked how long Turner had been "acquainted" with the property in question, to which Turner replied, "Since I was six years old. That's a long time." Turner testified that "as a boy, I was there all my life off and on. I have been there since I have been a young man. I've been there numbers of times since I have reached maturity age, and I have been there recently."[72] Turner testified that he had a degree in agronomy and horticulture from Clemson University but acknowledged that he had no professional experience in real estate: "I have done very little real estate buying and selling. I have observed a lot of prices and have heard of people making deals, but I haven't had much experience in resale value or purchasing value."[73] Nevertheless, he believed that he knew the value of the Weathersbees' property based on his history with it. At this point, William Sandifer, special assistant to the U.S. Attorney, objected, claiming that Turner's lack of technical knowledge of real estate transactions disqualified him as an expert witness. The judge disagreed: "Here is a man that says he has known this land since he was a child. He has been on it from childhood up through life, reared out in the country in this very neighborhood. . . . I'm not so sure but that some of these fellows that have lived in and by land and seen it and the crops produced on it aren't more competent to go and tell the value than some stranger that comes in that has some theoretical formula by which he appraises the land."[74] When asked about the per-acre yield of Weathersbees' cotton field, Turner referred not to any specific year or data but to common community knowledge and vernacular. "Easily a bale. . . . We spoke of it as 'a bale of cotton land.'"[75] If the jury had any reservations about Turner's qualifications, it nevertheless agreed with his conclusions and awarded the Weathersbees nearly double the government's offer. At the core of this legal conflict lay the disconnect between federal proposed use of the land (as space for construction) and the traditional local relationship to it (as space for living and working). Of course, the two sides would never meet, but this case reveals some success, however modest, in the local effort to assert value of the land beyond a simple, if efficient, market commodity.

The attorneys for the landowners drove home the residents' intimate relationship with the land. Clyburn Harley told the jury that her 1,220 acres had a name: "We called it the River Farm." Busbee, her attorney, also took pains to describe how this property, which Harley knew and had named, had become unrecognizable to her after the government got its hands on it. Harley described the way in which the property had been altered by the government. Though such changes really were not material to a determination of the land's value, the judge allowed this effective line of questioning. Busbee asked her about the landing on the river: Had anything changed about "the earth itself"? Had "the face of the earth . . . been disturbed"? Harley answered, "I wouldn't know my own farm, the government has done so much work down there, and piled up so much dirt until you cannot get right down to the landing." She also noted, "They've done quite a bit of damage. . . . [T]hey have destroyed some trees." She continued, "They have run numerous roads through there. They took the bulldozer and went right straight through the peach orchard, and dug up quite a number of trees. And they have roads everywhere. In fact, I got lost on my own farm." Busbee then asked whether "a very wide section of the ground had been changed and defaced." She replied in the affirmative, explaining that a valley had been created where none before existed. The government attorney, Yancey McLeod, confirmed that "the activities of the government that you have mentioned, all occurred after the government had acquired the property, after they had title to it," but landowners and the jury saw that fact as a mere technicality.[76] It did not matter. The construction—destruction— provided ample evidence of an entity that undervalued the land itself.

Lybrand, representing the Weathersbee family, likewise painted the government as a poor caretaker of the land and the accompanying dwellings. The Weathersbees' home had been built about 1828. When Lybrand asked if Albert Weathersbee knew the condition of the buildings on his land since the government seizure, he answered, "There have been a lot of tramps—I know of no better word to describe people who go about sleeping where they can—here and there sleeping in those houses. And, some degree of vandalism has gone on, because the old brass locks that were on those doors that were well over 100 or 125 years old, imported from England, have been stolen or removed from the house, from the doors." Weathersbee continued, "Of course, that's what takes place when a place is left abandoned and idle." The government's inattention and abuse was antithetical to a rural community that saw land as alive and productive. Weathersbee further elaborated, "Of course, the fields have grown up in weeds—fields that were highly productive last year and the previous years. They have grown up in weeds as high as your head or higher. As compared with what it looked like a year ago, it resembles . . . I think of it as 'Gone with the Wind.' It's gone." Finally, Weathersbee described tenant dwellings and other buildings as "abandoned," adding to the picture he painted of a desolate landscape. The government attorney objected that discussion of "changes during the past year would not be proper," but Weathersbee's point had been made.[77]

Attorneys for landowners also argued that not only were residents being deprived of their property, their children were losing their cultural and familial legacy. Such was the case for Louise Cullum, a widow who disputed the $38,300 the government offered for her 907-acre property. Busbee attempted to win sympathy for her by reminding the jury that its job was to determine the just compensation for this property based on its fair market value, but that this concept was complex and contested: "The fair market value of land is what a willing seller will take and what a willing buyer will pay . . . , the seller not being compelled to sell and the buyer not being compelled to buy. That makes it a voluntary transaction and that is the measure of just compensation." But, he added, "the landowners here didn't want to sell their land," so the jury was welcome to consider the fact that these transactions were being worked out under duress. The land in question had been held by the family for generations and in the absence of the government's involvement, would eventually have passed to Cullum's children. "The little boy is quite a young boy now, who is in school, a nice looking young fellow, but he could have farmed it. His mother couldn't of course. She says she lived too far away from there and she didn't know anything about farming. As a general thing, that is not a prerogative of our lady folk. That is something that men do. But young Robert Brabham will never farm that land, gentlemen of the jury." The U.S. government was spending billions of dollars to rehabilitate former enemies Japan and Germany, Busbee noted, so it was ludicrous, he argued, that "with respect to dealing with these people here, whose lands are being taken and many of whom are being driven from their homes . . . , dispossessed, run out of the country, and then to quibble with them on a few paltry thousands of dollars when their entire holdings and heritage is taken away from them." The jury ultimately awarded Cullum $64,762.60. The government appealed, and the U.S. Court of Appeals for the Fourth Circuit reversed and remanded the case for a new trial. Cullum and the government ultimately settled on $42,300. Five years of legal wrangling, attorneys' fees, and no doubt stress, resulted in only a $4,000 increase from the original offer.[78]

Not surprisingly at trials in which juries were expected to weigh the opinions of competing expert appraisers, each side took pains to gain any advantage it could. Sympathy for the landowners was the defendants' ace in the hole. Establishing their clients' patriotic credentials became standard practice for the landowners' attorneys. Lybrand pointed out that Albert and Frank Weathersbee were World War II veterans, noting Albert's rank of commander in the U.S. Navy. In questioning his client, Dr. A. H. Corley, who was disputing the government's offer for two tracts of land totaling twelve hundred acres, Thurmond sought to establish his client's patriotic sacrifices.

> THURMOND: Doctor Corley, I noticed this morning that you appear somewhat disturbed. I just want to ask this question: Has that condition been brought about since the death of your son in the war?
> DOCTOR CORLEY: Yes.
> THURMOND: Have you been yourself since your son was killed?
> DOCTOR CORLEY: No, I haven't.

Thurmond implied that Corley had already made the ultimate sacrifice. Thurmond also established that Corley's remaining son, A. H. Corley Jr., was employed by the Veterans Administration in Washington and could not attend the trial because "his government duties prohibit it." Corley testified that he had bought one tract of land and had "improved it from time to time. In fact, I bought it for my two boys. . . . I wanted to make farmers out of them. Of course, they both got into the Army and one was killed." With Corley's agrarian dream gone, the family lived on the land during the summer for a few years.

> THURMOND: You had the boys working on the farm, I believe?
> CORLEY: That's right.
> THURMOND: I believe you are a believer in the old school of thought of letting the boys work?
> CORLEY: That's right.
> THURMOND: And putting them out on the farm is the finest place in the world to raise boys, isn't it?
> CORLEY: Mine did work. I had to work.

Corley also testified that many changes had occurred on the property since it had been taken over by the government, including the destruction of "those large pecan trees." Moreover, the government had "taken from the main building there in the front door. . . . It had a plate glass door in it. That plate glass has been taken out." Thurmond then clarified that the door was "heavy plate glass with beveled edges?"[79] Attorneys for residents achieved some measured success, but few locals would have agreed that any compensation approached the true value of the land. In their eyes, "fair market value" had little to do with anything they would call "fair." The entire process felt wrong.

Along with the construction of plant facilities, the project also required the development of new highways. A planned four-lane highway cut through a portion of John Shaw Billings's property, taking out "2 rows of pecans, [and cutting] through my beautiful stand of long leaf pines." He was distressed. The new highway threatened his substantial investment and promised to undermine his plan for retirement. "Redcliffe becomes less and less the quiet secluded place for us to retire to. Right here at Redcliffe is where the Russians hit me—square on my land. Joe Stalin himself is now my personal enemy. . . . Imagine a four-ply super-highway as a Redcliffe boundary! With this of course will come noise and exhaust fumes and housing development and heavy trucks and the threat of fire in my woods. God damn Stalin, the Russians and Communism!"[80] Billings's reaction to the impending road construction provides an especially instructive window into the project's complexity. His venom is wholly directed at Moscow—not federal authorities, not Du Pont—although the location and implementation of the Cold War project arose from those entities. Billings betrayed no desire to undermine his support for what he clearly considered a war effort. But like other landowners, Billings would nonetheless take issue with some details of the appraisal of his land.

The surveying of the Redcliffe proceeded with no information given to Billings or to his cousin, Harry Hammond, who oversaw affairs at Redcliffe in Billings's absence and who had applied for work as a property appraiser with the COE. Despite his excellent connections, even Hammond admitted to "a sort of helpless feeling about the whole thing."[81] Prior to the appraisal, he attended a public hearing before a five-member board from the state Highway Department, during which he provided great detail concerning the value of Billings's condemned property.[82] Billings ultimately was offered and accepted two thousand dollars for approximately eight acres of his land. According to Hammond, neighbors who had a larger portion of property condemned for the road—approximately forty-two acres collectively—received a total of two thousand dollars, and Hammond credited his appearance at the public hearing in Aiken with resulting in the greater valuation of Billings's land.[83] Billings's neighbors begged him to join in a suit against the government, but he declined.[84] Throughout the process, Harry Hammond's doggedness, experience, and connections, as well as the Hammond name itself, made the condemnation and seizure process less painful. One phone call to the chief of the state highway commission, whom Hammond described as "a personal friend," resulted in a cut-through in the planned highway that would ease access to and from Redcliffe. "The cut thru will be put anywhere I want it," he boasted.[85] Billings even found himself at a luncheon with Du Pont president Crawford H. Greenewalt, who had come to speak with *Time* editors.[86]

Omitted almost entirely from receiving compensation were sharecroppers and tenants, though their fates can occasionally be glimpsed in the legal documents. In his testimony at a trial in which he contested the government's appraisal and offer, Albert Weathersbee acknowledged that he had received a letter from the COE notifying him that the government needed to acquire his property no later than January 15, 1951. "When that [letter] was received, I showed it to all the tenants and all except one moved away immediately."[87] Fielding Foreman commented that the workers who populated the Cassels and Foreman farms likewise "moved all over" when the government seizure began, although Fielding's father, Arthur, moved the tenants' houses to a new location.[88] Sharecroppers and tenants sometimes received compensation for unharvested crops. Earl Roberson, a tenant on land owned by Clyburn Harley, was paid $87.78 for crops destroyed by construction.[89] Waldo K. Keenan was awarded $316 for "destruction of crops and loss of labor" related to a tract of land owned by D. C. Bush.[90] Tenants R. L. McLean, Nathaniel Bell, and Willie Stallings received $431 "as the estimated compensation for the taking of said crops" they had cultivated on the Weathersbees' property.[91] The majority of the nonlandowners were African Americans. A team of researchers from the University of North Carolina sent to survey the removal and relocation process noted in late 1951 that only "the families of those Negro wage-earners who could pay their way were among the few non-white families who appeared to have worked out moving plans."[92] Contemporary observers estimated that nearly three thousand landless blacks would be affected by the seizure. One reporter noted that their plight was worsened by the fact that "their life has been crimped into a vestigial pattern of paternal discrimination." Negro county agent T. A. Hammond worried about the fate of the sharecroppers and tenants. "Since this thing happened, fifteen or twenty different counties around have . . . sent requests in . . . for sharecroppers. I don't know whether these people will go. They're bewildered, used to depending entirely on the white landowners. They still don't believe that they won't be loaded into a truck by somebody and moved on somewhere else."[93] One of Arthur Foreman's tenants, a man named Snow, was surprised to return from a weekend away "to find his house missing from its foundation and well on its way to a new site."[94] Many of the displaced farmers hoped to get jobs in the new plant.[95] One tenant farmer hoped that his knowledge of the land would aid him: "I want to be the chauffeur for a government official," the man told a reporter for the New Yorker. "I know a good fishing hole to take him to."[96] But knowledge of the land was not prized in this new enterprise. One journalist noted, "The man who commands a knowledge of the valley's history and of its terrain and waters is sure to stand in well with his neighbors. To know indisputably where Mister Walker lived before he lived where he lives now, to be able to guide a skiff around a submerged stump in the swamp—these have been immeasurable assets."[97] But no longer. The people most intimately connected to the land, not simply aesthetically but practically, the people most likely to hold the soil daily in their hands, were in the weakest position to keep it from slipping through their fingers and the least likely to have any compensation placed into those hands.

Militarization and modernization of the region brought not only financial hardship but cultural loss. The magnitude of the events swirling around them began to register with all residents, and they moved from a concern for receiving just compensation for their property to a realization that they were about to lose a way of life that could not be bought, could not be replaced. Would they be able to replicate the intimate relationship to the land that they had developed over generations? Could that be replaced? Vester Smith, plant superintendent at the Leigh Banana Crate Company, was doubtful. "What am I gonna do with my [hunting] dogs? Why, take the eight of them together and they're worth some real money." He figured that most residents in the plant area likewise possessed valuables suited for a pastoral way of life. "Three hundred and seventy-five thousand dollars," he exclaimed. "That's what I figure it at, if you took all the hunting dogs, all the rifles and shotguns, all those good cypress-bottomed fishing boats that nobody but folks around here know how to make anyway. . . . That's for 1,500 families, figuring every man has a shotgun and a dog and a boat, a reel, and some tackle. Now . . . how is the government gonna pay us back for all that? Where else can we get the use of it that we've been getting around here? . . . [W]here is the government gonna find us swamps like these to hunt and fish in, another Boggy Gut, another Bailey's Pond?"[98] Smith's questions evoke the painful loss of cultural identity for those within and in proximity to the site. But they were rhetorical questions. No answers were forthcoming.

Despite the drawing of boundaries and the intense process of removal and relocation, many locals devised their own solutions and continued to use the land, in violation of federal proscriptions. Men and women wedded to rural ways continued to hunt in the site's woods and fish in its ponds and streams. In September 1951, agents of the Federal Alcohol Tax Unit arrested four men operating a five-hundred-gallon-a-day still within the confines of the project.[99] Dispossessed of their homes, residents of the condemned areas nevertheless continued to engage in traditional pursuits, just as their ancestors had, as modernity pushed in at them at every turn.

In addition to the approximately eight thousand living persons, the Corps of Engineers also had to evacuate nearly six thousand departed souls from the region's numerous graveyards and cemeteries, some of which dated back to the late eighteenth century.[100] The disinterment of their loved ones upset the residents greatly. Ellenton resident Marion Brinkley recalled his encounter with Lorena Stark, owner of the Blue Goose café, who took steps to conceal her parents' graves from the COE. She asked Brinkley, "Marion, what are you going to do 'bout your folks?" Brinkley replied, "Well, I guess I'm going to move them." Stark retorted, "Well, I'm not moving mine!" According to Brinkley, Stark "got a colored fella and they went back [to the grave site] and she dug a hole, pulled up the tombstones, and buried them." She later told Brinkley, "I'll guarantee you, they'll never find them." And she was right.[101] Stark kept her ancestors' graves in place, forever tied to the land. But others would be forever separated from that same land.

In less than two years, the region was entirely transformed. Between January 1951 and June 1952, the more than two hundred thousand acres of land desired by the AEC had been cleared of its permanent inhabitants. As bulldozers moved across the landscape, it was divested of its idiosyncratic architectural heritage. The landscape had been home to a great variety of vernacular architecture, some of which was more than two hundred years old. Someone driving along the dusty county roads was certain to spot I-houses, shotgun houses, hall-and-parlor houses, cottages, and bungalows. Photographs reveal scores of outbuildings—sheds, corncribs, privies—some sturdy and well built, some ramshackle.[102] A few buildings within the plant's borders were preserved and used by plant personnel; others were moved by their owners; the rest were razed. Highways were lined with tractor trailers pulling uprooted houses on their way to Aiken, or Jackson, or Williston, or New Ellenton. Small towns that had once been full of life now were ghost towns, occupied only by hungry cats and dogs that had been left behind.[103]

While the procedure for assessing and acquiring the property within the site's boundaries was judicially defined, no similarly clear and consistent line of federal responsibility existed for the removal and resettlement of the displaced population. Those who wished to move their homes to new locations were responsible for contracting with movers and covering the expense.[104] The Farmers Home Administration of the Department of Agriculture set up a relocation center in Aiken but employed only one relocation agent—who was preoccupied with his own relocation efforts.[105] The Farmers Home Administration ultimately provided assistance to fewer than fifty displaced families.[106] South Carolina county agents likewise worked to compile information on available farmland and farm employment.[107] The sums dispossessed persons received for their property often were insufficient to set them up elsewhere, leaving many with few palatable options. One farmer exasperated by the process complained that "I didn't have enough [money] to buy a new piece of land until after I knew how much I'd get for the appraisal. They appraised the neighbors on my right, and the same day they appraised the folks on my left, but they passed me right by. So here I sit. I can't buy any land and all the good land is being bought up every day." Many residents acknowledged that despite their willingness to give up their homes as their patriotic duty, they expected something in return. One woman told a team of investigators, "I'll move now and I'd move again if our country needs it. But it does seem that they could be helping us out more since we didn't ask for this."[108]

Most residents stayed within the region, moving to existing communities such as Aiken and Jackson. Others created new communities. Many of Ellenton's former residents—120 black and 30 white families—created the town of New Ellenton, roughly two miles north of the plant perimeter on South Carolina Highway 19, which connects the town with Aiken. New Ellenton was constructed hastily in the wake of the announcement of the plant's location. According to the University of North Carolina researchers surveying the area in the early 1950s, "Immediately following the plant announcement, several of the business leaders of old Ellenton . . . began to acquire extensive land holdings along Highway 19, in a portion of what had been known as the Talatha settlement just outside the announced plant boundary. These men began to push for development of this site as a place where old Ellentonians could relocate their homes, where newcomers could park their trailers, and where business could prosper."[109] Despite problems with the soil and groundwater conditions, which held "little promise of yielding an adequate supply of water for any sizable growth in the embryo town," the group pushed ahead with the development. Although promoters called New Ellenton a planned community merely because it had been laid out on a gridiron pattern, the layout of the town gave no thought to topography: "The gridiron pattern was bulldozed into the hills and the street pattern took shape without regard to grades, drainage, soil erosion, or aesthetics."[110]

Ellenton's housing patterns had developed over decades and bore the racial patchwork quality of many rural communities, with no hard-and-fast demarcations between white neighborhoods and black. Not so with New Ellenton, which was created with racially segregated housing areas. One official from the National Urban League investigating employment and housing opportunities for African Americans as a result of the new Cold War enterprise in their midst noted this unfortunate feature of New Ellenton: "Black families set up along one side of the highway, whites on the opposite." Moreover, substandard living conditions characterized the black area: "Ramshackle shacks removed at great cost from the project site, outhouses, communal water pumps and wells, and outside boiling pots for clothes."[111] Groups of houses were served by a single water faucet, and severe soil erosion cut away usable portions of lots and created ruts in streets in some places while clogging them with sand elsewhere.[112] Those black tenants who were "moved" by the landowners for whom they worked faced a scarcity of housing far more drastic than that for whites. One historian notes that "new developments refused to sell to blacks or banished them to the least desirable property. Even then, few could afford the rising prices."[113] The federal acquisition program created two small communities. The Hollow Creek section about six miles west of New Ellenton, and Zion's Fair, a settlement north and west of New Ellenton, became home to concentrations of African American households, the majority of which had been moved from the plant area.[114] "Founded in part because of the barriers to land ownership in more prime locations and a desire to be 'somewhat independent of whites,' the communities ultimately could not escape racism. State and county authorities denied them incorporation and, thereby, eligibility for federal or state assistance desperately needed to provide the most rudimentary public services."[115] As one longtime resident caustically observed, "New Ellenton was the only town created with a slum already in place."[116]

The last of the land suits was settled on April 1, 1958, when Violet Green Cone of Charleston received payment for her 118 acres of land. Over seven years, the federal government had acquired more than seventeen hundred individual tracts, for which it paid more than seventeen million dollars. Most landowners accepted the government's offer on their property and moved on; others did not go so quietly. The government filed 696 condemnation suits, 251 of which went to trial and 445 of which were settled out of court.[117] Landowners could delay but not stop the inevitable. In the end, under the principle of eminent domain, the federal government would win.

Remnants of rural culture continued to rub up against this new conception of land use. Residents of the region abutting the plant regularly trespassed on plant territory to hunt, fish, graze stock, run stills, and cut wood. Trespassing remained a concern because of the potential for fires, risk to government-owned property, and interference by trespassers with certain scientific field studies.[118] Such anecdotal forays into the once-favored landscape did nothing to subvert the overriding reality. It was gone, all of it.

A TOWN DIES

I stood on a hill against the evening sky
Watching the town of Ellenton die.
Smaller and smaller it grew till at last
I knew it would soon belong to the past

Faces of men were of a hopeless resignation
To a fate which could promise no reconciliation.
Among the women was a strange hesitation
Betraying wounds of deep penetration.

Boys and girls, with their homes uprooted
Seemed to feel their lives had been looted
Of precious values they could never regain
Sad yet restless, they showed the strain

Even the dogs and cats seemed to wonder
Why their town was being torn asunder

Eyeing their owners with curious stares
They seemed at times on the verge of tears

A few buildings remain empty and bare
Streets are deserted, windblown, without care.
Vacant lots now blend with the fields.
A reminder of the power the Government wields

Churches are the same, with no less to give
But their members have gone elsewhere to live
So, empty, quiet and still they will be
Probably for eternity.

Ellenton is a town no more!!
I saw bulldozers push until they tore
Stately trees from out their chine
Victims of the march of Time.[119]

CHAPTER FOUR

"Bigger'n Any Lie"
Building the Bomb Plant

Pondering the vast construction project under way in rural South Carolina, one local reporter speculated breathlessly on its engineering and technological implications as well as its historical meaning. "The Plant is a Clark Hill dam, a Panama Canal, an Egyptian pyramid, and television," he wrote, "all rolled into one enormous package that means the future of America."[1] While overblown, the description conveyed a certain truth: the plant was an engineering and technological marvel. Nearly four times the size of Oak Ridge National Laboratory, the Savannah River Plant (SRP) was the largest construction project to date in American history.[2] The plant's physical requirements were vast. The project called for the construction of "nine integrated industrial plants" and included "research and development laboratories and process and service buildings for producing heavy water, deuterium, plutonium, tritium, and special products." Also required on-site were nuclear reactors, separations canyons, power plants, cooling basins, waste tanks, and administrative and ancillary buildings. The initial plans for the site involved only two nuclear reactors. However, after the outbreak of the Korean conflict, the number was increased to five. The final plans called for close to 250 separate structures.[3] The ultimate price tag: a staggering $1.3 billion.

The SRP was administered by both the federal government and Du Pont Corporation. The federal government owned the property and set policy. The Atomic Energy Commission (AEC) provided the overall supervision and direction of the project.[4] Du Pont designed, constructed, and operated the facilities that eventually would produce heavy water, fissionable and fusionable materials, and other products. The internal organization scheme and division of responsibility used by Du Pont was substantially that used in its commercial business and its previous war work. With Du Pont in charge, the construction

Figure 10. Construction administration area, early 1950s. Even from the air,
photographing the entire plant site is impossible. The whimsical pinwheel-shaped
buildings belie the deadly materials produced at the plant. Photograph courtesy of
Savannah River Site Cold War Historic Preservation Program.

and operation of the plant became a truly national endeavor. Du Pont sub-contracted with more than seventy-five different companies and purchased materials from more than four thousand firms nationwide.[5]

Basic construction materials began arriving on site on November 29, 1950, the day after the plant's location was announced. The nation's abundant natural resources were called into service to this new Cold War enterprise in capacities that boggled the mind. The amount of earth moved, the number of board feet used, the tonnage of steel consumed—all were cause for wonder. The AEC regularly astounded the public with figures to convey the enormity of the project: 80 million board feet of lumber; 126,000 railroad carloads of materials; 118,000 tons of reinforcing steel; 1.5 million cubic yards of concrete; 26,000 tons of structural steel; 85 miles of underground water lines; 82 miles of permanent railroads. AEC officials often illustrated the plant's immensity by converting these figures into commonplace examples designed to make them more comprehensible: "The 1.5 million cubic yards of concrete to be poured is enough to lay a sidewalk six feet wide and six inches thick from Savannah, Georgia, to San Diego, California." Or, "The 80 million board feet of lumber required could build 15,385 houses, enough to house a town of more than 46,000 people."[6] "The 126,000 carloads of materials required would, if placed in a single giant train, reach from Atlanta, Georgia, to the Pennsylvania Railroad Station in New York City. The 2,000,000 blueprints required is equivalent to a roll of paper 24 inches wide and would reach from Atlanta, Georgia to Seattle, Washington."[7] A local sharecropper contemplating the vastness of the project commented, "You can't tell no lie about this thing. This thing is bigger'n any lie."[8] Using images of postwar prosperity, modernity, and nation building, the AEC imbued the nuclear project with prosperity and growth while simultaneously asserting a sense of normalcy and everyday life. The SRP was the golden spike for the Cold War era.

What had once been a sleepy rural backwater overnight became a beehive of construction activity. Harry Hammond observed that the country road running through Billings's property "was crowded with trucks, dozens of workmen, tractors with drag lines, enormous gasoline steam shovels, and dozens more workmen."[9] Locals marveled at the dramatic changes to the landscape.[10] Harry Hammond wrote excitedly to Billings, "If you were here you would spend two thirds of your time watching the road machinery at work—eating down a hill and spilling it into a hollow. . . . One machine moves a three foot in diameter pine as if it were a match."[11] Watching the transformation of the land gave Hammond a "feeling of unrealness." "Like Alice," he noted, he felt that he had "stepped thru the Looking Glass."[12] Billings's uncle, Henry C. Hammond, former South Carolina Superior Court judge, was less enamored of the changes to the landscape as a result of what he termed the "major forest and earth operation." He believed that a project of such enormity that ultimately would create a weapon of untold destructive power could bring only trouble: "My personal view of this great undertaking grows darker every hour. It seems we have inlisted under a banner of predestined defeat."[13]

Changes to the earth itself were enough to give one pause, the operation so immense and transformative that only military metaphors would suffice. One observer described how "battalions of snorting earthmovers plunged into the fields. They ripped through swamp gum thickets that had sheltered some of the finest turkey and partridge coverts in the East, churned the rich red clay into a lifeless desert. Huge huts sprung up, weird cylindrical towers rose against the horizon."[14] The natural terrain gave way to a modern, militaristic landscape, but chroniclers searching for the right words to describe the process reverted back to the imagery and language of the natural world. The depth of wonder the plant's construction caused among local residents was surpassed only by their awe at the astounding speed of change. Trees felled by construction workers were replaced by "forests of huge tanks stretching into the sky."[15] The destruction of all that they had known and loved presented perhaps much more of an emotional challenge to residents than the financial and patriotic concerns. A landscape that they had considered full of life was being turned into a lifeless, secret world. It was hard to take. Ellenton resident Mike Cassels told a reporter for the *New York Times* that "so much has been happening around here that many nights I didn't know whether to take three slugs of gin, an aspirin, or go to prayer meeting."[16]

The natural resources mustered for the project were equaled only by the human resources required to construct the site. Du Pont and AEC officials estimated that more than thirty-five thousand temporary workers would be required to build the massive facility, while more than six thousand permanent personnel ultimately would operate the plant and make the region their new home. Thousands of potential workers flocked to Aiken and Augusta, crowding into employment service offices, drawn by rumors of project wages as high as seven dollars an hour.[17] The flood of new faces aggravated some of the locals.

Harry Hammond described the various blue-collar workers as "horrible look-ing creatures" who were "arriving in droves with no idea in the world when they will be put to work. The Salvation Army is having to care for some of them as they are absolutely penniless. They are disgusting and overbearing."[18] The influx of workers, the changes in landscape, left the self-proclaimed "slow going, country boy" deeply conflicted. "The quiet, lazy way of life has been completely changed. I don't like it, in one way, and—in another, it is making for progress. Whether that is good or bad remains to be seen."[19]

Across the region and the nation, observers speculated on the social and political changes that most certainly would accompany this latest Cold War venture. The urgency of the project and its voracious labor requirements in-troduced competing agendas and concerns as various groups struggled to as-sert their claims in the new and untested landscape. The plant's labor needs threatened to drain workers from local markets, which historically had been dominated by low-wage jobs in textiles and agriculture. The plant's con-struction would require the labor of tens of thousands of skilled and unskilled workers, and unions would certainly play an important role in labor recruit-ment. Construction workers might stay on the job for years and relocate per-manently to the region. How would that influx affect the region's states' rights politics? A large, unionized labor force might introduce liberal politics more in line with the national Democratic Party into a region that was decidedly conservative.

African Americans saw in the SRP an opportunity for advancement and hoped to use the Cold War crisis to their advantage. The plant's labor needs could not be met solely by white workers. Led by national civil rights organiza-tions, local blacks looked cautiously to the plant for economic salvation. Prom-inent organizations such as the National Urban League (NUL) and the National Association for the Advancement of Colored People (NAACP) regarded the SRP as the tip of the spear in their fair employment campaigns. Civil rights activ-ists descended on the region in late 1950, seeking to leverage the tremendous labor needs and recent federal antidiscrimination hiring initiatives to open up economic opportunities. Civil rights leaders couched their demands in the new language of national security, arguing that the failure to use African American workers at a moment of national emergency was dangerous and irresponsible. In addition, employment discrimination made for poor publicity abroad.

Civil rights supporters' demands were countered by the Du Pont Corpora-tion. A profoundly conservative company that saw its history and that of the nation as forever linked, Du Pont used the project's urgency as an argument against changing social patterns. The speed with which the plant had to be built also permitted the federal government to give lip service to antidiscrimination employment provisions and to rely on Du Pont's tepid assurances of fair hiring practices. Had existing and new government statutes been enforced, the door to African American advancement could have been kicked open. Instead, the Cold War emergency allowed Du Pont's corporate culture to predominate and to blunt most opportunities the plant offered for promoting rapid social change.

Large-scale hiring for the construction of the SRP began almost immediately after the plant's location was announced. Six months into the project, the AEC and Du Pont were hiring more than one hundred construction workers per day, and the frantic pace continued for almost a year.[20] Meeting the tremendous labor needs and tight construction schedule posed a number of serious obstacles for Du Pont and the AEC. The construction of the plant would require thousands of skilled carpenters, painters, cement finishers, electricians, plumbers, truck drivers, heavy equipment operators, and construction engineers as well a virtual army of common laborers.[21] Labor needs were complicated by the outbreak of the Korean War, with increased draft quotas and the recalling of commissioned and reserve personnel. The demand for common laborers aggravated an ongoing shortage in farm labor.[22]

AEC and Du Pont officials had to weigh conflicting demands. On the one hand, if the SRP offered higher wages than those offered by the region's traditional employers, it would drain the local labor supply; however, low wages would make it impossible to attract anyone from outside the area, and local people could not supply the plant's labor needs. Moreover, recruitment from outside the immediate area would result in massive in-migration that would burden already-inadequate community facilities.[23] Local industry leaders— particularly textile manufacturers, building contractors, and employers of farm labor—expressed great concern about wage rates and labor shortages.[24] Harry Hammond wrote indignantly to Billings that "backwoods ignoramus poor white trash in the [area near the plant site], persons who have done nothing but eke out a bare existence, are now working as laborers at the sand and gravel company and making $150.00 a WEEK, with overtime."[25] Employers worried about their ability to continue exploiting cheap, unskilled labor. R. K. Mason, local project manager for Du Pont, tried to assuage fears of labor pirating and announced that the company "would make an effort to discourage employing personnel from local industry without first securing release from their former employers."[26] Samuel Swint, president of the Graniteville Company, received regular updates from the AEC Savannah River Operations Office regarding its employment requirements and wages.[27] In February 1951, the Department of Labor noted that the technical nature of the work involved and the large number of skilled workers needed required the use of Atlanta wage rates at the plant to recruit the necessary workers.[28] Du Pont's wages remained consistently above those mandated by the Davis-Bacon Act, a 1931 federal law that required the federal government to pay no less than the prevailing wage on all federal construction projects.[29] For many unskilled workers in the region, therefore, giving up farmwork for even a common laborer's position at the plant was a vertical move. Rodman Lemon, president of the Barnwell Peanut Company, expressed concerns about the complete disruption of farm labor, although he noted that farm products were fetching higher prices than in the past and that many farm families had made money by taking in boarders.[30]

With nearly five thousand employees, the Graniteville Company, the region's largest employer, fell "directly within the shadow" of the SRP. Swint was particularly concerned about how the plant would affect his company's access to labor. What would it mean, Swint asked, to have "the most gigantic construction project of all time, breathing down its neck"?[31] Two weeks after the announcement of the plant, Swint telephoned the president of Cherokee Textile Mills in Knoxville, Tennessee, some twenty miles from Oak Ridge, to ask what he could anticipate in terms of competition. A. G. Heinsohn told Swint to expect severe difficulties during the peak of construction but encouraged him to remind his employees that "for the long pull they will be much better off sticking to their present permanent job than they would be by accepting a temporary job which at most could last only a couple of years."[32]

Perhaps acting on Heinsohn's advice, the Graniteville Company undertook a public relations campaign designed to keep its workers inside the textile plant gates. The company advertised in the area's newspapers, stressing its family nature and benefits package. Featuring long-term employees and their families, the advertisements heralded Graniteville's benefits and "steady work . . . all good reasons why so many people have been with Graniteville Company for such a long time."[33] The ads drew on Graniteville Company's one-hundred-plus years in the region and cast the SRP as untested and risky.[34] In a 1952

Figure 11. Construction workers attending a mandatory safety meeting, 1952. The vast size of the construction crew necessitated outdoor meetings using a public address system. Photograph courtesy of Savannah River Site Cold War Historic Preservation Program.

Figure 12. Shift change during the construction phase, early 1950s. Photograph courtesy of Savannah River Site Cold War Historic Preservation Program.

address to stockholders, Swint complained that since the arrival of the SRP, the Graniteville Company had suffered increased labor turnover and that new hires were less skilled than those in the past.[35] Although the pay rates for un- skilled labor at the Graniteville Company and at the SRP were roughly compa- rable, skilled workers at the SRP made wages more than 50 percent higher than those offered by the Graniteville Company, with the additional opportunity for overtime.[36] Swint appealed to Governor James Byrnes for help with keep- ing plant wage rates in line with local rates.[37] Swint kept track of the number of employees lost to the plant, and although that figure had reached only 275 by November 1955, he foresaw that new generations of white workers from the valley would now enjoy greater employment options.[38]

Local agricultural employers were particularly concerned about the flight of low-paid black labor. One irate farmer wrote to Senator Burnet Maybank complaining of the impact on wage rates and black workers: "Three Negroes, who have been with us all their lives, have quit, and are getting more for a week than we could pay for a month."[39] The town councils of Allendale and Fairfax feared the destruction of "agricultural interests" as their farm laborers left to pursue employment at the SRP.[40] Their fears were well founded. Although the wage rates for common laborers at the construction site were below prevailing union rates in other southeastern cities, they were substantially above local agricultural wages. Even in positions where pay was comparable with what local industry offered, the SRP provided the opportunity for overtime at time and a half, something unheard of in the agricultural sector. In the fall of 1951, farmers reported widespread shortages of cotton pickers, forcing employers to raise wages. The situation at times opened up new opportunities for those further down the labor ladder. One Augusta brick maker began employing African American women to avoid paying his male employees more. Black women working at the factory could earn about seven dollars a day, a substan- tial increase over the twelve dollars they earned each week for domestic work.[41]

But the promise of higher wages was not always sufficient to draw farm laborers from the fields. Recruiters for the SRP cited transportation costs as a major obstacle to satisfying project labor needs. Local buses could not take workers as close to their particular work areas as they needed to be, and car- pools cut into wage gains. Some potential employees stayed away because of the frequent accidents on overcrowded highways, while others cited union membership fees as a reason to stay with their current employers.[42] Employ- ers also used threats and coercion to control their laborers. Black farm wage workers and sharecroppers told one NAACP investigator that their employers threatened to fire them or displace them from their land if they filed applications for work on the site.[43] Monsignor George Lewis Smith, pastor of the St. Mary Help of Christians Parish and the Aiken Missions, told NUL officials that white employers of African American tenants, gardeners, and domestic and personal servants "are prepared to resist the movement of any significant number of Negroes into these new jobs which will pay from $2.00 an hour up."[44] He did not specify what form this resistance would take.

The majority of the skilled construction personnel came from outside the plant's fifty-mile "commuting area," although most workers employed on the site during the construction phase were from the Southeast. By November 1951, the project had drained the region of skilled white labor, and Du Pont began to recruit workers from across the country. To fill the gap, the SRP relied on what the *Atlanta Constitution* called "a new kind of migratory worker"—carpenters, electricians, steel workers, and masons "who have been towing their trailers with their wives and children from one big project to another, back and forth across the country" since 1941. "The wives like trailer camp life fine: its adventure, neighborliness, simplicity, and low cost." When asked whether the crowded conditions bred arguments, one wife responded, "Now, mister, those wheels are round. Anybody that doesn't like it here can just roll on somewhere else."[45] Ira Henry Freeman of the *New York Times* had a more derogatory term for these skilled workers: "high-caste Okie[s]."[46] Du Pont recruited the majority of these new migrant laborers through the building trades unions, which was the most expeditious means of obtaining skilled labor. According to union statistics, more than 90 percent of all building trades workers belonged to American Federation of Labor (AFL) unions, so recruitment through the unions was customary for large construction jobs. A few exceptions occurred. For example, between twenty and thirty displaced residents from Ellenton had been employed without union membership. One year after the announcement of the plant, well into the construction phase, twelve of nineteen internationals affiliated with the AFL were represented on the SRP. Most of the locals were located in Augusta, which had several highly organized unions: the carpenters (local chartered in 1899); bricklayers (1899); plumbers (1908); electricians (1948); and painters (1950). Outside of Augusta—for example, in Aiken—union organization was virtually nonexistent. Union rolls for truck drivers (teamsters), laborers, and operating engineers rose sharply during the first year of construction. Many of these first-time union members came from rural sections of South

Figure 13. The Savannah River Plant under construction, early 1950s. Photograph courtesy of Savannah River Site Cold War Historic Preservation Program.

Carolina, where labor council recruitment efforts had been vigorous. But these new union members seemed unlikely to become a political factor of any consequence, floating in and out of membership. They often failed to meet their union obligations after paying the ten-dollar initiation fee: roughly two-thirds of laborers were delinquent on dues within one year. The Teamsters reported the same fluidity in union membership, noting that unfamiliarity with union discipline and organization, illiteracy, and higher-than-average wages posed obstacles to long-term union growth.[47]

The project's spiraling cost and the recruitment of thousands of workers through unions rankled conservatives. In August 1951, Congressman William McDonald "Don" Wheeler of Georgia visited the site incognito to investigate reports of wasted manpower and allegations that jobs at the site could be obtained only through labor racketeers who charged exorbitant fees and perpetrated fraud through union kickbacks. Disguising himself as a common laborer in overalls, brogans, and a khaki shirt, Wheeler blended in with the construction crew and spent a day roaming around the project.[48] Claiming to have witnessed "loafing on the job, wasted manpower, feather-bedding and labor union racketeering," Wheeler demanded a full-scale congressional investigation.[49] In particular, Wheeler charged that the Du Pont was violating the Labor-Management Relations Act (the Taft-Hartley Act), which was passed by Congress in 1947 over President Harry S. Truman's veto and which severely restricted the activities of organized labor. Among other provisions, the act made it illegal to run a closed shop.[50]

When asked about Wheeler's accusations during testimony before an unrelated House Appropriations Subcommittee hearing in October 1951, AEC general manager M. W. Boyer scoffed. Boyer contended that by Wheeler's own admission, he had not gained access to secure construction areas but "more or less looked through the fence." Subcommittee chair Albert Thomas of Texas stipulated that "a man can see through the fence whether men are working or not," to which Boyer replied, "He cannot see over 200,000 acres."[51]

Wheeler's charges were echoed by Leslie Gould and Emanuel Doernberg, reporters with the *New York Journal-American*, who published a series of articles about union involvement in the plant. Doernberg mimicked Wheeler's ruse, donning overalls and posing first as a truck driver and then as a mechanic in an attempt to secure employment. Doernberg alleged that other workers repeatedly told him, "Don't waste your time applying for a job at the plant, go to the union hall, you'll wind up there anyhow."[52] Wheeler's and Doernberg's accusations were countered by Ray Shockley, state news editor for the *Augusta Chronicle*, who visited every area of the plant with the full cooperation of the AEC and Du Pont. He disputed Wheeler's claims, pointing out that "the Congressman could not have viewed the areas where the work is really going on because he was never issued a pass" and did not have an official escort. Shockley praised Du Pont's construction efforts, noting that the company "employ[s] the same systems of economy and efficiency on this project that it uses in its plants all over the nation."[53]

Area labor leaders roundly criticized Wheeler's "stunt." W. M. Tanner, business agent for a laborers' local, lambasted the congressman's "cheap publicity" designed to "create dissention and agitation in the country's most important defense project."[54] For its part, Du Pont claimed that Wheeler never completed a job application. Also, although Wheeler reported that the head of the carpenters' local had told him the initiation fee was $108, the fee was actually $50. Du Pont learned from confidential sources in the Augusta business community that the notoriously antilabor congressman was an "irresponsible" publicity seeker and that he had little power in Congress.[55] Du Pont officials also determined that several of Wheeler's first, second, and third cousins were employed at the plant site, where they had work ratings ranging from "satisfactory" to "very favorable." Du Pont confirmed that Doernberg had indeed applied for a position as a carpenter but found that when officials checked his work history, it had been falsified.[56]

Wheeler then returned to the plant site, where Du Pont and AEC personnel offered him a tour of the project. Wheeler refused, an action that one Du Pont official felt demonstrated that the congressman preferred bashing the unions to gathering facts.[57] Despite serious questions regarding Wheeler's methods and motives, the issue of waste and corruption at the plant had gained political traction. In early November 1951, a subcommittee of the House Committee on Education and Labor opened hearings to investigate Wheeler's charges. Headed by Representative Graham A. Barden of North Carolina, the committee subpoenaed twenty-one different AFL unions as well as several Du Pont and government officials. The hearings focused on allegations that Du Pont, the AEC, the U.S. Employment Service, and the labor unions had conspired to operate a closed shop.[58] The investigation of the nation's largest federal project amid the country's first military engagement of the Cold War gave the hearing a heightened sense of importance. Barden established a context in which union membership was painted as somehow unpatriotic and a national security risk.

Tying the construction of the plant to the ongoing war in Asia, Barden stated solemnly that the purpose of the hearing was to make certain "that the father of some boy in Korea might not be turned away at the gate for lack of a union card" and characterized the construction of the plant as "just as serious business as the boys in Korea are carrying on at the expense of 2,000 or 3,000 lives per week."[59]

Curtis A. Nelson, manager of the Savannah River Operations Office of the AEC, was the committee's first witness, and his testimony took all of the first day of the hearings. Not to be outflanked on the issue of national security, Nelson drove immediately to the heart of the matter, declaring that "the urgency of the construction work being performed at the Savannah River plant is of critical importance to the common defense and security of the Nation" and that "the very nature of the project has necessitated an extremely tight and compelling construction schedule." He clarified the relationship between the AEC and Du Pont, pointing out that "atomic-energy plants are not constructed and operated by the Government directly, with all workers Government employees, but by American industry operating with a maximum of responsibility delegated within a broad framework established by the Commission." Nelson noted that "when we contracted with [Du Pont], we bought their industrial know-how, including their personnel policies [and] industrial relations policies," which included their use of unions to recruit a large labor force. He emphasized that neither the AEC nor Du Pont "could meet its responsibility for manning the Savannah River job without resort to the unions as a primary source of labor supply." Granville M. Read, Du Pont's chief engineer, vigorously denied the allegation that Du Pont had an agreement with the craft unions to hold non-union employment to a token level of one hundred workers and bluntly told the committee, "We can't pour concrete and attend investigations." According to Read, "In the last two months we have had a total of eight overlapping investigating groups, either official or unofficial, occupying the time of our top people on this project." Senator Brien McMahon of Connecticut, chair of the Joint Congressional Committee on Atomic Energy, lampooned the hearings, declaring, "Investigations won't build plants.... I want the United States to build a hydrogen bomb before anyone else does."[60]

All officials from Du Pont and the AEC who came before the committee denied any collusion with the unions to create a closed shop. They likewise denied the existence of a work-permit system, whereby a job applicant was not permitted to join a union but had to pay money to the union to work on the job. Trumball Blake, an assistant manager in Du Pont's construction division, stated categorically that Du Pont did not hire solely union labor, although he did not know—and did not want to know—exactly how many union workers Du Pont hired. Other officials testified that they had made it clear to the unions that they planned to hire a certain number of nonunion craftsmen, although they could not agree on what the number was. The head of the local electrical workers' union stated that he referred nonunion men to the site. The congressmen were particularly interested in the degree of growth of union membership and how this growth affected union coffers.[61]

In the end, the committee was unable to prove collusion among the unions and Du Pont and the AEC; however, the hearings also appeared to show that Du Pont was doing just enough to stay on the right side of the Taft-Hartley Act. The subcommittee delivered its report in July 1952, concluding that a preferential hiring system for manual labor existed at the SRP and that prior to the project's opening, Du Pont and the unions had reached a verbal agreement under which Du Pont notified the unions of the number and type of employees needed and gave the unions adequate time to recruit and refer the workers. In addition, the committee report charged that Du Pont failed to use any other source to obtain workers. The subcommittee found that during the hearings, "Du Pont officials made studied attempts to confuse the facts of the situation, evade direct and pertinent questions, and generally mislead the subcommittee." Furthermore, Du Pont officials regarded the subcommittee with a "very thinly veiled arrogance." The AEC either knew the facts regarding Du Pont's employment practices and approved those policies or was negligent in not finding out the full facts. Either way, the subcommittee found that the AEC had failed in its oversight responsibilities and that the AEC and Du Pont had demonstrated utter disregard of the "fundamental rights" of American citizens to "seek and obtain employment in whatever field they may be qualified." The report recommended that "this and similar situations can and should be corrected immediately."[62] Du Pont and the AEC essentially ignored the committee's report, which, in the end, amounted to a congressional hand slap.

Despite the lack of punishment, concerns about organized labor's influence in the region abounded. Antiunion forces in particular feared the political impact of thousands of unionized workers and their families converging on the conservative southern state. In a series of articles that appeared in papers across the region, King Features Syndicate columnist Leslie Gould elaborated on the potential political impact of the influx of skilled workers: "South Carolina is the heart of the anti-Truman, anti–New Deal States' Rights movement. With the presidency at stake next year, an influx of 40,000 workers, plus one or two votes in each worker's family, could make South Carolina safe for Truman and also recapture for the New Deal control of the State Democratic machine. After 1952, the 6,000 permanent employees in the plant could give the New Deal forces 12,000 to 18,000 new votes."[63] Gould saw a definite attempt by organized labor and liberal democrats to violate federal laws, enrich the unions, and further the Truman administration's war on southern states'-rights conservatives. The *Columbia State* gave credence to Gould's four-part investigative series, barely concealing its contempt for the politicization of the working class. It disdainfully repeated a story of a grocer in a community within commuting distance of the plant who claimed "he had cashed checks running to upwards of $100 weekly for a fellow who had never worked in his life."[64] For southern conservatives and employers used to exploiting the region's vast unskilled labor pool, it was bad enough that unskilled laborers were making a living wage; far more serious was the possibility that they might become politicized.

Much to the relief of states'-rights conservatives, the nightmare of a politically active and liberal workforce slavishly devoted to the national Democratic Party never materialized. The construction phase, though intense and requiring tens of thousands of workers, was simply too brief for real political change to become a reality. As the project shifted to the operations phase, the vast majority of the unionized construction force moved on to the next project, the next town. The greater potential for regional change lay with the possible employment of thousands of African Americans at the SRP. The site's projected personnel needs signaled great opportunities for African American employment. The nation's two largest civil rights organizations, the NAACP and the NUL, immediately demanded equal employment opportunities for blacks at the site. Dedicated to addressing the economic, social, and political needs of blacks who moved to northern cities during the Great Migration, the NUL fought employment discrimination through education, persuasion, diplomacy, and subtle public pressure. More comfortable in corporate boardrooms than on the streets, the NUL "viewed itself as both an adviser and a partner to corporate America in the campaign for fair employment."[65]

Both civil rights organizations used the heightening tensions of the Cold War and the workforce needs of the nation's expanding military-industrial complex to their advantage. The NUL undertook a defense mobilization program following the outbreak of the Korean War and made the SRP the program's centerpiece. Harold O. DeWitt, NUL's industrial relations secretary, called the Savannah River project "one of the biggest jobs in industrial relations ever undertaken by the National Urban League or any of its fifty-eight affiliates." He repeatedly urged the organization to put more resources into opening opportunities at the SRP. This approach made good economic sense; given its size, focusing on the SRP would accomplish "more good for more people." The NAACP likewise made fair employment within the federal government and its contractors a top priority in 1949.[66]

Leaders of both groups took every opportunity to draw a connection between racial discrimination and the national security state. Clarence Mitchell of the NAACP warned that "many colored people have regarded the Atom bomb as a new device for maintaining white supremacy. It is easy for such ideas to flourish and spread when the colored citizens of the United States are shut off from full identification with Atomic Energy developments" through discriminatory hiring practices. Another NUL official warned that racial discrimination at a defense site would illustrate "a callous disregard . . . for obtaining the maximum utilization of the nation's manpower to stem the advance of Communist imperialism and slavery."[67] Speaking specifically about the SRP, Mitchell warned that the new plant "must not be handicapped by the petty prejudices of South Carolina."[68]

In fighting for equal employment opportunities at the SRP, the civil rights organizations were not entirely starting from scratch. For nearly a decade, the federal government had specifically forbidden its contractors to discriminate based on race, creed, color, or national origin. Antidiscrimination requirements originated with President Franklin D. Roosevelt's creation of the Fair Employment Practices Commission by executive order in 1941 and continued with Truman. In 1948, Truman signed Executive Order 9980, which forbade employment discrimination "within the federal establishment."[69] Although the plant's operation was managed by a private sector corporation, the overall complex fell under the AEC's auspices, thus making it a federal facility subject to Executive Order 9980. The success of the most recent fair employment provision resulted from federal officials' willingness to enforce its provisions.

The history of fair employment at federal atomic installations did not instill confidence. Julius Thomas, the NUL's director of industrial relations, was hopeful that the AEC would not repeat mistakes made at the Oak Ridge and Hanford atomic sites, where racial discrimination was rampant.[70] Despite their skill level and experience, he noted, African Americans at Oak Ridge "were assigned the most menial and unskilled tasks—as common laborers, janitors, and domestic workers." Thomas complained, "Blacks were ineligible for transfers to higher paying job categories or for promotion by the companies at Oak Ridge and were often discriminated against for skilled construction or production jobs." Even as Oak Ridge converted to peacetime conditions, black employment opportunities remained limited.[71] Hanford's racial record was equally dismal. Using pressing deadlines as an excuse, officials housed blacks in segregated quarters, defying the guidelines of the U.S. Fair Employment Practices Commission.[72] Given the precedent established at the Manhattan Project facilities, the NAACP and NUL demanded that all job classifications be opened to black applicants and that African Americans be placed in strategic employment positions before segregated hiring patterns became fixed. Civil rights activists knew that once African Americans had been excluded from certain jobs, it would be harder to reverse the tide.

NUL and NAACP officials focused on both the construction and operation phases of employment. Opportunities existed not only for persons in the skilled trades and for general labor during the plant's construction phase but, more important, for white-collar positions when the plant went on line. If blacks could acquire professional and semiprofessional positions on the operation staff, Mitchell argued, the plant could "completely revolutionize living conditions in this part of the South."[73]

Despite existing federal antidiscrimination initiatives, the civil rights activists faced a daunting task. They were operating in an environment where the job market was highly stratified by race. In the four-county area surrounding the plant, African Americans were employed primarily in agriculture and in domestic service. The region's major industry—textiles—was almost exclusively white. Changing this labor culture would be difficult, requiring persistence on the part of activists and a receptive audience at Du Pont and the AEC.

The NAACP directed its activities through its local branch and statewide organization. The NUL, which lacked a local branch, was at somewhat of a disadvantage and used its Southern Regional Office in Atlanta to orchestrate activities in South Carolina. A sense of competition and territoriality existed between the two groups. The NUL's Thomas noted that the NAACP "got the jump on us with this operation" and urged his organization to commit a "strong industrial person" to the region. With a firm commitment, the NUL would be poised to "move in . . . and carry the ball ourselves."[74] Ultimately, although the two organizations did not work hand in glove on the huge task, they did not stand in each other's way, and in this instance, the NUL ended up doing the lion's share of the work.

The NAACP made the first move, however. On January 5, 1951, a little more than a month after the AEC announced the location of the new plant, the NAACP hosted a meeting at Aiken's Friendship Baptist Church. More than three hundred people from the project area and nine active NAACP branches attended. Led by Aiken branch president and local mortician Robert A. Brooks and pharmacist C. C. Johnson, the group established committees to deal with problems related to employment, housing, and legal issues.[75] Mitchell set the campaign's mood, declaring, "When they take a man off his tractor, they have to give him a chance to work the reactor."[76] Mitchell again placed the racial conflict in a Cold War context, declaring that "too much of the propaganda used by foreign governments against the United States is true." Opening up employment opportunities to African Americans could "save America in the eyes of the world so that it will become a place where people may live together harmoniously."[77]

While the NAACP mobilized its members, the NUL's Thomas initiated the first of what would be many meetings with officials from Du Pont and the AEC. He urged them to open all job classifications to black applicants and to make fair hiring practices a reality.[78] The meeting did not inspire confidence that either the corporation or the federal agency would make nondiscrimination in hiring a priority. Despite the AEC's supervisory position, agency official Fletcher Waller told Thomas that it was unclear what role it would play in hiring. Waller also revealed that AEC officials had met with union leaders regarding fair hiring issues but expected some trouble. Despite the uncertainty regarding the extent of the AEC's involvement in Du Pont's hiring policies and union practices, the government agency certainly had control over its own staff, which, although tiny compared to Du Pont's, could set the tone for the project by offering opportunities for blacks. Thomas pushed Waller on this issue, arguing that if the AEC refused to take the lead, corporations and unions would feel free to discriminate. As Thomas later explained to a colleague, "The presence of a competent Negro man in an important spot on the Commission's staff would give assurance that the Commission intended to enforce a nondiscrimination policy." Waller responded tepidly that "he was not too sure that this was the proper thing to do." Irritated, Thomas pressured Waller to take a stronger stand: "Ordinarily, I probably would not have been so emphatic on this," Thomas later wrote, "but, knowing as we do how the 'brother' fares in some of these isolated southern areas, I am damn sure the Atomic Energy Commission will have to show a stronger hand than it has shown before."[79]

Put on the defensive by civil rights groups, the AEC and Du Pont conducted surveys of race relations and employment practices at federal facilities and in the private sector in the Savannah River region in early 1951. When officials visited Camp Gordon, Fort Jackson, the Augusta Arsenal, and the Clarks Hill Project, army personnel confirmed that incidents of racial tension at the facilities were few and that integrated work patterns instituted on site had not resulted in any backlash in the community at large. The AEC nevertheless disregarded that information and opted for a cautious course of employment that conformed to local discriminatory patterns. Hoping to snuff out criticism of its hiring practices, Du Pont conducted a similar investigation of racial hiring patterns, finding that voluntary segregation existed on the military bases and that private industry offered no instances in which whites and blacks worked in an integrated fashion in a professional capacity. Satisfied that a cautious hiring strategy would be in keeping with regional norms, Du Pont stated noncommittally that blacks would be considered for nonmanual positions "when [the] occasion arises."[80]

To appease civil rights groups, in February 1951, Du Pont brought in A. Julian Lee, an employment recruiter, to work in the Personnel Division and to oversee the hiring of black employees.[81] One NAACP leader noted that Lee was "the only white collar Negro employee" at the plant. Thomas commented that Lee appeared to be "a capable and straightforward chap who could be relied upon to do an honest job." But Thomas let Lee know that the NUL would be watching him, warning, "We would hate to get an apologist in a position of this kind."[82] Lee was anything but. He developed a close working relationship with the civil rights organizations and expressed frequent frustration over Du Pont's racial biases.

Lee worked under a number of constraints. First, although committed to opening opportunities for the region's black workers, Lee was not fully qualified for the position in which Du Pont had placed him. Despite Lee's earnest desire to help black people acquire employment, he had, as NUL officials noted, "no real training as an employment interviewer; has never used trade tests to test the validity of a person's statement as to his degree of skill in a trade; and more than likely finds it difficult to tell whether a person is fully qualified, partially qualified or unqualified." The more serious obstacle, though, was of Du Pont's making. Whereas whites sought out different employment interviewers based on job classification, Lee interviewed all black applicants regardless of skill level or job classification. He likewise never received a complete list of open positions but worked from a roster that included only the positions of truck driver, laborer, carpenter, and brick mason. Following local custom, Du Pont had "reserved" certain positions for blacks.[83]

Six months into the construction project, no African Americans had been hired in white-collar positions.[84] By June, the NUL's DeWitt noted that "Lee was rather despondent" and that "the discrimination being practiced made him sick all over." Lee offered numerous examples of employment discrimination. In one typical case, Lee reported, "A black teacher with a B.S. degree took a job as a laborer because he needed a job, while white high school graduates get their pick of jobs." Lee even inquired whether the NUL could help him get another job as an interviewer.[85]

During the first year of construction, NUL and NAACP representatives made monthly visits to Aiken and the surrounding region, holding meeting after meeting as part of an excruciatingly slow strategy designed to provide an opening wedge at the plant. They received a cool response. Du Pont and AEC officials stated repeatedly that they were reluctant to challenge the "local culture." Du Pont's construction supervisor, whom the NUL regarded as "timid" and "annoying," stated that "we have not come here to change customs and patterns that have been in existence for over ninety years." Those "customs and patterns," it seems, were not confined to the South. Dewitt characterized Du Pont's reputation for using nonwhite workers at its other plants as "weak." The NAACP and NUL's job was made all the more difficult by Du Pont's policy that the "decisions on racial employment would be made at the plant site." According to Du Pont's manager of personnel, "The home office in Wilmington did not intend to supersede the authority of the local operation management."[86] And the local leaders were exceedingly cautious and concerned about exacerbating racial tensions.

The AEC was no better, with officials remaining noncommittal when asked what they would do should Du Pont discriminate against black applicants.[87] When pressed again in June 1951, AEC director of personnel Arthur Tackman stated specifically that "when we hired Du Pont, we hired its employment policies."[88] Tackman also flat-out refused to hire African Americans on his staff. Halfway through the first year of construction, with hundreds of individuals being hired every day, no one at Du Pont or the AEC showed any inclination to honor fair hiring policies.

African Americans faced other obstacles as well. Information on job openings was not readily available through the black press.[89] Du Pont and the AEC were concerned that placing advertisements in the black press would enrage local whites. To their credit, Du Pont and the AEC avoided the practice common in larger urban dailies, which segregated their "help wanted" advertisements by gender and by race, a practice that clearly violated Executive Order 9980.[90] Even if black applicants learned of employment opportunities, they could not always apply for the positions. As a secure federal facility, the SRP needed guards. However, the AEC and Du Pont hesitated to employ black men in those positions. The NUL understood the importance of hiring black guards, for at other secured facilities, "the guards were responsible for permitting people to go to the personnel office and file applications for employment."[91]

Six months into the construction phase, very little progress had been made on fair hiring. NUL officials grew increasingly frustrated. Despondent, DeWitt lamented that "discrimination is rampant. Continuing to confer [with officials] seems to be accomplishing nothing. There is no evidence of any improvement. Moreover, I doubt if it is being given too serious consideration in spite of the statements of AEC officials" to the contrary. DeWitt argued that "the time has come to take a firm stand on this national disgrace," perhaps by going to the top of Du Pont's corporate ladder if necessary and by putting the matter before the public.[92] This direct approach was contrary to the NUL's typical modus operandi, which involved quietly working out agreements; however, AEC and Du Pont officials' intransigence led some proponents of civil rights to reconsider this approach. Thomas noted that "unless some fire is built under the AEC, there is little likelihood that Negroes will be treated fairly" on the project. It might be necessary, Thomas noted, to "make a national issue of this problem."[93]

The problem of African American employment was entangled with Du Pont's labor recruitment strategy, which was to rely on AFL unions to supply labor. In 1951, the AFL was not a bastion of racial liberalism. According to one historian, "Although the AFL constitution included a non-discrimination provision from the organization's inception, the federation had resisted pressure from civil rights activists to open its ranks to full black participation, and many AFL unions had policies of racial exclusion." In the Savannah River area, African Americans were excluded from numerous labor organizations, including the ironworkers', operating engineers', and plumbers' and pipe fitters' unions. Unions that did accept black members, such as the carpenters' union, relegated them to segregated locals. In occupations where blacks were the majority, such as bricklaying and cement finishing, they encountered few problems securing employment. Blacks gained easy entry only as common laborers, where they constituted the majority.[94]

Du Pont refused to challenge union referral policies. Lee complained to the NUL's DeWitt that the unions underreferred black workers. Fully qualified black carpenters were being referred as "helpers," while "helpers" were being referred as "laborers." NUL representatives tried to increase the numbers of African American referrals both by putting pressure on AEC and Du Pont officials and by attempting to persuade union leaders. Particularly obstructionist was William W. Holley, business agent for the carpenters' Local 283. When DeWitt inquired about the prospects for referrals of black carpenters, Holley screamed at him, "No damn body is going to come up here and tell me how to run the Carpenters' Local! No one looks out for Jews, Italians, or white people!" DeWitt regarded Holley as "a typical union boss with a minimum of education and a maximum of stubbornness." He had little hope that Holley would integrate the local but optimistically thought he might refer segregated crews of black carpenters.[95] During a later telephone conversation with Holley, the union boss "slammed down the receiver after exploding with 'go to hell you damn bastard!'"[96] The carpenters' situation was complicated by J. C. Artemus, union chief of the black carpenters' local in Columbia. He had a vested interest in maintaining his segregated group and was nervous about Holley accepting black applicants, seeking to make his local a referral point.[97] Despite Holley's hostile responses, he eventually referred crews of black carpenters to the SRP. By August, the site was actively employing black carpenters and cement finishers, but there were still no blacks in clerical positions, nor were blacks hired as electricians, mechanics, plumbers and pipe fitters, welders, heavy equipment operators, and ironworkers.[98]

As the first year of the construction phase drew to a close, African Americans had achieved only a small economic toehold at the plant site. Twenty percent of the construction force was African American, but about 91 percent of them worked as common laborers, with limited opportunities for advancement. The remaining 9 percent worked as cement finishers, carpenters, and truck drivers. Du Pont still employed only a single African American—Lee—in a white-collar position; the company had hired no black clerical workers. The AEC employed no black workers at any level. By the end of 1952, no African Americans had been hired as guides, messengers, security guards, firemen, clerks, electricians, ironworkers, heavy equipment operators, plumbers, metal workers, or painters, even though Du Pont was suffering from grave shortages in these job categories.[99]

The recruitment of applicants in the skilled crafts or in technical and professional positions was further complicated by the fact that few African Americans worked in those fields: in 1950, the country as a whole had "only 667 black chemists (1% of total), 3,236 electricians (1%), 8,290 plumbers and pipefitters (3%) and fewer than 700 engineers (.3%)."[100] NUL and NAACP leaders worked around the clock, cultivating contacts at the region's historically black colleges and universities in search of qualified black applicants for professional positions. One professor at South Carolina State University informed DeWitt that most of the young men graduating with engineering or business degrees planned to enter military service, which educated black men apparently saw as a more promising avenue for advancement than a federal facility in the South.[101] Neither the NUL nor college officials had anything to say about the career options deemed desirable to female students.

One of the most significant shortages for the plant was in the area of clerical workers. In a region where the most common occupation for white women was textiles and for black women was domestic work, skilled clerical workers— stenographers, typists, and clerks—were in short supply.[102] The shortage played into workers' hands; as demand for their services mushroomed, clerical workers employed in private industry saw their pay increase from $145 to $160 a month over a four-month period.[103] The NUL saw clerical positions at the plant as a potential economic boon for black women and put great effort into trying to open opportunities for them.[104] Despite the dearth of experienced clerical workers, neither Du Pont nor the AEC was eager to hire black women in those positions. The two entities' unwillingness to challenge local employment mores meant that black women had almost no chance of securing office jobs. Assumptions about what types of work were suitable for blacks and for whites, for women and for men, were deeply ingrained in southern and corporate culture.

In attempting to open office positions for black women, the NUL was fighting not just regional job discrimination but the systemic discrimination in the corporate world that reserved clerical and secretarial jobs for white women and relegated black women to service and janitorial positions. Racial exclusion from office work was the norm in the business world. By 1940, only 1.4 percent of gainfully employed black women nationally were office workers. Labor and gender historians have noted how, in the words of Sharon Hartman Strom, "the sexual objectification of women . . . was integral to office work culture."[105]

Jobs in the pink-collar office sector were reserved for young, white, single, and preferably attractive women.[106] As historian Michelle Brattain notes, "White collar workers—secretaries, stenographers, typists—functioned as more than providers of office services. Their work was also about sex. Office workers decorated offices with desirable young female bodies."[107] Historian Margery Davies argues that "the relationship between an employer and a private secretary remained very personal." The private secretary was "as a rule, an office wife."[108] The southern race/sex taboo made it almost impossible for black women to work in office positions.

Du Pont officials apparently took the notion of "office wife" quite literally. In May 1951, DeWitt complained of anecdotal evidence that Du Pont was training the wives of white male employees for office work rather than hiring black applicants. Moreover, although black applicants had passed the tests required of clerks and stenographers, the AEC had still refused to hire those applicants.[109] In May, DeWitt met with Arthur Tackman of the AEC, who reported that only about three out of two hundred black applicants had passed the clerical tests. DeWitt also noted a wide range of opinions within Du Pont regarding the use of black clerical workers.[110] He noted that "one party is hesitant about employing them while another person tested one applicant five times in an effort to qualify her. To date, however, no one has been employed and the community is concerned."[111] DeWitt was skeptical about the prospects for success in securing pink-collar clerical jobs for African American women: "It is safe to say that some progress will be made by the company in integrating Negro workers in jobs previously closed to them in this area; and it is equally safe to say that Du Pont will not try vigorously to integrate Negroes into so-called difficult areas such as clerical work unless organizations like the NUL and the NAACP continue to press an unending and uncompromising attack against this 'do-nothing' attitude."[112] By midyear, despite the NUL's efforts, DeWitt reported that "only four black women have been employed—as maids." Social patterns remained unchanged.[113]

Complaints about discrimination at the SRP reached the president. Lester Granger, the NUL's assistant executive secretary in charge of industrial relations, wrote to Truman in July 1951 charging the AEC with "bland indifference toward employment policies as they affect Negro job applicants." Granger further complained that Du Pont was "deliberate[ly] catering to racial practices in the Savannah River project area."[114] Lester H. Persells, southern chair of the American Veterans Committee, an organization of left-leaning veterans, likewise wrote to call the president's attention to discriminatory hiring practices at AEC's southern installations and to urge Truman to take action.[115] The committee also issued a press release describing as "reprehensible" such violations of Executive Order 9980 in "federal operations which are designed to build weapons for the defense of the very democratic principles which are being violated."[116]

Civil rights advocates' hopes brightened when they received some high-level assistance. Senator William Benton of Connecticut met with Truman in October 1951 to discuss civil rights measures and national security. Benton urged the president to issue an executive order to eliminate "discrimination in defense employment." Benton saw this issue as involving both civil rights and national security. "The Director of Defense Mobilization, Charles E. Wilson, has repeatedly called attention to the growing manpower shortage in [the] defense industry," the senator wrote. "In the coming year, [1.5 million] new workers must be found. Yet, today, as in World War II, evidence is mounting of failure efficiently to utilize millions of members of minority groups in the skills for which they have been trained." In states without fair employment laws, "the prevailing discrimination brings staggering and needless loss in defense production, in economic resources, in human values and in constitutional rights." Benton went on to make the Cold War connection. "There is a close relationship between the treatment of our minorities here at home, and the influence we can and must exercise abroad in the cause of peace and security."[117]

Executive Order 9980 forbade employment discrimination but did not include a system of uniform regulation or inspection. On December 3, 1951, from his vacation home at the U.S. Naval Station on Key West, Truman signed Executive Order 10308, creating the Committee on Government Contract Compliance. The eleven-member committee was charged with investigating allegations of racial and religious discrimination in hiring under government contracts. The committee's main responsibility was oversight—essentially, observing the degree of compliance exhibited by corporations and businesses with federal contracts and recommending to government agencies and departments how the procedures already in place might be strengthened.[118] The president regarded the creation of this committee as "one more step in the program I have undertaken to use the powers conferred on the Executive by the Constitution . . . to eliminate the practice of discrimination in connection with activities of the Federal Government." The reaction from southern lawmakers to the creation of this committee was immediate and critical. Alabama

Dixiecrat leader Horace Wilkinson denounced the order as "another effort on the part of Truman to usurp, overrule and override. This is adequate grounds for impeachment but I don't think there is anyone in Washington with guts enough to institute the proceedings." Senator Walter George of Georgia was less vitriolic than Wilkinson but no less critical, characterizing the creation of the committee as politically motivated: "The only thing I can make of it is that it looks like he may be preparing to run for President again. I will oppose [the antidiscrimination order], naturally."[119] For civil rights advocates, the committee's charge and power to sanction were less than they had hoped for. The new committee had no power to enforce the antidiscrimination clause and no way to punish violations.[120] The final responsibility for compliance lay with the contracting agencies themselves—in this case, the AEC. Responsibility for enforcing nondiscrimination was left to "the discretion of federal officials who had been less than enthusiastic about the program" to begin with.[121]

As difficult as the task of getting jobs for blacks during the construction phase of the project had been, Nelson Jackson, director of the NUL's southern field division, observed that "the 'nitty-gritty' is going to be getting colored people employed in production jobs with the Operations Division." Jackson predicted a "mad scramble" by the thousands of migrants for operation jobs. "Unless we act at once and continue to prod and follow through, the Negro worker will be confined to the inherited jobs in maintenance and personal service."[122]

Du Pont operations officials told the NUL that a large percentage of the operations personnel would come from transfers from the construction division. While such a policy made internal sense, it amounted to a gigantic roadblock for those hoping to use the plant to open economic opportunities for blacks. The NUL's Harry Alston made the obvious point that "the discriminatory policies of construction restricted the number of negroes who could qualify for transferral to many of the vacancies in Operations." Du Pont officials again shifted responsibility to the unions.

As hiring shifted to the second phase, Julian Lee began to work to place African Americans on the operations staff, yet he remained skeptical about Du Pont's willingness to move aggressively to hire blacks. And when hiring for the operations positions began, the NUL was dismayed to see that blacks were restricted to positions such as coal handlers, utility mechanics, maids, and janitors and were not being considered for the training program for more skilled positions. Du Pont personnel supervisors again expressed apprehension to Alston about integrating blacks into "white" positions. Alston reminded Du Pont officials that since these potential workers were nonunion, the company would bear responsibility for hiring or not hiring them. Union racism could not serve as an excuse. The company's assistant superintendent again reminded Alston that "Du Pont was not in South Carolina to change any social patterns."[123]

Both the NUL and Du Pont pressed their Cold War prerogatives in an effort to make their point regarding fair employment practices. In a meeting with NUL officials, Donald Miller, project manager for Du Pont's Operations Division, "elaborated on the broad and herculean responsibility placed upon Du Pont in the operation of the plant." The NUL's Alston responded that "the League was not necessarily interested in changing the 'social pattern' as such, but we were interested in American citizens having an opportunity to work on jobs which they were qualified for."[124] Alston's trips to the plant region became less frequent and focused more heavily on placing blacks in positions within the operations staff. Although blacks with higher-level qualifications continued to be referred to jobs in areas of maintenance, transportation, and service, some semiprofessional and professional positions had opened up. Further, Lee noted at the end of 1953 that "consideration was being given to the utilization of Negroes as laboratory technicians" and that he anticipated eight such applicants being referred within the month. By the end of 1953, roughly 5,000 of the estimated 7,000 permanent staff were in place; about 250 were black.[125] With the exception of one clerk, two laboratory technicians, and a research chemist, these African Americans were confined to the service and unskilled fields.[126]

By April 1953, Du Pont was demonstrating a greater propensity to hire African Americans in skilled and professional positions. Alston noted that two black chemists had been hired in the technical division. Lee remained concerned about the tiny pool of African American applicants for technical work and requested help locating people with the proper qualifications. Alston stepped up his recruiting by visiting and writing to more than twenty-five black colleges and technical schools in the region.[127] During a July 1953 visit, Curtis Nelson, the SRP's manager, informed Alston of plans for opening additional job classifications to qualified black applicants.[128]

By early 1954, Du Pont and the AEC had become if not aggressive in their recruitment of African Americans, at least not completely obstructionist. Still, the numbers remained small. The AEC had hired only one black clerk/stenographer, one clerk/typist, and one mimeograph operator. Du Pont had done slightly better, including one research chemist and eight lab technicians. Local black leaders told Alston that most qualified but rejected applicants had left the region.[129] Lee was more optimistic about the prospects of hiring African Americans in 1954, reporting that management had requested names of black women for clerical and technical positions, and he credited the NUL for the advances. By 1956, the plant had around eight thousand employees, approximately five hundred of them African American. Roughly twenty-five blacks were employed as chemical analysts and lab technicians, thirty-five were assigned to transportation, and one hundred were in what were termed "grade-A" jobs. The vast majority remained in unskilled, semiskilled, and service jobs.[130]

Despite the fact that by the mid-1950s, barely 7 percent of the SRP's workforce was black (with the vast majority in unskilled and semiskilled positions), the plant employed more African Americans than any other AEC installation. The NUL and NAACP had better success integrating the SRP facilities. By 1959, the Savannah River Operations Office reported "non-segregated cafeterias, lunch rooms, lockers, washrooms, water fountains, employment office, work areas and groups, medical and transportation facilities," as well as "non-segregated training for skilled and semi-skilled jobs." But actual economic opportunity available to area blacks was slow to develop. Following the passage of the Civil Rights Act of 1964 and the creation of the Equal Employment Opportunity Commission, the numbers steadily increased. Between 1968 and 1974, between 18 and 57 percent of new hires at the SRP were black. Yet even as production jobs opened up, much of this growth occurred in the most dangerous and least desirable positions. When Du Pont turned over management of the plant to Westinghouse in 1989, not a single black person was employed in an executive capacity.[131]

Employment opportunities steadily improved thereafter, and by the late 1990s, roughly 22 percent of Savannah River's 11,500 employees were African American, with a slowly increasing number in white-collar positions. Among those white-collar employees were Willar and Josephine Hightower. Willar grew up in Aiken County and attended South Carolina State University, where he graduated with a degree in mathematics in 1964. He undertook graduate work in theoretical mathematics at North Carolina College (now North Carolina Central University) in 1964–65, and there he met his future wife, Josephine. After graduating, Josephine took a job at Bell Labs in New Jersey, while Willar entered the U.S. Army as a second lieutenant. In 1967, Willar applied for and accepted a job at Savannah River as an engineer; Josephine was hired as a computer programmer two years later. The Hightowers enjoyed their positions immensely, but by the 1990s, they had become frustrated. Despite excellent performance evaluations, they seemed to have hit a career ceiling, while white employees they had trained were being promoted above them. The Hightowers were not alone in their frustration. In 1997, ten African American employees filed discrimination lawsuits against Westinghouse and three of its subcontractors. Within six months, eighty-nine additional employees had joined the suit, and the plaintiffs sought class-action status. In addition to wage and promotion discrimination, black workers alleged they were subjected to racist name-calling and jokes and that they were more likely than white workers to be exposed to hazardous working conditions. A study conducted for the plaintiffs showed that even when adjusted for years of education and experience, black workers made an average of twenty-six hundred dollars less per year than their white counterparts. Despite admitting that "statistically significant" disparities existed in some pay and promotion categories, Westinghouse denied that a pattern of discrimination existed and further argued that the use of racial epithets and other examples of harassment were isolated incidents. Much to the dismay of the plaintiffs, a federal judge denied class-action status.[132] Lamented Willar Hightower, "We were on our own." Within a year, more than half of the suits were settled out of court. In none of the cases did Westinghouse admit wrongdoing or disclose the amount of money paid.[133]

The creation of the SRP thrust western South Carolina into an exciting and uncertain future. But hopes (and fears) that the dramatic changes to the landscape brought about by the construction of the vast industrial enterprise would be matched by equally dramatic social or political changes were not realized, at least not in the way most of those concerned had envisioned. Thousands of unionized workers and their families flooded into the region, many bringing with them a support for organized labor and the national Democratic Party that was anathema to the area's traditional states'-rights leadership. Furious construction schedules determined by Cold War imperatives, however, meant that these workers left almost as quickly as they arrived, leaving no lasting liberal imprint on the state's politics.

Equally stunted was the employment potential held by the SRP for the area's African American citizens. Despite their best efforts to link economic opportunity for African Americans to national security and America's reputation abroad, civil rights advocates were outmaneuvered by corporate cold warriors quite willing to defy fair employment policies and by federal officials unwilling to take them to task. In the end, Du Pont and the AEC had the more compelling and immediate national security argument. With American troops fighting and dying in Korea and with knowledge of Soviet atomic capacities, the pressure to build the plant quickly was overwhelming. Arguments about equality and fairness were simply swept aside in the race for the superbomb.

CHAPTER FIVE

Rejecting the Garrison State
National Priorities and Local Limitations

Between 1950 and 1953, nearly 40,000 temporary and 6,000 permanent employees and their families—almost 180,000 persons in all—poured into the
relatively sparsely populated three-county region that played host to the Savannah River Plant (SRP). Many of these new residents chose to live close to
the city of Aiken, in South Carolina, some thirteen miles from the plant.[1] State
political leaders and industrial boosters heralded the arrival of the plant as just
the latest in what they hoped would be an endless succession of federal projects. Local residents likewise anticipated an unprecedented economic boost
from the plant and its high-paid scientific and technical personnel. But the
problems that accompanied the construction and operation of this massive,
high-tech facility were formidable, and the long-term changes to the region
that resulted from this and other defense installations constitute an important
yet mostly untold story of the modern South and Cold War development.

The development of critical defense areas, such as the tricounty region that
was home to the SRP, was profoundly shaped by the emergence of the national
security state during the early Cold War years. As the arms race with the Soviets accelerated and the conflict in Korea worsened, top administration officials
pondered a central question: Could the nation appropriately arm itself for a
permanent condition of total war without resorting to the creation of a garrison state in which the preponderance of resources were harnessed for military
and defense purposes, and in which ultimate power shifted from civilian to
military authorities? At the center of the national security state was the nation's
expanding nuclear arsenal. The creation of the SRP, then, forced administration
officials to confront this central issue of the Cold War. Wishing to avoid the
implementation of excessive governmental controls and planning that are fundamental to a garrison state, the Truman administration chose instead to rely

on existing infrastructure and private enterprise to prepare the country for and maintain a permanent state of war-readiness. Because the SRP was the largest installation operated by the Atomic Energy Commission (AEC), the experiences and problems encountered there would provide a blueprint for future Cold War communities.[2]

The SRP was the first large AEC installation created without an accompanying "company town."[3] The dispersal of this and other Cold War facilities to far-flung locations somewhat removed from large population centers brought rapid growth and development to areas poorly equipped to handle those changes. In the case of the SRP and the small communities surrounding it, Cold War necessities regularly ran up against the peculiarities and particularities of southern culture. Serious miscalculations by the AEC, underdeveloped rural infrastructures, and the traditional ambivalence of southern communities to urban planning and controls resulted in housing and sprawl problems that ranged from serious to disastrous. Such issues particularly plagued the city of Aiken, South Carolina, and its immediate outlying areas.[4] The specter of the garrison state, combined with the AEC's faith in private enterprise and the inability and unwillingness of it and other federal agencies to adequately plan for the human tidal wave that would descend on this region, foreshadowed the rapid modernization that would wash over large swaths of the South in the decades to come.

Citizens of the latest Cold War critical defense area eagerly anticipated the economic windfall expected to accompany the SRP's arrival. Likewise, they were willing to endure change in the interest of national security, but not indefinitely, and not for free. Faced with rapidly deteriorating and overburdened communities, residents of the counties affected by the SRP's creation became active in the marketplace of federal dollars, pressing their claims as citizens who had sacrificed for the good of the country but were unwilling to suffer prolonged deprivation because of it. South Carolina residents' demands for government intervention, controls, and assistance illustrate their level of comfort with the idea of the compensatory welfare state as well as their antipathy toward the garrison state. They interjected themselves into high-level discussions about the realities of the garrison state by insisting on butter along with guns. Their actions directly contradicted those called for by NSC-68, which argued that victory in the global struggle required American citizens to make sacrifices. Southern residents placed limits on those sacrifices and demanded benefits in return. Residents displaced by the plant and overwhelmed by the newcomers were left to fight for equitable treatment through the acquisition of federal funds; in doing so, they revealed the extent to which they had bought into a growth strategy that relied heavily on federal dollars and how they expected to benefit as residents of Fortress Dixie.

Aiken residents stood poised to welcome the new permanent arrivals, who they believed would be a "good class of people" since the plant "would require intelligent and trained personnel."[5] They were more anxious about the temporary construction workers who preceded the permanent operations personnel. One Aiken shopkeeper told a reporter for the *New Yorker* that residents were excited about the arrival of what he called the "right people—scientists, engineers, government officials." But, he added, "the winter residents have their houses and stables here, and I know they want to stay, but will they if these construction workers trespass on their estates?"[6] The well-heeled themselves seemed less concerned. Lillius Gilchrist Grace of the shipping and chemical family lamented the loss of Gracefields, a seven-thousand-acre hunting preserve that had been acquired by the government as part of the Savannah site. She took events in stride, however, putting them into context with other recent changes in her life: "This past winter, we had one of our coldest snaps and the camellias all" died, she noted. "And, of course, in New York the Ritz-Carlton's being torn down. I lived there for eight years."[7] Another winter resident noted that the wealthy in Aiken considered "inheritance taxes . . . a hell of a lot worse nuisance than this hydrogen bomb."[8]

Cautious optimism soon gave way to hard questions as residents and civic leaders began to contemplate the impact of the massive influx of workers on their community. Within days of the plant's announcement, AEC and Du Pont officials began fielding questions about housing for the approximately eight thousand workers expected to arrive over the first six months of construction. Most of these workers would eventually bring their families, expanding the population influx to more than thirty-five thousand. Moreover, the number of construction workers was expected to peak at forty-six thousand, and they would be augmented by a flood of concessionaires and tradespeople who would peddle their wares and services to the construction workers and their families.[9] Pere Seward, community facilities services commissioner for the Housing and Home Finance Agency, told a congressional committee that in addition to every worker, communities could expect three accompanying family members plus "the butcher and the baker and the candlestick maker."[10] Altogether, the number of new residents—both temporary and permanent— would total around 180,000.

Based on its experiences at the Oak Ridge, Tennessee, and Richland, Washington, facilities, and in response to concerns about creating a garrison state, the AEC decided against building and operating a company town.[11] For the duration of the war, both Oak Ridge and Richland (where Hanford scientists resided) were overseen by the military. Eventually, responsibility for the towns fell to the AEC. Historians John Findlay and Bruce Hevly note that "in a period of virulent anticommunism, government ownership and operation of [Richland] struck Americans as anathema." The towns fell under the scrutiny of a penurious Congress, and both the House and Senate conducted inquiries about runaway spending at Richland, Los Alamos, and Oak Ridge.[12] Seeking to avoid these political minefields, AEC officials chose instead to rely on the existing cities of Aiken and Augusta, Georgia, to absorb the new residents. The SRP was a critical component of the nation's long-term Cold War armament program. A government-run town, less than ideal for a hot war, was totally unworkable for a cold war, which might require a permanent state of war-readiness.

In choosing the Savannah River location, AEC and Du Pont revealed definite ideas about how growth would take place. They envisioned Augusta as the primary metropolitan center for the area, while Aiken, Williston, and Barnwell would become dormitory suburbs that would house the new employees. Indeed, a major factor that influenced the selection of South Carolina site was spatial: a large swath of rural land easily cleared and the proximity of nearby cities and towns.[13] Whereas before 1950 the various subregions within these counties—the agricultural regions, mill villages, and small towns—possessed distinct characteristics and rudimentary interconnections, the arrival of the plant reconfigured these functions.

Committed to relying on the adaptive resources of the surrounding communities and on the ability of private enterprise to meet the various needs of the newcomers, the Federal Housing Administration (FHA) filed a rosy report with the AEC on the region's housing market, the condition of its schools and medical facilities, and the ability of area banks to finance construction.[14] The AEC had seriously miscalculated. The Aiken-Augusta region was not prepared to house six thousand new permanent employees, let alone some forty-five-thousand-plus temporary construction workers and their families. In 1950, Aiken County boasted only fifteen thousand permanent dwellings, the majority of which were classified as "dilapidated" and "deficient," not a surprising characterization for rural dwellings but certainly inadequate to meet the housing needs of a highly skilled and educated workforce. Urban conditions were hardly more promising. More than a third of the dwellings in the city of Aiken were classified as dilapidated.[15] A majority of Augusta's twenty-one thousand residential units likewise were "substandard," lacking private baths and categorized as dilapidated.[16] In addition, by 1951, most available housing in Augusta had been occupied by persons affiliated with Camp Gordon.[17] By the middle of that year, with workers streaming in from across the country, the housing shortage was acute, and it would remain so until November 1952.

The enormity and novelty of the project undertaken and the likelihood that the SRP experience could serve as a blueprint (or cautionary tale) for future projects made the project the subject of intense study. In the early 1950s, the Housing and Home Finance Agency and the U.S. Public Health Service sponsored a study of the SRP's impact on the region. The study, conducted by a team of researchers from the University of North Carolina, found that despite the obvious and known infrastructure shortcomings, the creation of the plant went forward with no fixed policy or plan for housing, highways, or community facilities.[18]

The AEC regarded the government communities established at Oak Ridge, Richland, and Los Alamos "an unwelcome legacy" that hinted at the specter of the garrison state. For a nation facing a future of permanent wartime footing, the imposition of those types of government controls was deemed unworkable and undesirable. Officials were determined that the Savannah River Project would rely on private enterprise and construction to handle the housing needs of the new residents. Walter J. Williams, deputy general manager of the AEC, noted that "the Commission is counting on free enterprise to supply housing for its personnel to the maximum feasible extent. It desires to avoid being diverted from its primary responsibility of building and operating these new production plants by the distracting problems of providing and operating housing."[19]

Government officials quickly became aware of their miscalculations. In February 1951, Raymond M. Foley, administrator of the Housing and Home Finance Agency, reported that only "450 family units and 130 hotel-type rooms" were available for rent in Aiken.[20] In hearings before the Joint Committee on Atomic Energy, Foley admitted that "we have nothing we can really do in connection with the temporary needs created by the construction worker requirements."[21] The housing shortage was accompanied by inflation. Within weeks of the plant announcement, reports of rent gouging and inflated real estate prices abounded.[22] The town created its first real estate board in mid-December 1950, and the board agreed to hold the line on rents and on housing prices.[23] However, rents nevertheless skyrocketed.[24] Rent control legislation was one of the few federal programs that could meet immediate needs, but it did not go into effect until September 1951.[25] News outlets reported that farmland that sold for between sixty dollars and eighty dollars an acre in 1950 was being snatched up for ten times that amount in 1951, with buyers planning to turn the property into trailer parks. Just as in wartime communities, people made do with just about any type of shelter. Stories abounded of newcomers living in barns, tents, sheds, and converted dog kennels.[26] Everyone, it seemed, hoped to cash in. Hotel owners converted cavernous ballrooms into sleeping rooms, while absentee owners wrote to the Aiken County sheriff in hopes of settling up on their back taxes so that they could sell their property at inflated Cold War prices.[27] Du Pont used teams of "room scouts" to canvass the region, keeping lists of available housing for rent or purchase. But even this strategy encountered cultural obstacles. Property owners in smaller communities such as Barnwell lacked experience with transient populations and with renting and were not accustomed to such transactions. Residents tended to rent rooms only when approached by prospective tenants: it was not customary to fix up rental quarters in advance. Government observers noted that "pre-project renting was largely restricted to houses for tenant farmers, and when a prospective tenant saw a house he wanted to rent, he approached the owner and together they worked out the rent on the basis of what improvements were wanted."[28]

Harry Hammond described the problem of housing the construction workers as "a hell of a mess." He asked, "What in the H. did [Du Pont] expect[?] [For] labor to sleep out in the open fields?"[29] Others agreed. "There is no coordinated approach to the job," lamented Julius Thomas of the National Urban League (NUL). The result was "confusion and more confusion."[30] Mary Jane Willett of the YWCA reported on the problem in nearby Augusta: "Many of the people have two or three rooms rented in their homes. Servants are practically impossible to get and everywhere you go it is crowded. . . . There is a sense on the part of the community of the loss of a way of living which seemed to me as great as the reported reactions of some of the families whose homes are being taken over to make way for the Du Pont plant."[31]

In early 1951, with the arrival of construction workers imminent, the AEC became so concerned about the housing problems that it developed a program of its own. It authorized Du Pont to contract out for the construction of temporary barracks for single men and trailer units for workers with families. Du Pont eventually built temporary structures in Barnwell County to accommodate seventy-five hundred single men, but the first barracks did not open for occupancy until January 15, 1952, nearly a year after construction on the plant began. The barracks never reached capacity, but not because there were not enough men to fill them. The barracks themselves were spartan and contained no recreation rooms, lounges, or dining facilities, thereby limiting their appeal for unmarried newcomers to a small town with few or already overtaxed recreation outlets. Ultimately, about two-thirds of the young single men who came to work on the plant opted to live in Aiken. Also, Du Pont and AEC officials apparently underestimated the percentage of employees who would bring their families and so would have no use for barracks.[32] But housing problems reflected not only a lack of government foresight and planning but also local community prejudices. Community dynamics particular to Aiken County, where Winter Colony gentry were pitted against mill folk, seemed to dictate where the newcomers would live. Sylvia Bryant and Juanita Taylor, who were young women when the plant was built, recalled that newly arriving residents were warned to stay away from the textile mill areas, which had reputations as being rough, inhospitable places. "The Yankees, as we called them, were told 'Don't go to the [Horse Creek] Valley.'"[33]

To accommodate those workers who had brought their families, Du Pont contracted for the installation of four thousand trailer units in Aiken, Augusta, Williston, and Barnwell. Located on the rims of towns, the trailers were much more successful in attracting occupants than were the barracks. Each trailer was designed to accommodate a family of four, but 15 percent of trailer families had between five and seven people. Du Pont also built permanent housing, much of which was a failure. The AEC wanted to diffuse the impact on any single community and consequently spread the houses around. Some were located in tiny villages with no amenities or services, and these rural hamlets could not compete with Aiken or Augusta.[34]

Private enterprise attempted to meet this new housing need with projects throughout the area and particularly around the city of Aiken.[35] But just as the AEC and the FHA had been overly optimistic about the housing situation, so too did they overlook serious shortcomings in the regional infrastructure. In particular, subdivision developers encountered massive obstacles to the laying of water and sewer lines. According to Seward, Aiken and the surrounding communities could not afford to expand their infrastructures to service the new construction. The cities' "debt situation is more or less normal with communities in the South," Seward told a congressional committee. "Their bonded indebtedness is almost up to the limit in almost every case."[36] One local builder planned to construct some twelve hundred homes and a shopping center on 350 acres of land outside of the city of Aiken. But the property lacked water and sewer lines, and the one million dollars necessary to install them was prohibitive.[37] Any developer interested in building subdivisions in more remote, rural areas—Barnwell County, for example—would have to start from scratch, as Barnwell did not even possess a sewer system.[38] Despite the lack of services, workers continued to flood into the region. The tiny town of Williston in Barnwell County saw its population quadruple to five thousand in a matter of six months despite the fact that it had no sewage system and a water supply that could serve only twelve hundred people. The situation, the mayor reported, was "desperate."[39] Even in Aiken, an established city, some existing houses were not served by the sewer system, so new construction was unlikely to get service for quite some time.[40]

Compounding the problem of inadequate infrastructure was a shortage of mortgage money. By the summer of 1951, banks and insurance companies in the area had stopped issuing mortgages.[41] Particularly nettlesome to the AEC were credit restrictions imposed by the Defense Production Act of 1950, which strictly limited residential real estate credit and thus placed a stranglehold on the mortgage market, creating an unfavorable climate for developers. In 1950, the FHA insured fewer than sixty mortgages in Aiken, Allendale, and Barnwell Counties in South Carolina and Richmond County, Georgia.[42] In February 1951, Foley announced that the FHA "will relax the credit restrictions [imposed by the Defense Production Act] on the construction of new housing" in the Savannah River area "on a selective and carefully controlled basis."[43] Following this announcement, local entrepreneurs moved to fill the lending void. In June 1951, former governor and now Aiken attorney Strom Thurmond was one of several investors to found the Aiken Federal Savings and Loan Association, whose purpose was to "alleviate congestion brought on by the increasing population."[44] Even with these actions, however, the housing situation remained critical, for these measures addressed only the problem of permanent dwellings for permanent personnel, not housing for the temporary construction workers.

Federal officials were not the only group that could be accused of shortsightedness, for although local boosters exhibited boundless enthusiasm for recruiting federal projects, they proved ineffective in marshaling resources to deal with the housing problem. The efforts of the Western Carolina Council illustrate this shortcoming. Organized in May 1951, the council was a regional development organization composed of representatives from the eight counties within commuting distance to the plant. Members actively lobbied Congress for federal funds for the region but did nothing to address the housing shortage at the local or state level.[45] The state of South Carolina was no better. Neither the state's industrial recruitment organization (the State Research, Planning, and Development Board) nor any other agency took action to address residents' growth-related needs.[46]

Stymied by the lending squeeze, local entrepreneurs tried to meet the housing crunch with privately owned trailer parks. But because the operators did not know how long the workers would stay, these parks provided few extras. Most lacked amenities such as yards, playgrounds, and shade. The thousands of children who lived in these parks were forced to play in the small spaces between the trailers. Still, nearly 140 trailer parks were created in the tricounty region.[47] With names such as New Town and Here's Home, the trailer parks alleviated the housing crisis in part but contributed to the stress on community services. Trailers were not subject to property taxes; nevertheless, their residents—many of whom brought school-age children and stayed for nearly three years—used city and county services.[48]

The NUL and the National Association for the Advancement of Colored People (NAACP) knew that a project of this size would have a profound impact on the surrounding community, and they were determined to minimize the extent to which the new facility contributed to the extension of Jim Crow. Both organizations surveyed the region and observed that the city of Aiken and its surrounding communities were marked by relatively fluid housing patterns and boasted black businesses that served white customers.[49] Increased demand for housing from African Americans seeking employment at the plant raised the prospect of segregated housing projects. The NAACP and NUL had hoped to avoid the housing problems that had plagued Oak Ridge, where the government mirrored the housing practices of region's coal company towns and later the practices of the Tennessee Valley Authority. The government housing created at Oak Ridge imposed a system of racial segregation on a previously rural area "that had been a checkerboard of black and white farms and communities for generations." In addition, Oak Ridge officials segregated shopping districts and transportation.[50]

The housing of African American workers employed at the SRP presented a particularly sticky problem. White residents spread a rumor that barracks in Allendale would be turned into housing for black men; white residents also whispered that Mexicans and other non-Americans would eventually be recruited to meet the labor needs. The AEC denied both claims.[51] Still, housing for racial minorities remained a sensitive subject and was never adequately solved.

The government's decision not to create a company town helped the area avoid the overnight creation of government-sponsored ghettos; however, the alternative was hardly much better. The NUL charged that Du Pont and the AEC "had developed segregated housing facilities in areas which previously had followed a non-segregated pattern." In so doing, league officials believed, the AEC "had retrogressed . . . rather than progressed."[52] Civil rights groups hoping to use the Cold War crisis to further black economic opportunity and civil rights were dismayed to find that the crisis had the opposite effect on southern residential patterns.

Differences arose between the NAACP and the NUL regarding how to address the housing crisis. In the summer of 1951, NAACP representatives met with Du Pont officials about constructing segregated housing for black construction workers. The NUL disagreed with this policy, pointing out to local NAACP leaders "the danger of inviting a segregated housing pattern [that could] affect the housing pattern in Aiken."[53] The lack of housing ensured that the vast majority of African Americans hired on the project were local.

Alerted to the housing crisis, the Senate Banking and Currency Committee held hearings in January and February 1951. Chaired by Senator Burnet R. Maybank of South Carolina, the committee heard testimony from federal, state, and local officials as well as private citizens, illustrating the depth of the problem. Aiken mayor Odell Weeks and Sarah H. Busch, executive secretary of the Aiken Chamber of Commerce, highlighted the impact of the plant on that small city. These leaders noted that the announcement of the plant was "a staggering blow" that "struck like an ax." They characterized the housing crisis as "acute." In addition, these officials noted that the city lacked the water and sewer systems, schools, hospitals, recreation, and roads to accommodate the addition of some nine thousand permanent residents.[54]

The testimony of these and other interested parties highlighted yet another problem plaguing the region. The AEC and other government agencies had not planned for the housing crunch, nor had they anticipated the burden the in-migrants would place on the existing community facilities. Foley admitted in his February 1951 testimony before the Joint Committee on Atomic Energy that "the amount of permanent housing that will be needed for the operational staff of the installation in the Savannah River area cannot be provided and supported by the existing facilities in the communities in that area, water, schools, sewer systems, and so on." And, Foley grimly concluded, "there are no funds" for such services.[55]

The magnitude of the SRP project and the construction schedule made it eminently clear that "special action was imperative" to provide adequate housing.[56] The most critical problems—the need for housing, community facilities, and local planning assistance—demanded new legislation and appropriations. In response, on September 1, 1951, President Harry S. Truman signed the Defense Housing and Community Facilities and Services Act, with an authorization for expenditure of one hundred million dollars to meet some of these problems in the tricounty area and other sites of critical defense activity. These funds were available through 1953.[57] The Housing and Home Finance Agency and the Federal Security Agency would administer the funds.[58] Congress finally appropriated money to carry out the program in October 1951.[59]

The legislation sought to encourage builders to meet housing needs in more than forty critical defense housing areas.[60] Richmond County (Augusta) in Georgia, and Aiken, Barnwell, and Allendale Counties in South Carolina were designated as one combined critical defense area.[61] Under the act, the Federal National Mortgage Association (Fannie Mae) "received $125 million to buy up mortgages in critical defense housing areas, and the federal government was authorized to help finance various community facilities, including water and sewage."[62] Approximately six million dollars in aid was ultimately spent in the Central Savannah River Area.[63]

Improvements nevertheless came slowly. As late as 1953, many affected South Carolina communities still had not received federal grants.[64] Residents of the "critical defense area" wrote passionate letters to their congressional representatives and federal agency officials complaining of the slow pace of positive change. The writers indicated their willingness to endure change and sacrifice in the interest of national security, but only to a point. Well steeped in the belief that the road to positive growth and modernization was paved with federal aid, the residents expected the plant's presence to rebound in their economic favor. Busch noted that while Aikenites were willing to put forth the effort to accommodate the plant and the "newcomers," they wanted "good housing" and "good schools" in return.[65] Having made the initial sacrifice, public officials and private residents aggressively pressed their claims to services.[66]

Most insistent in their demands for federal funds were the inhabitants of New Ellenton, who often referred to themselves as the "DPs of World War III," evoking the displaced persons of Europe after the recent conflict there. Mayor H. L. McClain and Chamber of Commerce president Arthur Foreman did not hesitate to remind Maybank of their residents' sacrifices: "We feel that our cause is most just as we are the only 100% defense town in the area and the only one to date which has not received any Federal assistance for community facilities — save schools."[67] To the director of the Housing and Home Finance Agency, Foreman and McClain noted that as of July 1, 1953, New Ellenton contained 4,011 residents, half of them plant workers. The town contained 412 permanent dwellings and 8 churches, and was located 1.5 miles from the perimeter of the SRP site. Still, the town remained without water, which it needed "very, very badly."[68] Other residents asked only for what they felt was fair under the circumstances. Mrs. W. T. Phillips of Jackson complained of the "deplorable" situation of the public schools and the need for city water. "When we were forced to give up our homes" within the plant site, "we were told that adequate provisions of every nature would be provided to take care of unpleasant situations as they arose."[69] Mrs. Mack Foreman likewise complained about school overcrowding, noting that beginning with the fall 1952 term, "the school will run in shifts."[70] Mrs. B. D. Brinkley noted that enrollment in the schools in her community "is over 800 pupils and we have facilities for 500. . . . Also we have no auditorium or gymnasium." Like other residents, she pointed to the sacrifices made by the area's residents and their request for fair play: "It seems only fair that we should at least have what was taken from us in Ellenton and let our children enjoy normal school days."[71] Funding for schools was not included in the Defense Housing and Community Facilities and Services Act. Federal grants administered by the office of Education under Public Law 815 (School Construction), Public Law 874 (Operations and Maintenance), and a third supplemental appropriation allocated in 1951 funded the majority of school expansions. Eventually, most communities in the critical defense area received new classrooms built with federal funds. Aiken's school population grew from 13,400 students on the eve of the plant's construction in late 1950 to 15,000 the following fall. The town hired eighty additional teachers in 1952 and added forty permanent classrooms and thirty-six temporary classrooms. Even with the additional construction, many schools in the area operated in shifts to accommodate the new arrivals.[72] The federal government ultimately provided some $20.4 million through grants or loans to create or improve community facilities.[73]

Between 1951 and March 1953, twenty-three hundred new homes were constructed in twenty-seven subdivisions within commuting distance of the plant, and Aiken's population had ballooned to 20,700.[74] Mere construction, though, did not solve all of the community's problems. The Defense Act had no provisions for planning assistance to cities and counties.[75] Aiken and other South Carolina towns lacked adequate planning and zoning legislation and subdivision control powers, and the state had no enabling legislation to permit counties to perform these functions. Following the plant announcement, the South Carolina legislature passed an act authorizing counties in which "there is a sudden influx of large numbers of prospective inhabitants" to establish planning commissions and to enforce limited zoning powers. But Aiken leaders moved slowly, adopting only limited trailer park regulations.[76] Noted one study of the region, "In the absence of planning controls, hundreds of houses were constructed without regard to such basic considerations as topography, drainage, availability of sufficient and safe water supply . . . , accessible roads, garbage collection, [and] police and fire protection."[77] To handle the increase in traffic, Aiken built a four-lane highway connecting the town and the plant, and during this period, the plant and its accompanying housing developments added more than twenty miles of roads within the city of Aiken alone.[78] But even the new roads and corrections at the federal level could not solve all the problems. Traditional regional cultural hostility toward any perceived infringement on the rights of property owners hindered a smooth transition into the Cold War era.

This lack of preparation and control became clear with the rapid, haphazard expansion of permanent housing developments in Aiken County, where subdivisions grew up with little regard or respect for geography. Residential development took place in low areas with known histories of drainage problems. The Crosland Park development, Aiken's largest subdivision and home to many plant employees, was cursed with chronic sewage overflow.[79] Built on a two-hundred-acre tract north of the city, Crosland Park consisted of 542 homes, most of which were rented at seventy-five dollars a month to plant employees. The remaining homes were put up for sale at just under ten thousand dollars each.[80] Sewage problems were exacerbated by Aiken County's rolling sandy pine hills, which gave "rise to certain dangers of contamination of wells from sewage disposed of by means of open pit privies, cesspools, or septic tanks."[81]

Hastily planned suburban development directly contributed to traffic and safety problems. Developers gave little thought to street layout, disregarding critical elements such as topography, highway intersections, and future traffic volume. One survey of the region noted that "new houses were built with individual driveways opening on high-speed plant access roads." For Aiken, this lack of forethought resulted in an unusually high number of dangerous blind curves and traffic jams.[82]

Beyond their demand for housing, the newcomers burdened the city and county with health- and safety-related problems. During the period of plant construction, South Carolina's automobile fatality rate soared above the national average.[83] The city issued a rash of permits to taxi operators and bus operators and began discussions for a new bus station.[84] Traffic control and safety constituted a major problem at the installation. Although Du Pont employed a professional traffic engineer to design and construct "safe and modern" highway systems within the plant, traffic fatalities remained a major concern. Despite efforts to encourage carpooling, roughly twelve thousand private vehicles entered and left the plant daily at peak periods, "constituting an exceptional hazard." In one five-week period in 1952, five people were killed in plant-related traffic accidents.[85]

The housing situation for blacks worsened in 1952. Private-sector housing projects open to African Americans lagged behind those for whites. That year, developers planned thirty-six hundred permanent housing units for whites and only twenty-nine homes for blacks.[86] In April of that year, Harry Alston of the NUL noted that "Negroes are living in over-crowded facilities, many of which are substandard. Several of the displaced families have moved their tenant houses or shacks into Barnwell, Williston, New Ellenton and Aiken, adding to the number of inadequate housing facilities for Negroes in those areas, creating slum areas."[87] A Williston businessman reported to Alston that most blacks lived in rented housing with outside spigots and toilets and featuring coal oil lights; for these accommodations, they paid three dollars per room per week.[88]

Crime, particularly public drunkenness, also increased during the first year of the plant's construction.[89] In February 1951, Aiken's police department reported an increase in the number of transients, attributing that increase to the activity surrounding the creation of the plant and more particularly to the lack of housing. Many of the "transients" had arrived seeking construction work.[90] The city police expanded its workforce four times between March 1951 and August 1952.[91] The police department also reported an increase in complaints about juvenile delinquency, although because these offenders were not charged with crimes, it is difficult to tell how much of this "delinquency" was real and how much was mere perception. To deal with the problem of bored youths, the city recommended creating a "broad recreation program, social and educational activities for both races."[92]

The flood of new residents also challenged Aiken's public health infrastructure. City health officer C. M. Courtney found himself overwhelmed with the enormous task of inspecting the new trailer parks that seemed to pop up daily. He reported to the city council that complaints to his office had tripled since the arrival of the plant.[93] He was particularly concerned about the "influx of house trailers" and the sanitation problems they caused. Many of them, he reported in February 1951, simply used "an open hole dug in the ground beneath the trailer" as a privy. Courtney routinely reported on conflicts that illustrated the clash between rural culture and modernity. For example, he reported on the presence of livestock in trailer parks located in the city proper and requested that the city council pass an ordinance banning all hogs within the city limits.[94]

Most of the trailer sites were constructed without regard for public spaces and the need for recreation. The YWCA's Defense Services Division had an employee working to establish activities within the trailer courts.[95] The number of illegitimate pregnancies in the area grew, causing great consternation among public welfare officials.[96] To address the various public health issues, the National Committee on Social Work in Defense Mobilization called for more caseworkers and community organizers for the area.[97] A variety of public and private social welfare groups responded, including the American Social Hygiene Association, Travelers Aid Society, National Catholic Community Service, American Red Cross, National Federal of Settlements and Neighborhood Centers, and the YWCA.[98]

The SRP commenced operations in late 1952, and the first shipment of plutonium left the plant in December 1954. Beginning in 1956, the five reactors were operating continually and at full capacity. The final price tag for the plant topped $1.3 billion. By the late 1950s, Du Pont's operating force at the plant numbered 7,200, while the AEC employed another 230 or so. The combined annual payroll of Du Pont and AEC employees was roughly sixty-five million dollars.[99] The region, which at the close of World War II was categorized as underdeveloped and primarily rural, now represented an important outpost on the frontier of nuclear science as well as an integral component of the national security state. The process of creating the plant had been fraught with difficulty, as the needs of the nation and the decisions of federal officials collided with rural culture and the expectations of local residents.

The long-term changes to Aiken and the other surrounding communities, while not nearly as revolutionary, were nevertheless dramatic. By 1953, as a result of suburban development and annexation, the city of Aiken had more than doubled in size, and two-thirds of the plant's scientists, engineers, and managers chose to live there. Ken Kilbourne, executive secretary of the Aiken Chamber of Commerce, noted in 1957 that the arrival of the plant and the permanent employees brought not only economic benefits but cultural advantages as well: "Our schools and recreational facilities have been improved and enlarged. So have our civic and professional organizations. And here's something that seems significant to me: just the other day the *Encyclopedia Britannica* folks told me that they received more inquiries per family from Aiken than any other city in the country."[100] The profound changes that swept over this corner of the South were the direct consequences of the Truman administration's rejection of the garrison state model and faith in the ability of private enterprise to adapt to and meet the requirements of communities (and a nation) confronting the reality of living in a permanent state of war-readiness. The imperatives of the Cold War, the national security state, and the federal government's desire to avoid the garrison state entailed countless questions and decisions; too often, the proper questions were not asked soon enough, and the decisions were made too late to avoid some of the less savory aspects of growth and change. In the process, the region's physical, cultural, social, and political maps were remade. The destruction of huge swaths of countryside, the creation of significant defense installations, the granting of lucrative military contracts to large corporate entities, and the development of the space program fostered intense migrations that forever changed the character of the population, creating a middle class where none had before existed. Southerners coped as best they could with these profound changes, taking advantage of the economic opportunities and resisting prolonged sacrifice for what they figured was a permanent state of affairs.

CHAPTER SIX

"Better Living"

Life in a Cold War Company Town

Born in the Horse Creek Valley village of Graniteville in 1936, Ronnie Bryant's life followed the pattern typical of most valley boys. His family worked in textiles, and he figured he would do the same when he became an adult. When he entered Leavell McCampbell High School in 1950, word came from the Atomic Energy Commission (AEC) that Du Pont Corporation was going to build a massive facility some ten miles from the valley. Bryant graduated in 1954 and married his high school sweetheart, Sylvia, a few months later. He worked a summer job in textiles, but "it looked like there was no future in the Graniteville Company," he recalled. "All the good jobs were taken, or people were in line for the good jobs, so you had to look elsewhere for opportunity." Bryant put in an application at the Savannah River Plant (SRP) and was hired in the 400 area, where heavy water was produced, a job he landed because he had taken high school chemistry. It was a smart economic decision, as his starting take-home pay was almost 50 percent higher than what he would have made at the mill.[1] Bryant remained at the plant for the rest of his career, a move that placed him firmly within the region's emerging middle class. Bryant remained a resident of Graniteville, but in 1965 he built a brick ranch home on Laurel Drive, a newly constructed residential area that offered suburban features, a first for the valley. For six long suburban blocks, Laurel Drive parallels old Trolley Line Road, which connected Graniteville and the city of Aiken. Laurel Drive was an anomaly. It was not oriented to the mills, like all of Graniteville's other residential sections. Symbolically, Laurel Drive points out of the valley itself. In the 1960s, it became home to a new and expanding middle class, a transitional landscape between the old money of Aiken and the working class of the valley. A home on Laurel Drive probably would have been possible had Bryant stayed in textiles, but it certainly would have taken him longer to acquire. Ronnie and Sylvia's two children attended college and graduate school; their son, Ron Jr., is employed as an engineer at the plant.

The SRP not only remade the map of the region, erasing towns and roadways, but it also reoriented how the remaining communities interacted and, for that matter, defined themselves. It was a paradigm shift of sometimes abrupt, sometimes subtle characteristics. The altered trajectory of the Bryant family was by no means unique, as families throughout the region reconsidered their long-held assumptions about their place in the world.

Modernization of society and culture accompanied the militarization of the southern economy. The SRP employed thousands of highly skilled and educated scientists and engineers from across the nation who almost overnight created a vibrant middle class in a part of South Carolina where almost none had before existed. By the 1960s, the plant made the greatest single contribution to the economic base of Aiken, Barnwell, and Allendale Counties.[2] As historian Margaret Pugh O'Mara argues, "Policy choices made in the earliest years of the Cold War vested scientific institutions and industries with the power to transform regional economies."[3] Such was the case in South Carolina. Scores of suburban subdivisions and national retail outlets served the housing and lifestyle needs of these new white-collar residents and offered new opportunities to Ronnie Bryant and other longtime residents, thus helping to break down the intense localism that had characterized the surrounding area. For residents of the mill villages in Horse Creek Valley, the SRP was an economic godsend, enabling many of them to enter the middle class and giving them new opportunities to participate in the region's expanding mass consumer culture. Most native South Carolinians as well as newcomers proudly embraced their new roles in the nation's Cold War weapons program.

Together, this burgeoning middle class, the influx of national retail establishments and a flourishing consumer culture, and mass suburbanization introduced a larger culture heralding efficiency, rationality, consumption, technological innovation, and progress—all components of a vaguely defined notion of modernization—that threatened to displace the region's older rural culture. Much of this impact drew from the particular influence of the Du Pont Corporation.

Du Pont arrived in South Carolina ready to do battle in the Cold War. With 150 years of industrial experience, a complex product portfolio that encompassed a wide range of consumer products as well as nuclear materials, and a well-defined corporate culture, Du Pont fostered a local culture that privileged modernization, innovation, efficiency, and civic involvement. As historian Pap A. Ndiaye explains, "In the early 1950s, the majority of Americans still thought that the mass production of sophisticated goods under the apparently efficient and impartial aegis of engineers and managers had given them the best means of guaranteeing steady growth, defusing social tensions, and maintaining social peace." This belief was nowhere stronger than in the region surrounding the SRP, where both employees and nonemployees easily and readily adopted Du Pont's culture as their best hope for a peaceful and prosperous future.[4] The region's new emphasis on modernization and efficiency had wide-ranging consequences. The creation of the SRP decisively reordered the traditional rural landscape, not only through newly built structures such as suburban tract housing but also by blurring traditional geographic boundaries and by introducing a new understanding of land and space defined by Cold War imperatives. The emergence of the modern military state literally imprinted itself on the southern landscape. In a region where the relationship between town and country had once been relatively fluid, planners of the military-industrial complex introduced modern concepts of boundaries and land use that rendered the environment subordinate to technology and security. Aiken exhibited patterns that were in part merely the result of population growth but were also shaped by Du Pont's specific corporate culture and the nature of work undertaken at the plant.

The dramatic changes to western South Carolina were intimately tied to the wedding of science and government in the World War II and Cold War eras. The Cold War in particular instigated the era of "big science," in which billions of dollars of government funds were funneled to a wide range of scientific initiatives. With the advent and proliferation of generous research budgets, increasing numbers of American scientists signed on to work for their country. Involved in a range of projects that had broad application to American life in war and peace, scientists soon found themselves in a public spotlight that throughout the 1950s became increasingly politicized. Some, such as J. Robert Oppenheimer and Vannevar Bush, engineer, science administrator, and primary organizer of the Manhattan Project, became "scientific celebrities," chairing government committees, testifying before Congress, and offering commentary on a wide range of public issues. Bush became in effect the first presidential science adviser and had a significant hand in prompting scientists to embrace the role of public intellectual.[5] What Paul Boyer calls the "scientists' movement" became "a seminal force in American life." Undergirding this movement was a belief that "a commitment to science almost automatically gave one a global perspective and a unique ethical vantage point."[6] The power of the scientific community to shape national priorities made President Dwight D. Eisenhower uncomfortable, but he could do little to counter it. Historian Michael Sherry notes that "Ike could claim greater wisdom than generals and admirals, but for him to complain publicly about the pressures of scientists and other experts was virtually impossible—it would have smacked of the anti-intellectualism and cramped vision already imputed to Eisenhower and his associates too often for their political comfort. To challenge General Maxwell Taylor was one thing; to dispute Edward Teller was another at a time when so much wisdom and objectivity were attributed to scientists."[7]

Popular interest in science and scientists grew during the 1950s, so much so that *Time* magazine named fifteen American scientists its "Men of the Year" for 1960. Author and scientist C. P. Snow observed immodestly, "Scientists are the most important occupation group of the world today." Chemist William Libby, 1960's Nobel laureate, proclaimed, "We scientists are the only people who are not bored—the only adventurers of modern times, the real explorers—the fortunate ones."[8] Aiken, South Carolina, was the recipient of thousands of these adventurers, men (and a few women) who brought with them a passion for efficiency, research, and innovation that stretched beyond the laboratory and into their communities.

Just counting the numbers of migrating scientists and technicians does not convey the impact of the SRP on the region. As important in determining the shape of change was Du Pont's specific profile and corporate culture. Intent on promoting itself primarily as an innovator and creator of consumer products, such as nylon and cellophane, and downplaying its role in weapons manufacturing, Du Pont had crafted a culture that privileged scientific discovery, research, innovation, and creativity and that emphasized consumption and material well-being as the cornerstone of a free people.[9]

The Du Pont Corporation relentlessly encouraged the connection between the SRP and the achievement of the "good life." In fact, few corporations in the postwar era better represented the American Cold War promise of economic prosperity through mass consumption than Du Pont. By 1952, Du Pont offered more than a hundred products in a wide range of industries. The corporation created and promoted a patriotic self-image that relied not on military commitment but instead on its production of consumer goods. But the military and consumer components were inextricably intertwined, as Aiken County's experiences would demonstrate.

Du Pont aggressively melded its corporate history with that of the nation's. In an effort to refurbish its tarnished image from the Nye Committee investigations, in the 1930s Du Pont pioneered a new corporate public relations strategy: the company sponsored the radio show *Cavalcade of America*, an anthology drama centered on historical events that illustrated key elements of the nation's character. The events were told through stories of individual courage and achievement and emphasized human progress through technology. The show was broadcast weekly during prime time on CBS radio between October 1935 and 1953, with 781 episodes produced. In 1952, *Cavalcade* moved over to the new medium of television, where 202 episodes ran through 1958, first on NBC and then on ABC. The show employed leading actors and writers of the day, including Raymond Massey, Bette Davis, Errol Flynn, Agnes Moorehead, Ethel Barrymore, Arthur Miller and Stephen Vincent Benét. To ensure accuracy, the production team engaged the services of professional historians, most notably Arthur Schlesinger Jr., to edit the scripts.

The inaugural episode of *Cavalcade* dramatized, quite fittingly, the story of the *Mayflower*. Over the next twenty years, programs would focus on seminal events in the history of American innovation, such as the construction of the Erie Canal, the California Gold Rush, and the Louisiana Purchase, as well as the stories of famous Americans including Thomas Jefferson, Mark Twain, Abraham Lincoln, P. T. Barnum, and Elizabeth Blackwell. Also included were the stories of achievement in the areas of industry, science, and medicine. Viewers learned about the development of the smallpox vaccine; the successful application of quinine; the life and work of Charles Goodyear, the inventor of vulcanized rubber; and the history of the American dye industry. *Cavalcade* also included episodes on the life of Éleuthère Irénée du Pont and on Wallace H. Carothers, a Du Pont chemist who was a leader in the development of nylon, the "magic yarn" (this episode was shown twice); the "Story of Du Pont," a history of the company, was aired at least four times.[10] *Cavalcade of America* also introduced Du Pont's new corporate slogan: "Better Things for Better Living . . . Through Chemistry."[11] The brainchild of public relations specialist Bruce Barton, best known for his best-selling book depicting Jesus as the world's greatest salesman, the slogan is instructive regarding the underlying corporate goal of promoting consumerism and tying it to absolute confidence in scientific discovery, which leads to more commodities—"Better Things"—and thus better lives, the promise of postwar prosperity. The use of the ellipses forces readers to pause (for dramatic effect) before embracing the phrase that represents an article of faith within Du Pont: that the pursuit of happiness would be supported best "Through Chemistry."

Du Pont's focus on consumer products and its aggressive public relations campaign had the desired effect on the company's public image. In 1937, in the wake of the Nye Committee hearings, a survey commissioned by Du Pont reported that fewer than half of the ten thousand participants held a favorable opinion of the company, and 16 percent held the company in downright contempt. Twenty years later, in 1958, the same survey found that 79 percent of those tested thought well of Du Pont, while less than 3 percent were unfavorable. According to one historian of the company, "The merchants of death became a foggy memory, replaced by the smiling chemist."[12]

Du Pont's slogan clearly positioned the company not as the producer of a narrow range of industrial products or explosives but as the creator and guarantor of a more prosperous postwar lifestyle. This corporate identity was unabashedly promoted through Du Pont's employee magazine, aptly titled *Better Living*. The proliferation of consumer products developed by Du Pont was nothing less, the magazine declared, than "a reflection of the company's service to the nation."[13] The development of consumer goods, then, was not simply a smart business decision; it was a patriotic commitment.

Central to Du Pont's postwar identity was the belief that its development of a vast range of consumer products was key to demonstrating the superiority of capitalism and winning the struggle against communism. Victory in the Cold War would not be realized through the expansion of the nation's nuclear arsenal alone; it would also depend on American workers' ability to purchase homes, refrigerators, and pantyhose. *Better Living* regularly featured articles that compared the abundance of postwar America—and the good fortune of Du Pont employees in particular—with conditions experienced by workers in communist nations. Typical is a 1951 article, "Why We Eat Better," profiling Du Pont employee Steve Czekalinski. The article compares what a year's worth of wages bought for the American worker versus what a worker in a communist nation could afford or even have access to. The article includes a photograph of Czekalinski and his family surrounded by a year's worth of food and accompanying photographs with blank spots illustrating the absence of food and choices in communist nations.[14] Although the article does not reference

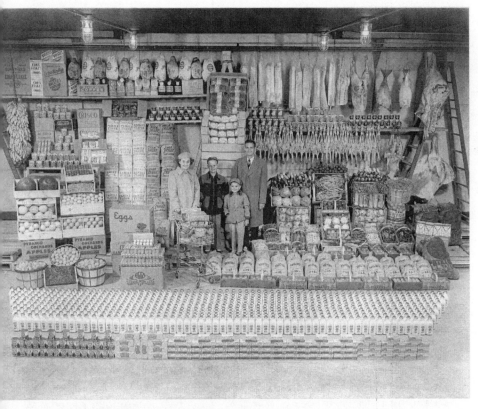

Figure 14. This photograph typified the ways in which Du Pont represented itself as
the guarantor of prosperity and the good life. From "Why We Eat Better: Industrial
Advances in U.S. Open the Way to Rich, Varied Diet," *Better Living*, November–
December 1951, 2–8. Photograph courtesy of Hagley Digital Images, 1972341_001,
Hagley Museum and Library, Wilmington, Delaware.

Czekalinski's ethnic background, few readers would have a hard time making the connection between his Eastern European surname and his American good fortune.

The following year, *Better Living* included a feature on John and Maylou Bonetti. He was a Swiss chemist employed at Polychem's Sabine River Works in Texas. Maylou had lived in Germany during the war before moving to Switzerland. The spread features photos of the Bonettis surrounded by brand-new appliances, clothing, and food as well as images of them enjoying holidays, sports, parks, libraries, and art galleries. Also included are photos of the Bonettis attending church and entering a courthouse, visual homages to religious freedom and the American criminal justice system. "What they quickly discovered as they became oriented to their new role as Americans was that the purchasing power of their adopted land had brought more than shiny cars and automatic washers," the article states. "In such fields as education, philanthropy, fine arts, and religion, the country's leisure and means and basic freedoms had nurtured advances equally as important as those in its material well-being."[15] In crafting this image, Du Pont was no outlier, as this perspective fit perfectly with the transformation of American liberalism during this period: it shed its redistributive features and replaced them with an emphasis on growth and mass consumption.[16]

To introduce Du Pont's carefully crafted image to its new South Carolina hosts, local theaters in 1951 ran *The Du Pont Story*, a sixty-minute melodrama produced to commemorate the company's 150th anniversary. The film opens with images from modern-day Waynesboro, Virginia, where Du Pont employees are taking the bus to work from their homes in the "new suburbs." The film then segues to a discussion of the vastness of the Du Pont industrial empire. With more than eighty thousand employees at plants across the country, the corporation's expansiveness mirrors that of the nation itself. Du Pont's story is America's story. From the opening frames, the film tells viewers that Du Pont's history is synonymous with that of the country. The historical narrative begins with the story of a failed hunting expedition. E. I. du Pont is hunting and his gun misfires, apparently for the third time. The culprit? Faulty gunpowder. His companion asks, "Why don't you go into gunpowder [production]? You will be making a great contribution to the country." Irénée's wife, Sophie, does not want him to pursue gunpowder production because it is too dangerous. Only when President Thomas Jefferson pleads with him does du Pont make his decision. "We need that gunpowder," Jefferson implores. "Not only for defense but for blasting. Clearing farmlands. Building roads." Jefferson tells du Pont that the state will not underwrite his business, as might be the case in France. "Here," Jefferson instructs, "citizens must take the risks and reap the rewards of free enterprise." Of course, the historical record tells a much different story. Du Pont had already formed his company by the time he sought help from Jefferson, although the U.S. government eventually became the company's first and most important customer.[17]

The film hurtles through the nineteenth century, as Du Pont powder heads west with the settlers. "Seeking a new independence, a new freedom, [the pioneers] were the vanguard of America. And with them went Du Pont powder, as indispensable as the food they ate. A force in the building of a nation." Throughout, the film highlights the company's emphasis on efficiency, innovation, and service to the nation. By the twentieth century, the consumer reigns supreme. "The public is the boss," proclaims Irénée du Pont. The film makes no mention of munitions manufacturing during World War I, no mention of the Hanford site of the Manhattan Project, no mention of Du Pont's role in the development of the atomic bomb or in the Cold War. The movie, of course, was meant not to be a complete record of the company's history but rather a dramatization of the "principles" that guided the company's leaders and, more importantly, an assertion of the shared, if reductive, American values prominent in popular and political culture. Such statements of beliefs and history transcended regional differences and antagonisms, thereby emphasizing the continuity of an American vision as the region was embarking on a remarkable transition.

Du Pont brought these principles to South Carolina and disseminated them regularly among its employees. The *Savannah River News*, the plant's employee newsletter, promoted this image of Du Pont, and, by extension, of the Cold War, as the provider of better living through the freedom of mass consumption. Employees—both newcomers to the region and longtime residents—embraced this new consumption-based American identity as the traditional rural and textile production-based identity faded into the past.

The company newsletter frequently published articles and photographs of employees enjoying their newfound prosperity as part of the area's new middle class, compliments of the Du Pont Corporation. Features regularly reminded readers and employees of the nation's high standard of living with statements such as "Many SRP employees have long known the joys that come with home ownership," the ultimate symbol of the American Dream in the postwar period. The newsletter also regularly equated freedom and consumption by reporting on employees' purchases. For a 1955 article, a group of employees were asked, "What outmoded possession do you next plan to replace?" Margaret Scott, who worked in communications at the plant, answered, "My next dream come true will be to trade in my old washer for a new automatic washer and dryer combination. I plan to do this through our convenient payroll plan for buying Savings Bonds." Other employees told of their plans to purchase homes and cars and to take exotic vacations.[18]

Shaping Du Pont's culture from the top was company president Crawford H. Greenewalt, a personification of the emphasis on innovation and achievement. Born into a world of opportunity and abundance, Greenewalt grew up in a family that valued creativity, learning, and exploration. Greenewalt's grandfather had invented a process that allowed typewriters to type in Arabic script. Crawford knew the Du Ponts from an early age and married Irénée du Pont's daughter, Margaretta, in 1926. He graduated from Massachusetts Institute of Technology with a bachelor of science degree in chemical engineering and embarked on what would be a lifelong career with Du Pont. He began as a chemist at the company's experimental station and was eventually appointed technical director of the Graselli Chemical Department. He was among a tiny group of civilians invited to the University of Chicago in 1942 to witness the first nuclear chain reaction. After Du Pont joined the Manhattan Project, the company's president chose Greenewalt to serve as liaison at Hanford between the production team and the physicists. When he took over management of the Hanford project, the nuclear physicists were suspicious because Greenewalt was not a nuclear physicist. However, he boned up so well on nuclear physics that in six months he could talk to the scientists in their own language. Greenewalt was such a quick study, in fact, that when Du Pont turned the operation of Hanford over to General Electric after the war, pioneering atomic scientist Enrico Fermi asked Greenewalt to quit Du Pont and devote his life to pure research. Greenewalt's wartime managerial success as well as his marriage thrust him into the corporate limelight; in 1948, he became one of the youngest men (as well as only the second nonblood relative) to become president of Du Pont.[19]

Greenewalt possessed a restless mind and creative spirit. An accomplished musician, he played the clarinet, cello, and piano; he built model steam engines, grew orchids, and developed high-speed photographic equipment to study hummingbirds. He built a time-lapse camera using an alarm clock. He eventually published three books studying hummingbirds, winged flight, and

Figure 15. Crawford H. Greenewalt, ca. 1945. Photograph courtesy of Crawford H. Greenewalt Photographic Collection, Part II, 1994333_001, Hagley Museum and Library, Wilmington, Delaware.

birdsongs and vocalizations. According to one family member, there was "no such thing as unproductive downtime" for Crawford Greenewalt.[20]

Greenewalt had a hand in crafting the company's corporate structure, which likewise reflected its emphasis on innovation. Composed of ten industrial departments directing such diverse projects as electrochemicals, explosives, and rayon, Du Pont officials frequently switched employees around to cross-fertilize the company and to broaden the employees' experiences. For example, an organic chemist might be put in charge of sales and left there to sink or swim. Within these positions, employees and managers received great latitude. If the manager did a good job, the general staff did not meddle.

Because of Du Pont's concerns about image, its desire to foreground its consumer products, and the exalted position of scientists in popular culture, Greenewalt maintained a very high profile. The public record of Greenewalt's thoughts concerning science, scientists, and society is voluminous. Science, Greenewalt proclaimed, was "the source of [our] national strength, of material progress, of added leisure, and of enriched cultural opportunities."[21] Science relied on creativity; it also was a communal effort in which no idea was ever lost or destroyed.[22] And the creative process, of course, relied on intellectual freedom.[23] As innovators and problem solvers, scientists, Greenewalt argued, had a duty to contribute to civic life.[24] This belief applied to Du Pont employees in particular. Greenewalt consistently remarked on the potential of research and innovation to improve Americans' material well-being, and encouraged his employees to expand their creativity to pursuits beyond the laboratory. Greenewalt and other corporate leaders put their industrial pursuits into a larger Cold War context. Humanity's material status could only improve in a free society, and innovation and creativity in science could take place only where no restrictions were placed on freedom of thought. This freedom extended beyond the laboratory to participation in democratic institutions. Greenewalt's philosophy regarding the scientists' role in society jibed with a general faith in scientists, a belief not only that they might legitimately offer expertise as scientists but also that they might weigh in on a number of policy issues. Greenewalt consistently maintained that industry and business leaders had a responsibility to involve themselves in political affairs, and Du Pont regularly urged its employees to be politically active.[25]

Potential employees were attracted to Du Pont because of its diverse industrial profile, its emphasis on research and development, and the potential for growth and experience within the company. Individuals recruited by Du Pont to work at the Savannah River facility received assurances that despite the more controlled and secret nature of their work, "initiative and ingenuity would be encouraged."[26] Two highly sought after young men, chemist Mal McKibben and nuclear scientist Walt Joseph, exemplify the Du Pont scientists of the 1950s and 1960s. With his bachelor's in chemistry from Emory University, McKibben considered offers from Union Carbide and Dow Chemical. Joseph, then a doctoral student in nuclear physics at the University of Pennsylvania, entertained thoughts of working for General Electric and Westinghouse. Both chose Du Pont because of its reputation as an innovator. For McKibben, the choice was easy. "Du Pont was a Cadillac," he analogized; "all the rest were Fords." Both men recalled the sense of excitement and discovery that imbued their work at the SRP. According to McKibben, "We were always encouraged to think creatively, and we were given the latitude necessary to solve problems." Many employees extended this creativity and problem-solving ability outside the plant.[27]

Of course, the SRP was different from Du Pont's other manufacturing concerns. Because the facility was dedicated to developing material for the hydrogen bomb, secrecy and security were paramount. Still, within the parameters laid down by the AEC, Du Pont remained dedicated to industrial cross-fertilization. Joseph was assigned to no fewer than six divisions within the plant during his long tenure. At one point, he was put in charge of plant traffic. McKibben was moved from heavy water production to fuel and target fabrication to separations—three extremely different processes—while employed by the company.[28]

Outside of the plant, employees were forbidden to talk about their work. Ronnie Bryant noted that he and his fellow workers in the heavy water production sector joked that when asked about their jobs, they would reply that they were making lipstick. Bryant also observed that the constant reminders not to talk about work outside the plant "made us feel that what we were doing was really important."[29]

Spouses and children were kept in the dark regarding the work at the site. Du Pont acknowledged that such secrecy could cause tension at home. In a "memo for housewives," Du Pont reminded spouses of plant employees that even dinner-table conversation about the plant was potentially dangerous. "SRP is not an ordinary plant," Du Pont cautioned; "Its mission is national defense; its job is important and secret."[30] Such extreme confidentiality at a time of heightened international tension caused stress for plant families. Children often came up with imaginative explanations for the secrecy that enveloped their lives. Joseph's son recalled that his father's "job and work were not the topics of conversation at our dinner table. He left in the early hours of the morning, riding with a group of other men in a carpool, and came home just in time for dinner. Some weekends there would be a late night phone call and he would leave for work in the middle of the night." Every few weeks, the rest of the family "would get in the car in the early evening and drive to pick my father up, and when we did we picked him up at a barber shop in a shopping center on the highway which ran from Aiken to New Ellenton. This was the only business I could associate my father with in the first six years of my life, so I made the logical assumption. My father was a barber."[31]

Everything about the plant dictated that it exist as an entity wholly separate from the surrounding communities. The boundary of the plant site was ten miles from the closest city. It was spread over 325 square miles of real estate—roughly the size of the city of Chicago. Plant operations and administrative buildings were secluded behind miles of wooded buffer. Traffic streamed into the plant in the morning and out of the plant at night. Employees needed identification badges to enter. It was a curious, secret place. As a vast military-industrial complex, it stood alone and aloof symbolically. As a place of work employing six thousand people, however, the SRP was never an entity unto itself. Its existence was immediately a powerful influence on the entire region and the everyday lives of everyone. An important facet of this connectivity came from the Du Pont employees themselves, especially those new to the area. Rather than isolating the employees and heightening the distance between employees and town, the insistence on secrecy and security facilitated community involvement. For many, the sense of mission that accompanied their jobs did not stop when they left the workplace. Many took seriously Greenewalt's—and Du Pont's—notion about their role in improving the standard of living. "Better living" was achieved not only through the acquisition of consumer goods but also through the creation and improvement of community institutions. Recalled Joseph, "It was expected that you were involved in civic affairs."[32]

Savannah River employees quickly immersed themselves in community life. Aiken attorney Buzz Rich recalled that "all those Du Ponters had a lot of energy . . . all that brain power, coming into that small southern town. They had time on their hands, in the evenings and weekends. . . . They got involved and started all of these activities."[33] Owen Clary, who grew up in the mill town of Warrenville in the valley and who eventually worked for the SRP before heading up a local food bank, remarked that many of the Du Pont employees were civic-minded. "They were generous with their time and always volunteered for fund-raising activities."[34] The activities of Du Pont employees were covered in the local newspaper and highlighted in the company newsletter. Du Pont employees founded a community theater group, the United Way, the Rotary Club, and a historical society, and they raised money for a new library. Plant supervisors and employees worked hard to relate their work—however secretive—to the community at large. Farmers of Aiken County flocked to a public program on radioisotopes and their applicability to agricultural research.[35] The YWCA sponsored a popular lecture series on subjects that ranged from the nature of matter to nuclear reactors. More than six hundred schoolteachers from around the region attended an all-day seminar on the incorporation of information about atomic energy into the school curriculum. Plant workers founded local chapters of their professional associations and made them relevant to the community. For example, the Savannah River Subsection of the American Chemical Society contributed $125 for science books for the local high school and counseled students on careers in chemistry and atomic energy.[36] Arthur Tackman, assistant manager of the plant, was named Aiken County Citizen of the Year for 1953. He had served as campaign chair of the American Red Cross–Community Chest, coordinator of committees of the annual Cotton Festival, and chair of the area Boy Scouts. He had resided in the area for only two years.[37] SRP employees provided volunteer labor to build a public swimming pool in Williston and organized and staffed various suburban fire departments. By 1955, Du Pont employees were either leading or participating in Aiken's major community institutions.

By 1968, Du Ponters and AEC folks were the in crowd. According to one employee, the social and cultural power of the Old Aiken/Winter Colony folks had been "diluted."[38] Almost overnight, Aiken's function and economic orientation changed from that of an upscale tourist town with rudimentary connections to rural communities into a modern space whose built environment and residents alike were reconfigured by the actions of AEC and Du Pont. Federal and corporate officials had envisioned Aiken and its surrounding small towns as dormitory suburbs for the new workforce. Augusta, Georgia, by far the largest metropolitan area in the region, they predicted, would serve as the commercial and residential center. They were wrong. Aiken became the region's new center of gravity for SRP employees and the rural and mill communities.

The construction, safety, and security requirements of the SRP had an immediate and dramatic impact on the local landscape, both inside and outside the plant boundaries.[39] The pursuit of federal dollars encouraged South Carolina leaders to adopt a more expansive and benign definition of *federal intervention* even as the economic salvation promised by outside investment complicated other traditional political boundaries. Although winning projects for South Carolina held the greatest political benefit for the state's elected officials, geographic realities, such as flood control, often dictated that states work together to secure federal aid. Through such combined efforts, the area surrounding the Savannah River basin acquired a regional identity tied to modernization and development and became known as the Central Savannah River Area, designating a metropolitan region that included not just South Carolina but Georgia as well. The militarization of the southern economy cemented this development-oriented geography and landscape, which blurred traditional boundaries and began to break down the intense localism of traditional communities. The new name, created by C. C. McCollum of Wrens, South Carolina, was chosen from among twenty-five hundred entries in a contest sponsored by the *Augusta Chronicle*.[40] The commandeering of this vast rural space for military needs meant that the SRP, and by extension the Cold War, quite literally imprinted itself on the landscape. Even a cursory look at a map of the area reveals that the SRP dwarfs other cartographical features such as state parks and city boundaries. Yet the plant site typically is rendered a pale neutral color, usually light gray or white, a stark visual representation of a vast, secret space. What cannot be represented on any map is how it reached far beyond its defined physical borders. That reach is no secret at all.

In nearby Aiken, the plant's impact on the landscape was almost as dramatic as the transformation within the boundaries. Most of the permanent operations staff—managers, scientists, engineers, and technicians—chose to live in and around Aiken.[41] By 1953, the city's permanent population had tripled. Ten years later, total real estate investment by SRP employees in the Aiken region had reached nearly sixty-five million dollars, while their annual payroll was slightly more than sixty million dollars.[42] Private developers created twenty-seven subdivisions to house this new middle class. The area surrounding the SRP, which at the close of World War II was categorized by AEC officials as underdeveloped and primarily rural, now embraced a Cold War suburban identity as an important outpost on the frontier of nuclear science as well as an integral component of the national defense state.

The creation of suburbs not only reflected a real housing need in the Savannah River area but also was driven by the security and larger industrial dispersion requirements of the Cold War state. O'Mara notes, "The ideal location for defense-crucial American industry, as defined by the president and by his chief civil-defense strategists, was in a small community that was at a certain distance from the central city but still connected to a regional metropolitan economy." Suburbanization and Cold War industrial dispersion went hand in hand.[43]

Developers of the new subdivisions marketed homes directly to plant employees, promoting the efficiency and convenience of the suburbs. In 1952, one developer touted its "really large, complete modern home[s] . . . ideally located only . . . minutes from the new Savannah River Plant."[44] Most of these middle-class houses were ranch style and measured about twelve hundred square feet. The subdivisions themselves were laid out along lines typical of 1950s suburbs across the nation, with large, elongated blocks and curving streets.[45] These developments sprouted like mushrooms after a summer shower. Quickly following on the opening of Crosland Park were Dunbarton Oaks, Aiken Heights, Aiken Estates, and Forest Heights, to name just a few, each ultimately annexed by the city.[46] These new subdivisions differed greatly from the rural landscape as well as the surrounding area's existing towns and textile mill villages, where the relationships among dwelling, workplace, and geography were intertwined.

Graniteville exhibited the layout and geographic logic of most textile mill villages. Built to harness the power of the swift-moving Horse Creek, the mill dominated its landscape, with rows of small company-owned homes ascending the valley walls but still oriented toward the center of production. Residents of the villages of Graniteville, Langley, Bath, Warrenville, and Vaucluse not only situated themselves within their villages proper but also regarded (and still do regard) themselves as residents of "the valley." Graniteville's individual neighborhoods bore names that resonated with a sense of time and place. Local lore contends that the Shakerag neighborhood earned its name during the influenza pandemic of 1918. During the outbreak, caregivers to the sick would hold rags over their mouths to protect themselves from the virus and could frequently be seen shaking these rags outside, apparently to rid them of the germs.[47] Battle Row designated a Graniteville street whose residents were particularly quarrelsome; Rock Town was a semicircle of homes so named because they were built of granite and sandstone; and New Town connoted those houses located up Breezy Hill, away from the valley, that were constructed after the central part of the village.[48] Residents of the mill valley landscape were enmeshed in a web of history and geography. The newer subdivisions built to accommodate the influx of plant employees possessed no such orientation and engendered no such connection with local geography. The housing boom of the 1950s severed connections with the land itself and brought about the loss of a traditional sense of place and history.[49]

Like Ronnie Bryant, other young valley residents entered this emerging middle class. E. C. Thomas, who returned to work at the Graniteville Company following his service in World War II, recalled that local textiles could not compete with the wages offered at the atomic plant.[50] The son of a carpenter and a self-described "badass valley boy," Owen Clary worked summers in the corduroy division of Gregg manufacturing. His future might have been in textiles had the SRP not come along while he was in high school. After receiving a degree from Furman University, Clary taught history at the Coast Guard Academy and eventually took a job as an industrial engineer with the SRP. His college education and white-collar employment allowed him to purchase a home in the Kalmia Hill subdivision, located halfway between Graniteville and Aiken, a lovely neighborhood with winding streets and towering magnolias near the spot where William Gregg had chosen to build his home a century earlier as he developed the Graniteville Company.[51]

Although the SRP did not hire nearly as many African Americans as whites, over time, black residents of the region benefited economically from the new opportunities provided by the Cold War development. For example, after eleven months as a janitor at the SRP, Shepherd Archie moved to the transportation department, eventually working his way up to a supervisory role "over all the heavy equipment in roads and grounds." Although African Americans started at lower rungs on the economic ladder and thus faced a longer climb into the middle class, Archie recalled that their "lives changed tremendous from poor to middle class. They got a better life out of that, by this plant coming. . . . Now most of them own homes."[52] Black plant employees were the target customers for the Harlem Heights subdivision, located 1.5 miles outside the Aiken city limits and offering potential buyers city water and "nice wide streets." Promoters of the development, which was eventually renamed Pineland Terrace, urged black home buyers "not [to] confuse this [subdivision] with the low, poorly located home sites generally offered to colored people. . . . This is for the discriminating home seeker who wishes to give his family the best, rear their children under the very best of conditions and frankly, don't you think you owe that to them?" Among those who bought property in this subdivision were National Association for the Advancement of Colored People leader Dr. Charles C. Johnson and community activist Josie Hazel.[53]

Whereas the majority of scientists and engineers tended to make their homes in Aiken, Du Pont records indicate that production operators, maintenance mechanics, and traffic and transportation personnel gravitated toward the smaller communities of New Ellenton, Jackson, and Barnwell and eventually made up a significant portion of the populations of these small towns.[54] This residential division by social class mirrored developments surrounding Washington State's Hanford Engineering Works, with the town of Richland housing a disproportionate share of the scientists and engineers and nearby Pasco and Kennewick becoming home to lower-status employees and African Americans.[55] Du Pont officials noted that New Ellenton and Jackson in particular "have no other economic reason for their being except to support the SRP by providing homes for employees of the SRP."[56] North Augusta, a town resurrected near where the town of Hamburg once stood, grew tremendously as a result of the plant—182 percent. Located directly across the Savannah River from Augusta, Georgia, North Augusta was almost exclusively a residential community, with the second-largest concentration of SRP employees and their families.[57]

Like so many newcomers to the region, Arthur D. Rich, an attorney in Strom Thurmond's Aiken law firm whose wife worked as a nurse at the SRP, lived in the new suburb of Aiken Estates, located on the south side of Aiken and at the time the closest subdivision to the plant. Aiken Estates was developed from a portion of Hitchcock Woods, ancestral property of the Hitchcock family and beloved horse country. The original plans for the subdivision called for two hundred homes and included Mitchell Shopping Center. Rich recalled that almost all of his neighbors were Du Pont employees. "Most of them had bought a temporary house at Crosland Park. And then, as they worked and made money, they built in . . . the south-side area." Rich's son, Buzz, recalled with amusement the regularity of the Du Pont families. "Most of the kids I grew up with—their parents were Du Ponters. . . . Dad would come home from work at 4:30 and mom would have dinner on the table at 5:00."[58]

Accompanying the new suburbs and developed during the course of the 1950s were shopping centers; chain department stores such as J. B. White, Sears, and J. C. Penney; chain drugstores; supermarkets; a drive-in movie theater; an expanded McCrory's five-and-dime; and scores of restaurants.[59] Plans for area suburbs frequently included adjacent shopping centers to serve the new residents.[60] The local newspaper heralded the retail establishments that accompanied economic development and population growth in the 1950s as "tribute[s] to the progressive spirit of Aiken."[61] Du Pont officials estimated that by the early 1960s, approximately ten thousand persons in the Aiken region drew their livelihood from retail and service businesses catering to the burgeoning community.[62] The arrival of national retailers reoriented the residents. Aiken's previous major retailers were small merchants. Working-class residents of the valley, as well as residents of Aiken County's rural communities, preferred Augusta's larger, more affordable chain department stores.[63] But the arrival of expanded commerce drew valley shoppers to Aiken, where they were more inclined to patronize the new establishments than the small shops, thus drawing them closer to Aiken and making it less necessary to travel to Augusta. Sylvia Bryant recalled that "once White's was built, we started shopping" in Aiken.[64] The arrival of the plant and its employees ultimately began to break down the fierce divisions separating Aiken and the valley by bringing along the trappings of a more modern cosmopolitan lifestyle that benefited the entire region and drew its people together. Graniteville resident Lenwood Melton speculated that the arrival of scientists and engineers somehow brought the region into the modern era. To Melton and others, despite the myriad problems associated with the plant, being a resident of Fortress Dixie paid off in the end: the plant and the new permanent residents "upgraded things, really, because we had never had that level of people amongst us. When you got those types coming in, and of course, they were more well-to-do [than the millworkers], and they built some fine houses, they brought the shopping malls, they started new churches, they started doing things like big city folks. . . . As far as the community of [greater] Aiken is concerned, it grew up into a very respectable area."[65]

City planners facilitated this retail expansion by remaking the built environment in service to automobile consumers from the suburbs and surrounding towns. In November 1951, about ten months into the construction phase, Aiken began rezoning downtown blocks from residential to business to allow for commercial growth.[66] Two years later, merchants from the downtown business section petitioned the city council for additional parking. The council voted to narrow several of Aiken's beloved boulevard green spaces, thereby widening the streets and creating more parking for shoppers.[67] This decision to sacrifice aesthetics for commerce, to substitute a landscape of consumption over a landscape of leisure, drew harsh criticism from longtime residents of the City of Parkways, led by fixtures of Old Aiken, such as the headmaster of the prep school and Eulalie Salley, the city's best-known real estate agent to the Winter Colonists. In 1956, city leaders made another concession to retailers and a more cosmopolitan population when they moved to amend Sunday blue laws. In a scathing editorial, the *Aiken Standard and Review* lambasted the city council for "plac[ing] the almighty dollar above Almighty God."[68] One resident lamented the changes economic prosperity and expansion had brought to Aiken. In "A Tale of Two Cities," Thomas H. Williamson contrasted old and new Aiken:

> Two cities are growing
> In the boundaries of one,
> One city of sadness
> And the other of fun.
>
> One the old city
> The other one new,
> One where serenity
> Reigns the year thru.
>
> One where the hustle
> And bustle remain,
> And we have little choice
> Betwixt pleasure and pain.[69]

Williamson's poem captures the core tension of modernization. Such anxieties certainly played out throughout the nation in the 1950s and 1960s, but the rapid pace of the shift combined with the particular history of Aiken itself made the situation there much more dramatic and transformative. Williamson laments the loss of choice in the face of this change, though he concedes that it was unstoppable. Many agreed with his concerns, but many others embraced the shift. They agreed that choice was an issue: the SRP offered them one.

The city council increasingly found itself burdened with proposed regulations suggested by suburban residents concerning noise and aesthetics, and for the first time the council adopted subdivision regulations.[70] But the newcomers' desire for order and progress often rubbed up against the sensibilities of the older residents. For example, in 1956, the city council was debating whether to require all dogs within the city limits to remain on leashes. Opposing the new ordinance quite boisterously were the Winter Colonists. Their objection? They used packs of hounds for fox hunts and other sports and feared that a leash law would endanger their hounds and ruin their sport. Mrs. Robert J. Harrington lodged her protest before the city council, claiming that "the hounds have never been able to wear collars because of the danger of being caught on bushes in the woods and hung."[71] Conflict arose again in 1962, when the council was deciding which city roads to pave. For most communities, paved roads were a sign of modern life, but in Aiken, wealthy horse owners resisted paving as detrimental to the animals' welfare.[72] Throughout the 1950s and 1960s, as the city council struggled to accommodate itself to population growth and residents' increasing commercial demands, it regularly encountered resistance from a sector of the population that was increasingly feeling out of step with its new neighbors.

Although Aiken merchants welcomed the spending power of the new white middle class, social acceptance of the Du Ponters was slow to materialize. To Old Aiken, those restaurateurs, merchants, real estate agents, and lawyers who made their living off the Winter Colonists, the plant employees were Aiken's "new Negroes," according to Pat Conroy—"technological Negroes to be sure, but Negroes, nevertheless," segregated in their suburban enclaves on the city's perimeter and spurned by the established social networks.[73] Du Pont wives organized the Town and Country Club after being shunned by local women's clubs.[74]

By the early 1960s, the social character and built environment of Aiken County had changed significantly. The number of professional and technical workers had tripled in the course of a decade. In 1950, the vast majority of the population was employed in agriculture and textiles; by 1960, the number of men and women employed in nonagricultural industries represented 93 percent of the workforce. Aiken County's clerical workforce doubled, as women moved from textiles to office work at the SRP. "Engineers Technical" appeared as a local employment category for the first time in the 1960 Census.[75] With a burgeoning middle class and a massive high-tech facility that reordered the community's economic and social life, modernity had overtaken the region. With these profound changes, the "progress" Governor Thurmond had sought back in the late 1940s had arrived.

With the dawn of the Cold War, the city of Aiken changed its civic marketing strategy. No longer billed merely as an enclave for elite tourists, Aiken had transformed itself into a dynamic and progressive example of the modern South. Festival programs and other promotional materials highlighted Aiken's progressive government and its modern conveniences, its "fine, up-to-date shops" and "multiple shopping units adjacent to the city proper." Aiken adopted a new city seal in the mid-1950s; it is divided into quadrants depicting golfers, a thoroughbred, an antebellum mansion, and the atomic energy symbol with the word *Progress* emblazoned across it. Furthermore, Aiken's boosters began promoting the area as a place to live, not just to visit. The arrival of the Bomb Plant encouraged further industrial development, and by the end of the decade, Owens-Corning Fiberglass Corporation; Pyle National, a Chicago-based manufacturer of electronic and electrical equipment; and paper manufacturer Kimberly-Clark had built plants in Aiken County.[76] In 1967, the University of South Carolina opened a regional campus in Aiken.[77] By the 1960s, the city's brochures no longer heralded the "Sport Center of the South"; instead, Aiken's new slogan was "Charm and Progress," illustrating attempts to meld tradition and modernization, to find that ideal middle landscape between pastoral ideals of agricultural and premodern simplicity and modern ideals of efficiency and technological innovation. The covers of promotional brochures bore photographs of a modern brick ranch home rather than the earlier image of a polo player with jodhpurs and whip, highlighting the middle-class suburban lifestyle rather than the celebrations of elite recreation. Instead of colorful descriptions of upscale sports, marketing literature featured data on housing costs, public schools, health care, and churches.[78] Aiken's recreational offerings and focus on the wealthy and on nature, while still plentiful, became

Figure 16. Aiken City Seal. Image courtesy of City of Aiken.

complementary to the new primary emphasis on progress, community, and technology.

In 1960, ten years after the AEC made the decision that changed this corner of the South forever, Aiken celebrated its 125th anniversary. In a commemorative brochure, Ken Kilbourne of the Chamber of Commerce composed a descriptive narrative of the hypothetical Aiken in the year 2000. Like most time-traveling flights of fancy, scientists play a key role in this future. By 2000, Kilbourne believed, local scientists would have transformed Aiken into a model city that embodied the perfect mix of technology and mass consumption. Declaring the natural environment dangerous, scientists had by 2000 rendered it irrelevant by creating a protective shell over Aiken, allowing them to exert maximum control over the environment. The result, the scientists argued, would be "less physical fatigue, [fewer] colds [and] miseries" that threatened human existence and productivity. The same scientists who had launched the nuclear project that had suddenly thrust this region of South Carolina into the center of an unstable, chaotic world would bring security, control, and certainty. In Kilbourne's utopian dream, Aiken would be entirely rezoned; gone were the beautiful boulevards and nineteenth-century homes that lined the streets of the central city. The suburbs and consumption would define the community; "suburban interests" and "shopkeepers" would share power in City Hall, and the central city would be given up completely to retail.[79]

Kilbourne's prognostications, like other futuristic imaginings, reveal much about the contemporary mind-set, especially the vision of the Chamber of Commerce. Although such city planning celebrating suburban sprawl has since become discredited for its inefficient use of space, in 1960 it seemed unequivocally logical and sustainable. Moreover, it reveals a community brimming with confidence. Still, Kilbourne's future Aiken is striking for the complete nature of its transformation. The Winter Colony, which had once provided the livelihood of so many as well as defined the city's character, plays no role. From his perspective, such a development might not have seemed much of a stretch. By 1960, the demands of the Cold War and the arrival of a multinational corporation threatened (or promised) to erase what had been distinctive about Aiken. Such was also the case in other southern communities in which Cold War militarization took hold. Most residents of these communities now deemed critical defense areas embraced the opportunity to partake in a middle-class lifestyle and welcomed the benefits that their new militarized economy would bring. Yet they remained mindful of the costs. Like those promoting Aiken's "charm and progress," most southerners eagerly grasped the promise of the future while hoping to retain the best of the past.

CHAPTER SEVEN

Shifting Landscapes
Politics and Race in a Cold War Community

From 1941 to 1948, Aiken County was represented in the South Carolina state senate by Fred Brinkley, a physician from the tiny town of Ellenton. In addition to being one of the town's two doctors, Brinkley was also a part-time farmer and owner of the one of the town's gristmills. A longtime resident of Ellenton, Brinkley was closely tied to the region's agricultural rhythms and was active in community affairs. And like every other state senator, Brinkley was a Democrat in a state that reviled Republicans. In the early 1950s, after Ellenton was condemned to make room for the Savannah River Plant (SRP), Brinkley moved to the city of Barnwell. He died relatively soon after the evacuation, in June 1952, with his passing serving as poignant symbol of the larger transformations under way in the area.[1]

The influx of thousands of new residents from communities across the nation altered not only the region's demographics, built environment, economic profile, and cultural identity but also its politics. In 1968, fifteen years after operations commenced at the SRP, Aiken County voters elected George Mc-Millan to represent them in the State Senate. A Republican and former Du Pont supervisor at the SRP, McMillan was just one of a growing number of Republicans elected to public office in Aiken County and in the expanding suburban regions across South Carolina and other southern states in the 1960s and 1970s. The origins of the Republican Party lay in the communities housing the plant employees; the party drew strength from their conservative, middle-class values, forged not only by opposition to certain New Deal–era programs and staunch anticommunism but also from notions of efficiency and modernization as they applied to the political process. Such values were also deeply engrained in Du Pont's corporate culture.

The growth of the Republican Party in Aiken County coincided with and at times appeared synonymous with the acceleration of school integration. Although the passage of the Civil Rights Act of 1964 and the Voting Rights Act of 1965 motivated thousands of white southerners to vote Republican, the party's roots in South Carolina went further back and were tied to the changes brought on by the Cold War. Integration in this region was in part shaped by Du Pont's corporate culture. Although the company encouraged employees to participate in local and state politics, there was an understanding that employees were not to engage overtly in the desegregation debate and were to let the issue run its course. As with its employment strategy, Du Pont preferred to follow local custom rather than challenge it directly.

School integration proceeded as slowly in Aiken County as it did in other towns across the South, but without the extreme public acrimony and outright violence present in some communities. Although whites in Aiken County—both longtime residents and newcomers—were content to drag their feet on the issue, the impending threat of a loss of federal funds as well as the judicial dismantling of freedom-of-choice school-assignment plans in the late 1960s finally brought desegregation to the region. When meaningful integration finally came to the county in 1970, white resistance died with a whimper.

The relatively uneventful process of integration partly resulted from factors related to Aiken's particular historical development as well as the more recent changes brought about by the Cold War. White resistance in this corner of South Carolina was muted by a variety of factors, including changing demographics, the influence of Du Pont's particular corporate culture, the central role given to large corporations for securing prosperity and security, the reputation of black schools, and the presence of Winter Colony residents. The intense backlash and white flight to private academies found in other communities simply was not present in Aiken. While not exactly welcoming of the prospect of integration, white parents also were unwilling to take extreme measures to stop it.

Following company president Crawford H. Greenewalt's advice, Du Pont employees became involved in the city's political institutions, initiating innovations that were based on their desire for modern, efficient, representative government, something that seemed lacking in this one-party region. The majority of Du Pont's permanent operations staff took up residence in Aiken's burgeoning suburbs and in the highly suburbanized town of North Augusta.

To bring order and efficiency to the development chaos that was the result of rapid residential expansion, residents of these suburban enclaves organized civic associations that would regularly and collectively bring particular neighborhood issues before the city council. The first such group organized was the Crosland Park Civic Association. By the early 1960s, every suburb boasted a neighborhood association.[2]

These new civic associations were in the forefront of promoting a change in city government from the commission form to a city manager system. Crosland Park Civic Association took the lead among newcomers in supporting the transition to a full-time city manager system, which, members believed, would promote "sound principles of efficient city administration." A full-time city manager would be better equipped to handle the problems associated with rapid growth, something Crosland Park residents knew only too well. The five-hundred-plus-home subdivision was cursed with chronic sewage overflow, a complaint regularly brought before the city council.[3] Crosland Park residents likewise supported the "appointment of city employees on the basis of merit apart from political considerations or influence," as well as "planning and zoning provisions which provide for orderly growth, stabilize property values, and protect the citizens of Aiken from the inconvenience, danger, and expense which can result from irresponsible real property development." Finally, the association called for "a carefully developed system of public hearings which assure that the citizens of Aiken shall have the opportunity to be heard in matters of basic policy determination." By calling for a merit system and a transparent decision-making process, the new residents were advocating not only for a more democratic and representative government but for a process that in many ways resembled the scientific process, in which all variables are carefully weighed.[4] With the new neighborhood associations in the lead, Aiken residents overwhelmingly approved the adoption of the city manager system.[5]

Du Pont employees likewise were instrumental in bringing two-party politics to what had been a one-party state. Du Ponters took the lead in promoting Republican candidates in national elections and in organizing the first county-level Republican Party, joining other white-collar suburbanites around the state and region in developing a viable second party. South Carolina's one-party system had grown out of historical racial and political animosities. Since Reconstruction, the Republican Party had been anathema to South Carolina's white voters, synonymous with "negro control." The return to Democratic Party rule in the 1870s was marred by violence, perhaps nowhere worse than in Aiken County, which had seen two of the worst race riots in state history in 1876. Throughout the first half of the twentieth century, South Carolina was the region's most reliably Democratic state, refusing to bolt the party in 1928 and polling huge numbers for Franklin Roosevelt in the 1930s and 1940s. The Republicans rarely fielded candidates for office even at the state's highest levels, and Democrats dominated local politics in all forty-six counties. According to one account, by midcentury, "the South Carolina GOP was merely a quaint relic of the past, widely accused of graft, corruption, and gross mismanagement."[6] Republican conventions were derided as "the semi-annual gathering of the pie brigade" where the spoils of party patronage were distributed.[7]

Dissatisfaction with the national Democratic Party began to emerge in the 1930s and 1940s as changes brought on by the Great Depression, New Deal, and World War II began to chip away at a southern caste system grounded in low-wage labor and white supremacy. By the late 1940s, a growing number of whites were becoming increasingly hostile toward the national Democratic Party's position on civil rights. In 1948, outraged at President Harry S. Truman's civil rights initiatives and the inclusion of a civil rights plank in the Democratic Party platform, South Carolina Democrats joined white conservatives from several other southern states and bolted the national party, throwing their support behind the States' Rights Democratic Party, more commonly known as the Dixiecrats. Led by presidential candidate and South Carolina governor Strom Thurmond, the Dixiecrats hoped to wrest enough votes from Truman to throw the election into the House of Representatives. In the end, the Dixiecrats won only four states, but their campaign constituted a shot across the political bow, serving notice to the national Democratic Party that white southerners' political allegiance could no longer be taken for granted. Still, despite their misgivings about the direction of the national party, wrenching a majority of southern whites away from the Democratic Party was going to be extremely difficult. Once "liberated," where would they go? By the early 1950s, the South still had no meaningful Republican Party organization. Southern whites unhappy with the direction of the Democratic Party continued to express their displeasure in presidential elections, voting in unprecedented numbers for the Republican candidate, but not as members of any local Republican organization. The existing party apparatus was too weak, too corrupt. Any viable Republican Party would have to be built from scratch by individuals free of the historical political baggage carried by white southerners.[8]

Much of the impetus behind the growth of the Republican Party was the particular economic change that accompanied the Cold War. Between 1950 and 1970, 90 percent of growth in employment in industry in the South took place in high-wage industries, many of them considered part of the military-industrial complex.[9] These white-collar employees, housed in expanding urban and suburban areas, increasingly identified their economic interests as resting with the Republican Party.[10] South Carolina's employment profile changed dramatically. Aiken County was one of the state's fastest growing in terms of industrial expansion. In Aiken County in 1940, 31.5 percent of adults were employed in agriculture; by 1970, that percentage had dropped to 2 percent. In 1940, Aiken County was roughly 18 percent urban; by 1970, 44.4 percent of the population lived in metropolitan areas. Over the same period, the percentage of Aikenites employed in white-collar jobs shot from 15 percent to 41 percent. As part of this transition, the county had become wealthier. From 1953 to 1962, purchasing power in the county rose by five hundred dollars per capita and two thousand dollars per household, and retail sales doubled in dollar volume.[11] Such changes were not limited to Aiken. Overall, South Carolina's suburban population grew by nearly 400 percent between 1950 and 1970.[12] Aiken joined rapidly expanding counties such as Richland (Columbia), Greenville, Lexington, and Charleston in the white-collar suburban boom.

Profound political change followed this economic transformation. From 1946 to 1963, South Carolina had the lowest level of party competition in the South. Between 1964 and 1974, however, it moved into first place in the Deep South and seventh overall in the region. No other Deep South state experienced increasingly competitive two-party gubernatorial elections between 1960 and 1975.[13]

The expanding metropolitan areas were the source of the reborn Republican Party. In 1952, Dwight D. Eisenhower drew support from wealthier whites in the urban and suburban areas of South Carolina, as well as more race-conscious whites in the majority black lowcountry who were disturbed at the role of civil rights in the Democratic Party platforms of the late 1940s and early 1950s. By 1956, skeleton Republican Party organizations existed in roughly half of the state's forty-six counties. Between 1956 and 1963, the party had no paid staff and no official, continuing central headquarters. Party leadership came from a mishmash of businessmen, disaffected Democrats, and newcomers, most of them political novices.[14]

The early leaders of South Carolina's retooled Republican Party were recent transplants. Gregory D. Shorey Jr., for example, was born in Massachusetts and educated at Boston University, ultimately earning a graduate degree in public relations and marketing communications. He served in the U.S. Navy during World War II and subsequently became active in the Massachusetts Republican Party. In 1950, he moved to Greenville, South Carolina, where he founded a company that manufactured marine safety and water sports equipment and moved quickly to the top of the state Republican Party hierarchy. He served as state chair of Eisenhower for President in 1952 and 1956, a Republican elector in 1952 and 1956, state executive chair from 1954 to 1956, and state chair from 1956 to 1962.[15] The renascent GOP received financial backing from Roger Milliken, president of the family owned Deering-Milliken Textile Corporation, the world's third-largest textile firm. Milliken had contributed extensively to the national Republican Party but had avoided the dysfunctional state party until the revamped version emerged in the 1950s.[16] Still, even with Milliken's support, the party operated on a shoestring budget. While serving as state chair, Shorey paid his own travel, office, and campaign expenses, which totaled nearly sixty thousand dollars. Since the party lacked a formal headquarters, he often convened party meetings at his office or home.[17]

Support for Eisenhower in 1952 was the first solid sign of the potential of Republican Party fortunes in the South. Not yet ready to become full-fledged Republicans, disaffected Democrats calling themselves Citizens for Eisenhower actively campaigned for the former general. Republicans and Citizens for Eisenhower combined to give the eventual winner 49.3 percent of the voting population, only slightly less than the 50.7 percent Democratic candidate Adlai Stevenson received. In the presidential election of 1956, in the wake of the *Brown* school desegregation decision (a case in which the Eisenhower administration submitted an amicus curiae brief supporting the NAACP's position), Eisenhower lost support from lowcountry whites. Dissatisfied with the president's position on race, whites living in majority-black counties threw their support to unpledged electors. But expanding suburban areas in majority-white counties farther upstate responded differently. The only South Carolina county Eisenhower carried in 1956 was Aiken. Led by the county's new residents, the Republicanism of Aiken County was shaped by an opposition to New Deal–style liberalism and a staunch anticommunism. The party leadership reflected the more cosmopolitan nature of the rank and file, with most key leaders having moved to South Carolina from elsewhere in the country, bringing their Republican sympathies with them.[18]

Although the burgeoning suburban areas of Aiken County were starting to flex their Republican muscles, the mill villages of Horse Creek Valley remained solidly Democratic. Owen Clary, who grew up in the tiny textile mill village of Warrenville, was something of an oddity in his family and community. Despite his father's warning that "no son of mine is going to be a Republican," Clary embraced and acted on his conservative sympathies. He organized a High School Students for Eisenhower group at Graniteville High School; only five other students joined. In 1952, he passed out Eisenhower literature door-to-door in the mill villages and was greeted with a hail of rocks.[19] Despite Clary's experiences and the hard-core Democratic support in the valley, Aiken County was changing.

Between 1956 and 1960, Republicans made major strides in attracting party members in Richland, Lexington, and Aiken Counties. These successes really resulted less from a concerted effort by state party officials to organize these counties specifically than from indigenous political rebellions that grew out of changing local economic and social demographic circumstances and the changing national political environment.[20] By 1960, the state Republican Party had been transformed, drawing strength from expanding urban and suburban areas in Aiken, Richland, and Charleston Counties and their middle- and upper-middle-class residents. Contemporary commentators observed that presidential Republicanism in South Carolina was stronger than that in any other southern state.[21] The party drew the support of prominent disenchanted Democrats, such as former governor James F. Byrnes.[22] In 1960, Republican presidential candidate Richard Nixon lost the state by fewer than ten thousand votes, with 63.2 percent of all city and suburban residents voting Republican. South Carolina Republicans adopted a brand of conservatism that mirrored in important respects the conservatism growing in the country as a whole during this period. Popular conservative themes included concerns about the influence of organized labor, the conduct of the Cold War, and the expanding and increasingly disruptive civil rights movement. Republican senator Barry Goldwater of Arizona was the face of this new conservatism, and he enjoyed widespread popularity among South Carolina Republicans. With Nixon's defeat in 1960, Aiken Republicans heralded Goldwater as "our jet-pilot" and "the political strongman of our times."[23] Governor Ernest Hollings confirmed the changing political tide, noting in September 1960 that the majority of South Carolina voters supported the Republicans.[24]

Not content to express their Republican sensibilities in presidential elections alone, Republicans in Aiken County, led by Du Pont employees, built the party from the roots up. Harber "Mac" MacClaren was one such Republican foot soldier. Born in the Middle Tennessee county of Hickman, MacClaren was the son of schoolteachers. His father, a staunch Democrat, served two terms as the county superintendant of schools, and MacClaren often joined him on his politicking. Recalled MacClaren, "I grew up not knowing there was anything but a Democratic Party or elected Democratic Party officials." MacClaren describes his early political leanings as decidedly ambivalent and even remembers feeling a little sorry for Herbert Hoover, believing that the president had been unfairly scapegoated for the Great Depression. MacClaren graduated from the University of Tennessee in 1942, joined the U.S. Army Signal Corps, and served in the European theater until early 1946. After returning to Tennessee, he got married and began searching for employment. His wife's family was friendly with the personnel supervisor at Oak Ridge National Laboratory, and MacClaren was hired in the health physics area, which was responsible for radiation detection. While at Oak Ridge, MacClaren took advantage of every opportunity to pursue his education, taking courses in mathematics and physics. It soon became clear, though, that he would have difficulty advancing at Oak Ridge because most of the positions above him were secured for the long term. The coming of the SRP provided a welcome opportunity. He applied for a position with the new plant and was hired by Du Pont in 1951. He spent a few months in Wilmington working on designs for the plant's radiation detection facilities and arrived in Aiken in 1952. MacClaren's first home was in Crosland Park, and he was instrumental in organizing the subdivision's civic association. MacClaren, who had supported Republican Thomas Dewey in the presidential election of 1948 and Eisenhower four years later, soon became involved in organizing the local Republican Party. According to MacClaren, the "movers and shakers" of the local and state GOP were newcomers to South Carolina. In Aiken, that meant Du Pont employees.[25] SRP employee and nuclear physicist Walt Joseph remembers the first meeting of the Aiken County Republican Party in March 1956: "The law required political conventions to be held in public buildings so the group reserved the courthouse for the designated evening. When the small band of party faithful arrived for the convention, they discovered the courthouse dark and locked. Repeated attempts to phone the building custodian and other political figures were unsuccessful. Finally, in desperation, but within the letter of the law, the convention was held in the courthouse parking lot."[26]

The small but tenacious group of Republicans moved quickly to make their presence felt in local politics. The organization sent a delegate to the Republi-

can National Convention in 1956, and the following year, David Dows, an Aiken Winter Colonist and local Republican activist, became chair of the South
Carolina party. Also in 1957, Republicans in the town of North Augusta nominated candidates for mayor and city council, garnering about 30 percent of the
vote. Two years later, for the first time in Aiken's history, Republicans contested
seats on the city council.[27] The three candidates, two of whom were raised and
educated outside the South, were chemical engineers at the SRP. Although all
three were defeated, they collectively garnered 28 percent of the vote.[28] Having
taken the leap into local politics, the area's Republicans began reorganizing
precincts in early 1960.[29]

The grassroots growth of the Republican Party in Aiken County was as
much ideological as practical: many newer residents of the area saw the local Democratic Party as a closed body of established elites, so the Republican
Party simply offered a vehicle for political involvement. Eugene England, a
Republican candidate for the Aiken City Council in 1959 and an SRP employee,
argued that party competition offered voters the best opportunity for effective, efficient government.[30] In 1961, three Republicans ran for seats on the city
council. Collectively, they criticized the Democratic Party for regarding municipal offices as "a closed private club."[31] They also labeled the city government
"stagnant" and unresponsive, citing issues such as a lack of a fire station near
the newer subdivisions and a failure to properly map storm sewers.[32] To acti-
vate the party's base, the Republican Club of Aiken held seminars on practical
politics and grassroots organizing.[33] The three Republican city council candidates won 40 percent of the vote.[34] By 1962, Aiken County Republicans had
organized ten of the county's forty-one precincts, with many of them captained
by plant employees, one of whom was Walt Joseph.[35]

By 1962, with healthy activity at the grassroots and durable party support
in the suburbs, the state Republican Party felt confident enough to take on
three-term U.S. senator Olin D. Johnston. Johnston possessed formidable political credentials. Elected governor in 1934 and again in 1942, he had served
as the state's senator since 1945. A reliable New Deal Democrat, Johnston was
a strong supporter of the rights of labor and championed a limited welfare
state. Johnston had remained a loyal—if not enthusiastic—Truman supporter
in the 1948 presidential election, when many states'-rights conservatives in
South Carolina bolted the Democratic Party. Johnston also had not abandoned
the Democratic camp during the tumultuous 1950s, when many disgruntled
southern Democrats voted as independents.[36]

South Carolina Republicans nominated well-known syndicated newspaper columnist William D. Workman to run against Johnston. The forty-seven-year-old Workman had no previous political experience and had always maintained a politically neutral position. However, in a letter to Senator Barry Goldwater, chair of the National Republican Senatorial Committee, Workman revealed that he had "opposed the [national] Democratic tickets since Roosevelt's second term."[37] Devising a winning strategy proved difficult for the South Carolina Republicans. They considered trying to yoke Johnston to liberal president John F. Kennedy and the increasingly disruptive civil rights movement, but painting Johnston as a racial liberal was futile. Although hardly a virulent white supremacist, Johnston had established his segregationist credentials in the 1940s and had never wavered. He also deftly kept his distance from certain elements of Kennedy's program, assuring South Carolina's white voters that he never supported civil rights measures or "wasteful foreign aid give-aways."[38]

Although this was his first try at public office, Workman's conservative criticisms of the civil rights movement and the welfare state were well established. In 1960, Workman published *The Case for the South*, in which he explained the white South's opposition to integration. Declaring his position to be that of "the man in the middle," he lambasted the U.S. Supreme Court's decision in *Brown v. Board of Education*; engaged in a chapter of head-scratching over what he considered African Americans' "obsessive" concern with semantics, such as their overly defensive opposition to the use of such terms as *Auntie* and *Uncle*, "which formerly were used by white friends and neighbors with genuine affection"; and in general argued for a states'-rights approach to the race question. Workman found African Americans unprepared for and lacking the proper character for full equality: "The average Negro will find a stopping place of relative contentment far short of anything which will suffice for the average white man. . . . Offer a white man more pay for more work, or harder work, or longer hours, and he generally will have it. Make the same offer to a Southern Negro, and he will find some way of avoiding the extra effort, particularly if the rewards offered are beyond those to which he has geared his way of life. The Negro has his virtues, but too seldom do they include foresight, thrift, and perseverance—those factors by which the white man builds a better life for himself." Workman's "case" was built on the tired, timeworn southern racial apologist arguments: that hundreds of years of cohabitation had given southern whites special insight into the nature of African Americans; that blacks as a group were an adolescent race only recently moving into civic adulthood;

and that southern whites were most capable of directing their own racial affairs without interference from the courts or the federal government.[39] Having made his position clear, Workman stated confidentially on a number of occasions that he did not wish to bring race into the campaign.[40] His hesitation did not result from any particular squeamishness about raising the issue: he likely wished to avoid discussions of race and integration because they were not issues on which he could attack Johnston.

Unwilling to take on Johnston directly, Workman attacked liberalism generally and Washington liberals in particular, calling them a "group of arrogant intellectuals surrounding the Kennedy clan."[41] Workman railed against the evils of an activist federal government with its expansive, meddling bureaucracy, which he considered one step away from communism.[42] He opposed federal aid to education as well as any federal involvement in health care for the elderly. The expanding welfare state had become "a cradle to the grave protection," an "indulgence by the federal government at taxpayers' expense."[43] He endorsed "national defense to whatever degree and at whatever cost is essential to the security of the United States" and championed an unrelenting resistance to world communism. One Workman advertisement criticized Johnston for supporting arms control and disarmament, warning voters that by advocating arms reduction, Johnston threatened national sovereignty and supported the notion of a Soviet superstate.[44] Such heated rhetoric was red meat to local defense workers on the front lines of the Cold War. An arms agreement threatened the livelihoods of folks who developed materials for nuclear weapons. Workman did his best to craft his message in the Goldwater mold, making his campaign part of the broader push for "a new conservatism which is spreading throughout America," a political movement that sought to stem "the liberal tide which has been sweeping the United States toward the murky depths of socialism."[45]

Contrary to his stated desire to keep race out of the campaign, Workman tried to make political hay out of the civil rights movement's increasing momentum and the mounting resistance from southern whites. Workman opened an October 2 speech in Walterboro, South Carolina, by referencing the riots that had rocked the University of Mississippi campus the previous day in the wake of James Meredith's enrollment. Workman praised "the virtues and the courage of Ross Barnett," the Mississippi governor who was "trying to stand firm against the federal pressures which are beating him to his knees."[46] As elsewhere, Workman's guns were trained on the liberals in Washington and not Johnston specifically.

In Aiken County, employees of both the SRP and the Atomic Energy Commission played key roles in the Workman campaign. Gus Robinson, who worked in the commission's Office of Public Information, and Don Law, editor of the *Savannah River Plant News*, provided key information on the political temper of plant employees, telling Workman that they predicted "a good Republican vote" for Workman from among the plant's personnel.[47] Joseph served as a precinct captain for Workman, while North Augusta was considered a lock for the challenger.[48] Workman also enjoyed the strong support of Ken Kilbourne of the Aiken Chamber of Commerce.[49]

Workman made an impressive showing in an improbable race, garnering 44 percent of the statewide vote from an electorate that only a decade earlier had possessed an almost visceral distaste for all things Republican. Aiken County was one of only three counties to give a majority of its votes to Workman.[50] Workman's most lopsided victories within the county came from precincts in Aiken and North Augusta heavily populated by SRP personnel.[51] Workman was not the only Republican candidate that year to garner respectable support at the polls. Also challenging the establishment in 1962 was state representative Floyd Spence of Lexington County, a former Democrat who withdrew from the party in mid-April 1962 and announced his candidacy for the Republican nomination for Congress from the Second District, which included all of Lexington County and parts of Aiken County, skirting the northern edge of the city of Aiken. He secured the nomination and in November won Aiken County but lost the race to Albert Watson.[52] Watson's defeat of Spence was largely credited to the support the Democrat received from Strom Thurmond. After winning reelection in 1964, Watson switched parties and ran as a Republican in 1966. Spence ultimately took the seat in 1971, when Watson vacated the office to run for governor. Spence remained in Congress for the next thirty years.

Although defeated in 1962, South Carolina Republicans continued to make tremendous strides in building their party. In 1963, two Republican candidates won seats on the North Augusta City Council, the first Republicans in the county to be elected to municipal office.[53] State Republicans built off the momentum of Workman's challenge and looked forward to the presidential contest of 1964. Goldwater, the Republican candidate in that election, received support from an unlikely source: former governor and now U.S. senator and Aiken resident Strom Thurmond. In 1950, Johnston had defeated Thurmond's bid for the U.S. Senate seat, and Thurmond had temporarily retired to private life. As a new resident of Aiken, Thurmond appeared regularly in the local press, most prominently as an attorney representing landowners displaced by the SRP. In that capacity, he burnished his credentials as an advocate of local citizens fighting for what they considered fair market value for their property. Thurmond's triumphant return to public life coincided perfectly with the uproar over the *Brown* decision. In September 1954, well after the state Democratic Party primaries, Senator Burnet Maybank died suddenly of a heart attack. In a meeting held only hours after Maybank's funeral, the South Carolina State Democratic Executive Committee named state senator Edgar Brown of Barnwell, a powerful national Democratic Party loyalist, as the party's nominee instead of convening a special primary election. South Carolina's rank-and-file Democrats immediately reacted with anger. Capitalizing on this wave of public outrage, Thurmond declared himself a write-in candidate on September 7 and pledged that if elected, he would resign from office before the 1956 Democratic primary, allowing South Carolina voters to choose a senator to serve the remaining four years of the term. With this bold stroke, Thurmond transformed himself into a candidate of the people, a political outsider bravely challenging the draconian dictates of the state Democratic Party, whose leaders had met behind closed doors and deprived the people of their rightful voice. To a group of white southerners still reeling from a Supreme Court decision they considered unjust and oppressive, this was an exhilarating development. In just two months, despite the obvious practical obstacles facing a write-in candidate, Thurmond engineered a huge upset victory, garnering an astounding 63 percent of the vote. He was easily reelected in 1956.[54]

In September 1964, two months after President Lyndon Johnson signed the Civil Rights Act (which the Aiken paper denounced as a "legislative monstrosity" that "creates extraordinary rights for some, at the same time extending Federal control over the liberties and property of everyone"), Thurmond announced he was leaving the Democratic Party and joining the Republicans to support Goldwater. Thurmond's party switch was a tremendous coup for South Carolina's Republicans. The state's most popular politician lent the fledgling party instant credibility. The Aiken County party vice-chair stated that he was "caught completely by surprise by [Thurmond's] action, but I'm tickled to death."[55] Many observers have since credited Thurmond with bringing two-party politics to the state; however, a closer look demands that more credit be given to local and state party operatives, changing demographics, and the 1962 campaign, factors that combined to make his party switch something less than suicidal. Ever the astute politician, Thurmond no doubt had observed the changes in the political terrain wrought by the Cold War. Even while technically a private citizen, Thurmond was never out of the public eye, appearing frequently at community events. His professional and possibly his social circle came to involve individuals from the SRP. And although it is impossible to know the extent to which he was influenced by Aiken's burgeoning Republican sentiment, he most certainly was aware of it. Within this context, then, Thurmond's switch seems less an example of political soothsaying than a well-timed and logical political accommodation. Although Thurmond and his aides always maintained that the senator's high-profile switch was a singular act of political bravery, former aid Harry Dent confided to Thurmond's biographer that Workman's 1962 challenge to Johnston provided "a pretty good poll" of potential Republican support.[56]

South Carolina Republicans enthusiastically supported the Arizona senator in the 1964 presidential election.[57] Aiken County went heavily for the Republicans, with voters supporting Goldwater over Johnson by a nearly three-to-one margin.[58] Despite his monumental and historic defeat, Goldwater's—and conservatives'—ascension within the Republican Party energized grassroots activity in South Carolina. Aiken was no exception. In 1965, six Republican hopefuls entered the city council primary, marking the first time a South Carolina city had held a Republican primary for a municipal election.[59] The election also witnessed the candidacy of the first African American to be nominated in a South Carolina municipal election, the Reverend Norman L. Bush of Friendship Baptist Church, the city's most prominent black congregation.[60] The heaviest Republican primary vote came from Precinct 4, at Mitchell Plaza, located near a large subdivision of plant employees on Aiken's southern edge. Bush won the second-highest number of votes among the Democrats, but the three Republican candidates swept the election.[61] According to MacClaren, Aiken "has never been the same since we elected Republicans to the city council and blew away the Democrats. That is where the breakthrough was."[62]

By 1967, Aiken had expanded to include six voting precincts and had developed distinct geographical voting patterns. Precincts 2 and 4 were heavily African American; Precinct 3 included Crosland Park; Precinct 6 encompassed South Aiken, where many of the new suburbs housing SRP scientists and engineers were constructed. Precincts 3 and 6 were heavily Republican.[63] North Augusta elected its first Republican mayor, Cecil Collins, in 1965 and reelected him four years later.[64] In 1967, Aiken County became the first county in South Carolina to hold a Republican primary.[65] The following year, Gilbert

McMillan was elected state senator, serving in that capacity until 1980. The Arkansas-born McMillan had graduated from Auburn University with a degree in chemical engineering and later joined Du Pont as an industrial supervisor. In 1953, McMillan joined the workforce at the SRP. He became active in Republican Party politics, serving as the chair of the Aiken County Republican Party in 1968.[66] Three Republicans, including two incumbents, were elected to the Aiken City Council in 1969.[67]

The Aiken County GOP benefited from the Republican Party's national resurgence throughout the late 1960s. In 1966, Aiken County voters elected five Republicans and one Democrat as their representatives in Columbia.[68] That year was important for the GOP across the state. Drawing heavily on the white backlash against the legislative successes of the civil rights movement, the party produced candidates for 22 of the state's 50 Senate seats and 70 of 124 spots in the General Assembly. Although party leaders stated that they would have considered ten wins a major victory, they won seventeen contests.[69] Thurmond ran for reelection to the U.S. Senate as a Republican in 1966 and won handily. The Republican presence continued to grow in the state during the late 1960s and into the 1970s. In 1972, the state legislature approved the creation of the Aiken County Commission, providing home rule for the county; later that year, all positions on the commission were filled by Republicans. The commission's chair, Harold V. Graybeal, was an engineer for Du Pont.[70] In 1975, Republican political novice James B. Edwards defeated General William Westmoreland in the party's gubernatorial primary and went on to defeat longtime Democratic congressman William Jennings Bryan Dorn in the general election, thus becoming the first Republican elected governor in the state since Reconstruction. The Republican Party, whose rebirth and growth was fueled in part by changes precipitated by the Cold War, had become a force in South Carolina's political life.

The arrival of the SRP, the growth of a militarized and modern economy in the South, and the emergence of the Republican Party coincided with the quickening pace of the civil rights movement and growing white resistance. The influx of SRP employees strained local schools at the same time that black South Carolinians were seeking access to those schools. Like many communities across the South, Aiken County was already sorely pressed for school facilities. Prior to 1950, public education for black children was abysmal. Local resident Frank Roberson recalled that "the county only gave us three months of school. [The teachers] would stay over, more or less volunteering to teach us."[71] Expenditures for students were four times greater for whites than for blacks. As a result, black schools often lacked the basic amenities afforded white schools, such as lunch programs.[72] Well into the twentieth century, Aiken County had no free public high school for African American children. Those students with the financial means could pursue education beyond the eighth grade at one of three private high schools: Martha Schofield Normal and Industrial School, which had originated as a Freedmen's Bureau school; Bettis Academy; or Haines Institute.[73] Educational opportunities for the county's poor whites were only marginally better. In 1953, the Schofield School was deeded to the county and from that point on operated as a public school. On the eve of the construction of the SRP, the county had nine public high schools for white children and two for African Americans. Aiken County also was home to a number of private schools, including a Catholic elementary and secondary school; Mead Hall, an eight-grade school sponsored by the Episcopal Church; and Aiken Preparatory School, which educated the children of the wealthy Winter Colonists.[74] By the early 1960s, enrollment in nonpublic schools was 898 county-wide.[75]

The racial inequality that defined South Carolina's segregated school system came under attack in the late 1940s in the case of *Briggs v. Elliott*, in which Harry Briggs sued Robert Elliott, the school board supervisor in Clarendon County. Briggs's legal challenge began as a complaint over unequal school transportation and soon grew into a desegregation case. The NAACP filed suit in 1949. *Briggs* eventually became combined with four other cases and was decided by the Supreme Court as part of *Brown*. Fearing an adverse judicial decision, South Carolina governor James Byrnes, elected in 1950, embarked on a massive school construction program that he hoped would forestall court-mandated desegregation. With money raised by a 3 percent sales tax, the state ultimately committed seventy-five million dollars for the construction of new schools, with three-quarters of that amount going to facilities for African American children. "South Carolina need have no fear that white children and colored children will be forced to attend the same school," Byrnes declared in late January 1951 in his first message to the state legislature. "The white people will see to it that innocent colored people will not be denied an education because of selfish politicians and misguided educators."[76] Under Byrnes's program, eight new schools were constructed in Aiken County.[77]

The Byrnes construction program dovetailed with the massive migration to Aiken County that accompanied the construction and operation of the SRP. Once the operations staff began arriving, the county received federal funding to construct additional schools. Other improvements, such as the addition of cafeterias, libraries, and gymnasiums, were made to sixteen existing schools.[78]

Following the *Brown* decision in 1954, desegregation of public schools in the South generally moved at a snail's pace, and Aiken County schools were no exception. Ten years later, only 137 African American students attended formerly all-white schools in South Carolina under various pupil placement plans.[79] The Aiken County Board of Education operated under a transfer request system popularly known as freedom of choice that was approved by officials with the U.S. Department of Health, Education, and Welfare (HEW) in September 1965. The application and transfer process was extremely slow and ineffective. School officials stated that choice would be denied only in the case of overcrowding, but for the 1965–66 school year, the board approved only 121 transfer requests, a miniscule fraction of the 24,000 students enrolled in the county.[80] By the start of the 1967 school year, only one of South Carolina's 106 school districts was in compliance with HEW guidelines for desegregation.[81]

James Gallman, a lifelong Aiken County educator who was teaching math at all-black Jefferson Junior High School when the freedom-of-choice policy was in place, recalled that very few students took advantage of it. Those who did tended to be the children of educators or of professional people. The few who received transfers did well academically but were socially isolated among their white classmates. The mass of African American students remained in segregated schools.[82] Among the African American students who were granted transfers during the freedom-of-choice era was Patricia Abney, who integrated Langley-Bath-Clearwater High School in Horse Creek Valley. Her presence at the formerly all-white school brought forth some name calling, she recalled, but also a few smiles from students. She suffered some retaliation from whites. Her mother was pelted with debris while attending football games to watch Patricia play in the band. According to Abney, this hostility did not last more than a year or two.[83]

But as in so many communities, the freedom-of-choice system did not result in sufficient integration, and in 1967, only seventeen thousand black students were enrolled in previously all-white schools statewide.[84] Most of the state, including Aiken County, was found to be in violation of Title VI of the Civil Rights Act of 1964.[85] If the Aiken County school district failed to take steps to comply with the law, it risked losing more than $650,000 a year—25 percent of its operating budget—and thus funds to pay more than 130 teachers.[86] According to HEW officials, Aiken County schools, like schools across the state, suffered from "severe problems."[87] The agency's Civil Rights Division criticized freedom-of-choice plans, saying that nowhere in South Carolina had they produced a desegregated school system. Moreover, the state had a peculiar grade system that made transferring difficult. White elementary schools offered grades 1–6, junior highs offered 7–9, and high schools offered 10–12; most black schools offered either grades 1–7 and 8–12. Furthermore, the burden of integration was assumed exclusively by African Americans. As of April 1968, no white children in South Carolina attended formerly black schools.[88]

The future of freedom of choice for Aiken County and the nation's schools was decided on May 27, 1968. In a unanimous decision, the U.S. Supreme Court essentially ruled that those plans must be abandoned. The Court ruled that these plans, which by that time were used in about 90 percent of all southern school districts, would be permitted only under extremely limited circumstances. Senator Thurmond called the ruling "appalling."[89] School boards across the region had to go back to the drawing board. Aiken proceeded with a modified freedom-of-choice plan for the 1968–69 school year that included some consolidation of grades. During that year, 28 percent of the county's black students attended integrated schools, fifty black teachers taught in previously all-white schools, and thirteen white teachers taught in formerly black schools.[90]

Aikenites and other whites throughout the South seeking to delay desegregation looked hopefully to the election of Richard Nixon as president in 1968. In particular, Thurmond's support for Nixon was predicated on the president's commitment to a go-slow approach to school integration. Thurmond told school districts they should hold off on radical changes toward integration to see whether the new administration would be more lenient.[91] The local paper ginned up the anxiety, contending that desegregation that would satisfy HEW would occur only by a "massive relocation of population on the Nazi pattern."[92] South Carolinians, like much of the southern population, wondered what position the new Nixon administration would take. Would the Justice Department be as aggressive as it had been under Lyndon Johnson?

The answer was no. The Nixon administration scrapped its predecessor's deadlines for complete school desegregation by September 1969, favoring a "more flexible" policy that would mean still more delay.[93]

Aiken County received approval of its 1969–70 school plan from HEW in mid-July 1969. Under the new plan, the elementary schools in Aiken would operate by geographic zones, as would the junior highs. For the time being, the high schools would continue under freedom of choice.[94] The closing of some elementary schools and the integration of other schools brought complaints, mostly from white parents, but unlike other regions in South Carolina and the rest of the South, Aiken did not experience extensive white flight into parochial schools and private academies.[95]

A plan for complete desegregation of all grades and faculty was in place for the 1970–71 school year. Gallman was moved from the previously all-black Jefferson Junior High in the valley to Langley-Bath-Clearwater High School, a formerly all-white high school also in the valley. Gallman remembered "very little strife or conflicts" when integration finally occurred: "It was just accepted that this was going to happen." Gallman continued to teach at Langley-Black-Clearwater until 1976, when he became the assistant principal at Kennedy Junior High in Aiken. Two years later, he became the principal of New Ellenton Junior High. Gallman encountered few racial incidents over the course of his career. Most parents, he recalled, simply "wanted someone who cared about them and about their children."[96]

Looking back, Aiken resident and former SRP employee Willar Hightower compared the integration process in Aiken County to a car race in which Aiken never took the lead but instead drafted, positioning itself in "the draft that is created as race car drivers get close behind the lead car and allow the car ahead to pull them along." Still, as Hightower recalled, the process was not entirely free of conflict. The consolidation of the high schools presented the biggest obstacle and brought the black community closest to demonstrating.[97] At the time, Aiken supported two high schools: historically black Schofield High and the formerly all-white Aiken High. Schofield had long served as a central cultural institution and source of pride for the county's African American residents. Teachers, administrators, parents, and students lauded the school's academic standards and rallied around its sports teams. According to Gallman, the school offered particularly strong science, math, and language arts programs. Schofield teachers and the community expected their talented alumni to continue on to college. Gallman, for example, pursued his undergraduate degree at Claflin College in Orangeburg, majoring in math not because he was interested in the subject but because he wanted to prove to a particularly influential teacher from Schofield that he could do it. His college math classes paled in comparison to those he took at Schofield.[98]

Desegregation brought challenges for Aiken's black community. The Aiken County School Board sent all eleventh- and twelfth-grade students to Aiken High, while Schofield offered grades 9 and 10. The principal at the formerly all-white high school became the principal of the newly integrated Aiken High, while the principal of Schofield became the assistant principal. Similarly, and particularly upsetting to the black community, was the decision to make Aiken High's football coach the head coach at the integrated school and to make Bill Clyburn, head football coach at Schofield, the assistant coach. In 1975, when the head coaching position became available, the school board again bypassed Clyburn in favor of a nonlocal white candidate. Hightower, one of the first African American professionals hired at the SRP, noted that the coaching decision "created a big, big stir. The black community did all but demonstrate." The situation was defused when Clyburn "stepped forward and said, 'I accept the school board's decision.'" There would be no demonstrations. Shortly after he was bypassed for the head football coaching position, Clyburn became principal of Aiken Elementary School. Hightower also recalled that despite a relatively peaceful transition, some persistent problems accompanied integration. In particular, he noted that when black students violated school rules, they received harsher punishments than did white students who had committed similar infractions.[99]

Although numbers and photographs do not tell the whole story, they give some insight into the desegregation process. By 1974, roughly four years after Aiken schools were integrated, the high school faculty contained roughly equal numbers of African American and white teachers and administrators, with both races found in all fields of instruction. African American students appeared on the cheerleading squads, joined hobby and academic clubs, were chosen as campus beauty queens, and participated in a wide range of extracurricular activities.[100] As Gallman noted, it appears that once the final decision to integrate was made, and after legal delays had been exhausted, key individuals were determined to see that it worked with as little conflict as possible.[101]

Demographics played a significant role in determining the level of resistance to integration in Aiken County. Between 1930 and 1960, racial ratios underwent extensive change and reversal. Aiken County had become significantly whiter. In 1930, there were six whites to every five nonwhites in the county; by 1960, that ratio had more than doubled to fourteen whites for every five nonwhites. In 1960, Aiken County's population was only 26 percent black, a change that resulted mostly from the massive influx of whites for the SRP, although out-migration of African Americans played a role as well. Between 1930 and 1950, as the region's agricultural economy entered a state of transition, Aiken County's black population declined 10 percent. Between 1950 and 1960, the white population grew by nearly twenty-six thousand, compared to only two thousand for blacks.[102] Historic housing patterns likewise mitigated fears regarding desegregation. Although majority-black sections certainly existed, the city's older neighborhoods exhibited more of a checkerboard quality. Aiken did not have a ghetto, and achieving integration would not require busing. Whites' fears of being outnumbered did not find fertile ground in Aiken.

Safely in the majority, Aiken's whites also did not harbor the cultural fears of African Americans found in more volatile communities.[103] Schofield High School's academic reputation and its graduates' success rendered moot arguments about the academic unpreparedness of black students that whites in other communities used to block integration. Most of the teachers at Schofield had degrees from four-year institutions, and the principal, James A. Taylor, was universally respected. Black employment in the opulent homes of Winter Colonists lent a cosmopolitan air to a certain segment of the black community. Hightower recalled that the Royal Aikenites—those men and women employed by the Winter Colonists—made livable salaries and "therefore saw no need to overtly push for quick integration. They were already integrated because they had a feeling as being 'a member of the family' for the whites they worked for."[104] Likewise, Aikenites prided themselves on the genteel reputation that accompanied the presence of the Winter Colonists. The children of the Winter Colonists had for years been educated in expensive private academies. Winter Colonists had no personal stake in the dispute over desegregation, but they put a premium on community harmony.[105]

Finally, as one black Aikenite phrased it, integration proceeded relatively peacefully because "there were some people who were going to make sure that this was going to work. They were leaders in their schools, and in the community, and so they said it was going to work, and it just worked." Among these community entities that inadvertently aided the cause of integration was the SRP and its thousands of transplants. Serious discussion of integration came about roughly fifteen years after the SRP arrived on the scene. During that time, Du Pont and its employees had imbued and energized the region with a notion of progress and growth that the greater population had adopted. The influence Du Pont and its employees exercised on the region was not solely based on demographics but was also characteristic of the regard with which Americans had come to hold large corporations. Although criticism of corporate America had not completely disappeared, citizens seemed reconciled to its existence and had in the postwar era assigned corporations a central role as guarantors of prosperity and security.[106] By 1965, profoundly shaped by the arrival of the plant, the area thought of itself as modern and forward thinking.

Although whites' notion of what a modern community looked like and how it responded to certain social and political challenges did not include a progressive and proactive approach to integration, neither did it mean violent resistance to desegregation. Boisterous opposition had no place in this landscape of progress. Hightower commented that many of the "plant people with PhDs tended to focus on the technical aspects of a problem rather than what your color is."[107] And Gallman matter-of-factly stated SRP leaders helped desegregation "by focusing on what can make the area grow. Strife over schools won't help economic growth."[108]

Integration of African Americans into Aiken's political life came about slowly, but without the rancor and overt hostility encountered in other southern communities, a development Hightower credited in part to the leadership of Aiken's long-serving mayor, Odell Weeks. First elected in 1946, Weeks held the office until 1953 and again from 1956 to 1991. According to Hightower, Weeks "was somewhat liberal in his decision-making process. [He] knew a large number of Blacks because of his business, which was primarily homeowner's insurance. His office treatment of blacks caused him to thrive in his insurance. The word was out that Mayor Weeks was a good person. His conversations with Blacks were not of a condescending nature. This made for a feeling among Blacks, mainly in the rural areas of Aiken, that demonstrating was not necessary to move forward. Patience was the order of the day."[109]

But patience alone could not overcome structural and demographic hurdles. Not only did white voters outnumber blacks by a ratio of four to one, but African Americans also had to contend with local and state laws that required political parties to put forth slates of candidates at election time. Voters had to vote for as many candidates as there were vacancies in multiseat races. If five vacancies existed in a city council race, for example, a ballot would be voided if it included votes for only three candidates. This rule forced blacks to vote for candidates whose positions they did not support if they wanted their votes for other candidates to count. The full-slate law was repealed in 1972, and in November 1973, Clyburn became the first African American elected to the Aiken City Council. In the city's predominantly black Second and Fourth Precincts, the overwhelming majority of voters voted only for Clyburn. Although the support of black voters made Clyburn the top vote getter among the candidates, he enjoyed support in the predominantly white precincts as well. Hightower, who served as Clyburn's campaign manager, credited his victory in part to door-to-door campaigning by black and white football players coached by Clyburn. When asked in 1973 about his status as Aiken's first African American elected official, Clyburn said that times had changed; moreover, he had "always thought there wasn't any animosity between the races in Aiken as some people thought."[110] When Clyburn ran for reelection against three Republicans in 1977, he again received the most votes.[111] Clyburn served on the Aiken City Council until 1981, when he was elected to the Aiken County Council, a position he held for five years. From 1983 to 1986, he served as principal of Aiken High School. In a special election to fill Clyburn's vacated seat on the city council, Hightower defeated Jane Vaughters, a white Republican, by nine votes.[112] Hightower was elected to the Aiken County Council in 1986, defeating white Republican Owen Clary, to fill the seat vacated by Clyburn.[113] To fill Hightower's former seat on the city council, Aiken voters chose Lessie Price, a nineteen-year employee in the SRP's personnel department, over Republican Etta Findley, a white real estate agent. Price, the first black woman elected to the Aiken City Council, has remained on the council for more than twenty-five years. In 1995, Clyburn was elected to the South Carolina House of Representatives, where he still serves.[114] And between 1988 and her retirement in 2011, Clyburn's wife, Beverly, served on the Aiken City Council.[115]

Sometimes overtly, sometimes clandestinely, residents' desire to build a modern southern community had helped usher in a competitive two-party system and had muted overt, violent resistance to integration. The arrival of the SRP reconfigured the region's social, cultural, and political maps. The particular corporate culture fostered by Du Pont, the overwhelming presence of SRP employees in the region, and the particular racial dynamics that developed in Aiken County do not fit neatly into the dominant historical narrative of southern change. But given the importance and prevalence of federal Cold War installations in the South, perhaps the story of the SRP and Aiken County is not so exceptional. Paying closer attention to the relationship between the local and the national, the influence of specific corporate or military cultures, and the interplay with specific historical dynamics within individual southern communities may ultimately yield a more compelling narrative of southern history in the post–World War II era.

EPILOGUE

The 1980s brought significant changes for the Savannah River Plant (SRP). The partial meltdown of a reactor core at the Three Mile Island plant near Harrisburg, Pennsylvania, in 1979 created a climate of increased fear and trepidation regarding the nuclear power industry. Although it is considered the worst nuclear accident in U.S. history, the events at Three Mile Island did not result in loss of life, nor was there a significant release of radioactive material into the environment. Still, the incident put the federal government and the nuclear industry on the defensive as an energized environmental movement and a nervous public demanded greater regulations.

The decision to temporarily restart the SRP's L reactor, previously shut down in the 1960s, ignited objections from environmentalists and disarmament advocates alike. The Senate Armed Services Committee, chaired by Strom Thurmond, held local hearings on the issue in February 1983. Representatives of the South Carolina Wildlife Federation, the Sierra Club, and Physicians for Social Responsibility took strong stands against further plutonium production and warned of the threat of possible radioactive releases, the thermal effect on the Savannah River, and the potential health risk to children. One representative from the GrassRoots Organizing Workshop argued that the government that wanted to restart the L reactor was "the same Government that . . . was willing to napalm children, women and old men in Vietnam, and is now willing to support the massacre of people in Central America." A representative of the National Academy of Sciences, however, provided data showing minimal impact from the L reactor on river organisms. The restart had strong support from area political leaders, including Aiken County's representatives in the state legislature and the mayors of Aiken, Augusta, North Augusta, Williston, and Allendale. In the end, the Department of Energy renovated and reconditioned the aging reactor. It was activated in 1985 and was deactivated in 1988.[1]

The 1986 explosion and fire at the Chernobyl Nuclear Power Plant in Ukraine forever changed the game plan for the nuclear power industry worldwide. The explosion released huge quantities of radioactive particles into the atmosphere. Deaths from the initial explosion and from prolonged radiation exposure have run into the hundreds of thousands. Considered the worst nuclear power plant accident in history, the disaster at Chernobyl brought the industry under intense scrutiny.

A year after the Chernobyl accident, Du Pont announced that it would not renew its contract to operate the SRP. These changes had been precipitated by more than just nuclear crises; the international scene had shifted dramatically. The fall of the Berlin Wall, the collapse of communist regimes in Eastern Europe, and the demise of the Soviet Union signaled the end of the Cold War and with it a new mission for the SRP. By 1988, all reactors at the SRP had been deactivated. The Department of Energy, which had assumed federal oversight of the facility from the Atomic Energy Commission, announced the following year that its primary mission had changed from weapons production to a comprehensive program of environmental compliance and cleanup. Also in 1989, Westinghouse Savannah River Company, a subsidiary of Westinghouse Electric, assumed operation of the site. Reflecting its new emphasis, the facility's name was changed from the Savannah River Plant to the Savannah River Site. Its mission transitioned from the production of nuclear materials to assure supremacy in the Cold War arms race to the safe and secure stewardship of the nation's nuclear weapons stockpile, nuclear materials, and the environment. The Cold War had ended, and along with it the SRP's role as a key production component in the country's nuclear weapons complex.[2]

The Savannah River Site's new mission of stockpile stewardship and cleanup highlights growing concerns in the 1970s and 1980s regarding the Cold War's environmental legacy. Waging the Cold War required not only massive financial resources but also a remarkable amount of land. By the end of the twentieth century, Cold War facilities covered some twenty-seven million acres across the United States. Vast acreage was required in particular in the American West for nuclear weapons and missile testing. Forty years of fighting the Cold War created what have become known as "national sacrifice zones," areas so contaminated that they remain uninhabitable and pose a continued threat to public health. Anthropologist Catherine Lutz notes that "military target practice, atomic bombing, and toxic washing have created a surreal landscape, particularly in the West, of bomb craters, spent missile noses jutting out of the pierced earth, and giant pits of animal carcasses poisoned by radiation."[3] In their study of the communities linked to the Hanford Engineering Works, historians John M. Findlay and Bruce Hevly state that "by the early 1990s, the Hanford Site was commonly identified as one of the most polluted places in the United States. The U.S. Environmental Protection Agency, noting the 440 billion gallons of liquid radioactive and chemical wastes released into the ground and distributed about the place after 1943, ranked Hanford as 'the most contaminated site in the nation.'" But Findlay and Hevly highlight a peculiar environmental juxtaposition within the confines of the Hanford site. The Hanford Reach, a fifty-mile stretch of the Columbia River that flows through the nuclear reservation, was set aside as a national wildlife refuge because of its natural attributes. They further note that other portions of the nuclear reservation have been set aside for ecological research and wildlife preservation. Such conflicting forms of land use epitomize what they call a "hypercompartmentalized West," a region in which land and water resources had become increasingly fragmented. But the juxtaposition of nuclear waste site and pristine wilderness also highlights the Cold War's highly ambiguous environmental legacy. While carefully documenting the damage done by the work at Hanford, Findlay and Hevly also point out that the Atomic Energy Commission was the first government entity to set aside land for explicitly environmental reasons.[4]

Similar contradictory forces of environmental threat and environmental protection existed and continue to exist within the boundaries of the Savannah River Site. As at Hanford, the production of highly radioactive materials and the storage of radioactive wastes pose serious environmental concerns. From 1953 until the reactors were deactivated, around thirty-six metric tons— 40 percent of the plutonium in U.S. stockpiles—was made at the SRP. The waste materials generated by this and other production remained at the site, housed in massive underground storage tanks. In the 1970s, leaks were discovered in the tanks, although no detrimental effect on the off-site civilian population was found. Natural areas closest to the complex's manufacturing facilities were not always so lucky. Lost Lake, located within the site's boundaries, had been heavily damaged by contamination from an industrial seepage basin. Steel Creek, a tributary of the Savannah River, received hot water effluent discharge from the L reactor and was considered a sacrifice zone. A 1988 Department of Energy report noted that a primary aquifer within the Savannah River reservation had been contaminated with solvents. Wildlife at the site was likewise affected. Researchers discovered that reactor seepage basins that had received radioactive contaminants, including strontium 90, had contaminated turtles on the site. In addition to radioactive emissions into the air, ground, and water, ecologists studying the area surrounding the site were greatly concerned about the impact of elevated water temperatures on natural habitats. Large quantities of water from the Savannah River were used to cool the site's nuclear reactors. The water eventually flowed down cooling canals into reservoirs, streams, and a swamp before returning to the river. Elevated thermal temperatures have had some detrimental effects on area habitats, including higher rates of certain parasitic infestations, the destruction of original swamp forests, and reduced body weight in fish during the summer months—"skinny bass." By the mid-1990s, the cost to clean up Savannah River and other Cold War sites had reached into the hundreds of billions of dollars.[5]

The impact of the SRP on communities outside the plant's boundaries appears to have been less than the damage caused by other Cold War facilities. A fourteen-year, $10.3 million study undertaken by the Centers for Disease Control reported in 2006 that the fifty-year-old plant delivered a negligible amount of radiation to thousands of residents in the counties around its boundaries and therefore posed little health risk to the area communities.[6] The Centers concluded that cancer rates in communities surrounding the plant were about the same as in similar communities.[7] But while the study provided some level of comfort to area citizens, in the course of collecting data, scientists received declassified documents that revealed safety mishaps at the site. A 1960 memo revealed an accidental tritium leak that was classified as "moderate." Workers repairing the leak were briefly exposed. Also in 1960, according to documents, a rapid restart of the L reactor resulted in extreme heat that came within forty seconds of a potential fuel meltdown if a shutdown had not been performed. After the incident, the rapid restart of reactors was prohibited. In 1970, a neutron source, used to generate plutonium, was held too long with cooling after being removed from the K reactor. The incident resulted in significant contamination inside the reactor building, which was shut down for three months.[8] Although the study ultimately confirmed that citizens' health had not been compromised, it also reminded area residents of the potential dangers posed by the site.

The health of workers at the Savannah River Site and other Cold War plants was another matter. By 2007, more than seventy-two thousand workers, retirees, and family members of workers who staffed facilities at Savannah River, Hanford, Oak Ridge, the Nevada Test Site, the Rocky Flats Complex in Colorado, the Paducah Gaseous Diffusion Plant in Kentucky, and elsewhere had sought damages from the Energy Employees Occupational Illness Compensation Program to treat a range of cancers and other ills thought to be related to hazardous materials in their workplaces. Proving that a certain level of exposure caused a particular illness is extremely difficult, and more than half of the claims have been denied.[9] In 1997, ninety-nine African American employees filed discrimination suits against Westinghouse Savannah River Site and three other site contractors. In addition to claims concerning wage and promotion discrimination, black workers claimed they were more likely than white workers to be exposed to hazardous working conditions. The story was covered on CBS's Sunday news show 60 Minutes in 2000. Robert W. Warren, an attorney who represented dozens of Savannah River workers, observed that employees there stood less chance of having claims accepted because they lack the organization and lobbying advantages found at some sites where more workers were white and where staff were represented by strong unions: "Black workers. . . . were put in high-exposure areas without proper protection or monitoring. They worked in some of the most dangerous places, but there are no records today to show that." Wayne Knox, a radiation-safety expert who was a contractor at the SRP for nearly two decades, confirmed that blacks were often employed in menial tasks—cleaning spills, scraping paint, removing waste—and were sometimes sent to the most dangerous parts of the plants, without being told of the risks they faced.[10] A former epidemiologist with the Centers for Disease Control hired by the plaintiffs to conduct a study on radiation exposure rates found that black workers at the site were exposed to 1.7 to 1.8 times more radiation than were whites. An unrelated study by a professor of epidemiology at the University of North Carolina found that black nuclear workers were four to five times more likely than whites to die of multiple myeloma, a rare blood cancer.[11]

Like Hanford, the Savannah River Site has a complex environmental legacy. While it has produced massive quantities of toxic substances and wastes that require careful stewardship, the site also has been a boon to the study of ecology. In 1951, a team of scientists undertook environmental baseline studies to inventory the terrestrial flora and fauna and the general ecology of the area. Biological baseline studies of the region's waterways were conducted by the Academy of Natural Sciences in Philadelphia under the direction of Dr. Ruth Patrick. These scientists conducted comprehensive surveys of the Savannah

River at three- to five-year intervals and found that biological change to the river stemmed from a variety of sources, including dam projects, industrialization outside the boundaries of the plant, sewage treatment, and dredging. In addition, virtually no biological alterations had occurred to the river environment as a direct result of the activities at the Savannah River Site. Also undertaken in 1951 were benchmark radiation surveys. From 1955 to 1961, University of Georgia researchers at the site began studying radioecology—the fate and effects of radioactive contaminants on the environment and the use of radioactive tracers to follow ecological processes. In 1961, the Savannah River Ecology Laboratory (SREL) was established within the reservation, and in 1972, the Atomic Energy Commission designated the SRP reservation as the nation's first National Environmental Research Park, an outdoor laboratory for investigating the effects of energy technology and production on the environment. Off-limits to the general public, the research area was large and possessed a high natural diversity of species, creating an ideal environment for conducting uninterrupted, long-term ecological research. Over the years, scientists with the SREL have published more than three thousand articles in peer-reviewed scientific journals.[12] Retired SREL ecologist J. Whitfield Gibbons conducted the longest uninterrupted study of freshwater turtles in the world, spanning twenty-six years and involving more than twenty thousand turtles. Gibbons calls the laboratory "an ecological researcher's paradise," and notes that the SREL has produced more ecologists and has done more to further the study of ecology than any other facility in the world.[13] Any assessment of the legacy of the Cold War must take such accomplishments into account. The impact of the SREL and other projects within the site's boundaries focused on environmental stewardship is clearly visible from outer space. A satellite image of the site reveals not a hellish deathscape but a lush, verdant island. Outside the plant's boundaries, the land clearly shows the environmental damage that is the result of the more traditional ways by which humans have affected the natural landscape.

More than half a century has passed since the Atomic Energy Commission and Du Pont Corporation made the decision that set this region on the path to modernization. The Savannah River Site is today the state's largest industrial employer, and its wide-ranging impact on the region remains unrivaled by any other single entity. Like the antebellum cotton plantations, the arrival of the

Winter Colonists, and the coming of the textile mills, the creation and impact of the SRP during the Cold War has become an integral and celebrated part of the region's history. In 2005, former employees of the SRP, led by scientist Walt Joseph, founded the Savannah River Heritage Foundation. Its goal is to build a heritage center and museum at the site to educate the public on the technical, social, and ecological impacts of the Cold War. The foundation also hopes to create a walking tour through the former town of Ellenton, complete with exhibits recognizing the sacrifices of its residents. On August 27, 2010, the Savannah River Heritage Foundation commemorated the discovery and confirmed existence of the neutrino. The smallest of particles, the neutrino has no electrical charge and only the smallest mass. It is, according to Joseph, "the closest thing to nothing that is still something." The neutrino, Italian for "little neutral one," was calculated to exist in 1931 by Austrian theoretical physicist Wolfgang Pauli. In 1956, Clyde Cowan and Frederick Reines, two physicists working in the SRP's P reactor, detected and confirmed the neutrino's existence. Cowan died in 1974, but Reines accepted the Nobel Prize in both of their names in 1995 for the discovery, the only Nobel Prize awarded for scientific work conducted in South Carolina. The commemoration of the discovery of the neutrino was a fitting tribute to the Cold War forces that had so dramatically transformed the South. The 2010 celebration included a scientific conference, a banquet, and the unveiling of a historical marker commemorating the discovery.[14] The marker stands across the street from the Aiken Chamber of Commerce, an appropriate placement given the importance of the SRP in the city's growth, development, and modernization. The Savannah River Site, still commonly referred to by locals as the Bomb Plant, remains rendered mostly as a vast blank space on maps. It is anything but. The site, embodying the powerful economic, social, cultural, and political forces that accompanied the Cold War, has left an indelible imprint on the landscape of the modern South.

NOTES

Abbreviations

ACC Minutes	Minutes, Aiken City Council, Aiken County Government Complex, Aiken, South Carolina
AED Records	E. I. Du Pont de Nemours and Company, Atomic Energy Division Records, Gregg-Graniteville Library, University of South Carolina at Aiken
ASR	*Aiken Standard and Review*
BRM	Burnet R. Maybank
BRM Papers	Burnet R. Maybank Papers, Special Collections, Marlene and Nathan Addlestone Library, College of Charleston, Charleston, South Carolina
CAN	Curtis A. Nelson
HLA	Harry L. Alston
HH	Harry Hammond
HOD	Harold O. DeWitt
HST Papers	Harry S. Truman Papers, Harry S. Truman Library, Independence, Missouri
JAT	Julius A. Thomas
JSB	John Shaw Billings
JSB/FWB Papers	John Shaw Billings and Frederika Wade Billings Papers, Manuscripts, South Caroliniana Library, University of South Carolina at Columbia
NCJ	Nelson C. Jackson
NUL-SRO	Papers of the National Urban League—Southern Regional Office, Library of Congress, Washington, D.C.
SHS	Samuel H. Swint
SHS Papers	Samuel H. Swint Papers, Gregg-Graniteville Library, University of South Carolina at Aiken
SRPP	E. I. Du Pont de Nemours and Company, Atomic Energy Division, Savannah River Plant Papers, Accession 1957, Hagley Museum and Library, Wilmington, Delaware
WDW	William D. Workman
WDW Papers	William D. Workman Papers, Modern Political Collections, South Caroliniana Library, University of South Carolina at Columbia

Introduction

1. Schulman, *From Cotton Belt to Sunbelt*, 141. For military spending and the South, see also Markusen et al., *Rise of the Gunbelt*; David L. Carlton, "The American South and the U.S. Defense Economy," in *South, the Nation, and the World*, ed. Carlton and Coclanis, 152–53; Hooks, "Guns and Butter."

2. For the impact of the Cold War on western development generally, see Hevly and Findlay, *Atomic West*; Lotchin, *Fortress California*; Nash, *American West Transformed*; Nash, *Federal Landscape*; McGirr, *Suburban Warriors*; Fernlund, *Cold War American West*.

3. See Findlay and Hevly, *Atomic Frontier Days*; Gerber, *On the Home Front*; Sanger, *Working on the Bomb*; Hunner, *Inventing Los Alamos*; Fishbine, *Children of Usher*; Litchman, *Secrets*; Shroyer, *Secret Mesa*; Charles W. Johnson and Jackson, *City behind a Fence*; Olwell, *At Work in the Atomic City*; Leland Johnson and Schaffer, *Oak Ridge National Laboratory*; Hales, *Atomic Spaces*; Fischer, *Los Alamos Experience*.

4. Schulman, *From Cotton Belt to Sunbelt*, 149. For examinations of southern military bases and their impact on their host communities, see Myers, *Black, White, and Olive Drab*; Lutz, *Homefront*; Phillips, "Building a New South Metropolis."

5. The historiography of the civil rights movement is large and ever-expanding. Key older works include Dittmer, *Local People*; Carson, *In Struggle*; Payne, *I've Got the Light*; Chafe, *Civilities and Civil Rights*. More recent works have expanded the parameters of the movement beyond the traditional 1954–65 framework, putting greater emphasis on activism during the New Deal and World War II eras. For civil rights activism in the 1930s and 1940s, see Sullivan, *Days of Hope*; Egerton, *Speak Now against the Day*; Frederickson, *Dixiecrat Revolt*; Brooks, *Winning the Peace*; Kruse and Tuck, *Fog of War*.

6. See Lassiter, *Silent Majority*; Kruse, *White Flight*.

7. Sullivan, *Days of Hope*; Egerton, *Speak Now against the Day*; Gilmore, *Defying Dixie*; Tyson, *Radio Free Dixie*; Woods, *Black Struggle, Red Scare*; Dudziak, *Cold War Civil Rights*.

8. Stewart, "*What Nature Suffers to Groe*," 12.

9. Mart A. Stewart, "Southern Environmental History," in *Companion*, ed. Boles, 414–15.

10. The respective roles of race and class in the rebirth of the Republican Party in the South are topics of fierce scholarly debate. For those arguing for the primacy of race, see Carter, *Politics of Rage*; Carter, *From George Wallace to Newt Gingrich*; Black and Black, *Rise of Southern Republicans*; Black and Black, *Politics and Society*; Frederickson, *Dixiecrat Revolt*. For arguments supporting the class-based origins and success of the GOP in the South, see especially Shafer and Johnston, *End of Southern Exceptionalism*. Complicating this dichotomy is an intriguing study of the evolution of "suburban politics," which involved elements of both race and class. See Lassiter, *Silent Majority*.

Chapter One. "This Most Essential Task"

1. Rhodes, *Dark Sun*, 363, 372–74. The Soviet nuclear test was conducted in Kazakhstan. See Cirincione, *Bomb Scare*, 19. "Report to the President by the Special

Committee of the National Security Council to the President," January 31, 1950, in *Foreign Relations of the United States*, 513–23; McCullough, *Truman*, 763.

2. ASR, September 14, 1949.

3. Gaddis, *We Now Know*, 96; Cirincione, *Bomb Scare*, 17.

4. Gaddis, *We Now Know*, 99.

5. Buck, *History*, 1; Gaddis, *We Now Know*, 99.

6. Gaddis, *We Now Know*, 91; Gaddis, *Cold War*, 54; Flank, *Hell's Fire*, 330.

7. Gaddis, *Cold War*, 36; York, *Advisors*, 41–42.

8. Craig and Logevall, *America's Cold War*, 103–5.

9. Donovan, *Tumultuous Years*, 150, 152, 153; Rhodes, *Dark Sun*, 371, 378. Rhodes has written the definitive work on the scientific and political background of the development of the hydrogen bomb.

10. Cirincione, *Bomb Scare*, 22.

11. Gaddis, *Cold War*, 61; Bird and Sherwin, *American Prometheus*, 416–30; Craig and Logevall, *America's Cold War*, 106.

12. Gaddis, *We Now Know*, 231; York, *Advisors*, chapter 4.

13. Gaddis, *Cold War*, 61.

14. Gaddis, *We Now Know*, 231. For a discussion of the role of the military in Truman's decision-making process, see Rosenberg, "American Atomic Strategy."

15. "Memorandum for the President," November 18, 1949, File: Atomic Energy: Superbomb Data, Box 175, President's Secretary's Files, HST Papers; Rhodes, *Dark Sun*, chapter 20.

16. Wells, "Sounding the Tocsin," 119; "Memorandum by the Joint Chiefs of Staff to the Secretary of Defense," January 13, 1950, in *Foreign Relations of the United States*, 503–11. According to Herbert York, very little congressional opposition arose in response to Truman's decision (*Advisors*, 70–71). See also Rhodes, *Dark Sun*, 406–7.

17. McCullough, *Truman*, 761.

18. Joseph Alsop and Stewart Alsop, "Matter of Fact: Pandora's Box I," *Washington Post*, January 2, 1950, File: Atomic Energy: Superbomb Data, Box 175, President's Secretary's Files, HST Papers.

19. Roy Valencourt to President, January 27, 1950, "An Open Letter," January 29, 1950, Ann S. Hedges to Harry S. Truman, January 29, 1950, Horace L. Friess to Truman, January 29, 1950, all in File 692-J Misc., Box 1533, White House Central Files, Official File, HST Papers.

20. McCullough, *Truman*, 763–64.

21. Harry S. Truman to David Lilienthal, January 31, 1950, NSC-Atomic Weapons—Thermonuclear file, Box 202, President's Secretary's File, HST Papers.

22. Statement by the President on Announcing the First Atomic Explosion in the USSR, September 23, 1949, in *Public Papers*, 485.

23. Leffler, *Preponderance of Power*, 326; Donovan, *Tumultuous Years*, 78, 83; Wells, "Sounding the Tocsin," 117; Hogan, *Cross of Iron*, 297. Truman signed off on NSC-68 in September 1950.

24. Gaddis, *Cold War*, 43.

25. Ibid.

26. Buck, *History*, 2. In the short term, General Electric started producing quanti-

ties of tritium at the Hanford Site in Washington State. See Carlisle and Zenzen, *Supplying the Nuclear Arsenal*, 73.

27. Holland, "Steward of World Peace," 18.

28. Bebbington, *History*, 5.

29. E. I. Du Pont de Nemours and Company, *Savannah River Plant of the U.S. Atomic Energy Commission*, 3; "Wizards of Wilmington," 94.

30. Mosley, *Blood Relations*; Dorian, *Du Ponts*; Zilg, *Du Pont*; "Wizards of Wilmington," 98; Ndiaye, *Nylon and Bombs*, 8.

31. Zilg, *Du Pont*, 151, 156–59; "Wizards of Wilmington," 98.

32. Hounshell and Smith, *Science and Corporate Strategy*, 221–86.

33. Crawford H. Greenewalt, Diaries, vol. 2, December 16, 1942–December 31, 1943, 2, Hagley Museum and Library, Wilmington, Delaware.

34. Martin, "Corporate Cold Warriors," 174–77.

35. Bebbington, *History*, 5.

36. Harry S. Truman to Crawford H. Greenewalt, July 25, 1950, Greenewalt to Truman, October 17, 1950, File 1, Box 42, Series III, Accession 1814, Crawford H. Greenewalt Papers, Hagley Museum and Library.

37. S. L. Abrams to Crawford H. Greenewalt, August 15, 1950, in ibid.

38. Ndiaye, *Nylon and Bombs*, 191.

39. Ibid., 211.

40. Similar to the Hanford arrangement, Du Pont undertook the new assignment on the basis of cost plus a fixed fee of one dollar. Furthermore, any patents resulting from work at the new plant would become the property of the federal government. See Bebbington, *History*, 7–8. See also "History of Negotiation of Contract AT (07-2)-1," in File 1, Box 5, Subseries A, Series II, SRPP.

41. Crawford H. Greenewalt to Stockholders of E. I. Du Pont de Nemours and Company, October 18, 1950, File 1, Box 42, Series III, Accession 1814, Greenewalt Papers.

42. "Opening Statement by Crawford Greenewalt, President of Du Pont," Hearing Held before the Joint Committee on Atomic Energy, August 4, 1950, in Bebbington, *History*, 250.

43. C. H. Topping, Engineering Department, E. I. Du Pont de Nemours and Company, "Plant 124 Site Survey," November 27, 1950, Box H-10-1, Series 43, Records of the Atomic Energy Commission, Record Group 326, National Archives and Records Administration, Southeast Region, Morrow, Georgia; Lang, "Our Far-Flung Correspondents," 42. See also H. F. Brown to Heads of Departments and Branch Offices, Works, and Divisions of Explosives Department, July 11, 1950, File 7, Box 6, Subseries C, Series II, SRPP.

44. O'Mara, *Cities of Knowledge*, 34.

45. Topping, "Plant 124 Site Survey," 31.

46. Ibid., 23, 27; Bebbington, *History*, 12; Du Pont Explosives Department to Executive Committee, November 8, 1950, File 9, Box 6k, Subseries C, Series II, SRPP.

47. "Plant #124 Memorandum Site Report," August 24, 1950, 1, 16, File 4, Box 9, Subseries A, Series III, SRPP.

48. "Report to the President by the Special Committee of the National Security Council to the President," January 31, 1950, in *Foreign Relations of the United States*, 513–23; Topping, "Plant 124 Site Survey"; H. F. Brown to Heads of Departments and Branch Offices, Works, and Divisions of Explosives Department, July 11, 1950, File 7, Box 6, Subseries C, Series II, SRPP.

49. Tindall, *Emergence of the New South*, 700–701; Schulman, *From Cotton Belt to Sunbelt*, 72; Reed et al., *Savannah River Site at Fifty*, 103; Goldfield, *Cotton Fields and Skyscrapers*, 183.

50. James C. Cobb, "World War II and the Mind of the Modern South," in *Remaking Dixie*, ed. McMillen, 10.

51. Ibid., 9; Reed et al., *Savannah River Site at Fifty*, 108; Goldfield, *Cotton Fields and Skyscrapers*, 143.

52. Cobb, "World War II," 5.

53. Edgar, *South Carolina: A History*, 517.

54. Frederickson, *Dixiecrat Revolt*, 171.

55. Cobb, *Selling the South*, 1.

56. Edgar, *South Carolina: A History*, 503; Reed et al., *Savannah River Site at Fifty*, 100–103.

57. WDW, typescript for broadcast, "Inside South Carolina," December 3, 1950, Topical File: Energy, Nuclear, SRP, Box 29, WDW Papers.

58. Reed et al., *Savannah River Site at Fifty*, 136–37; Workman, *Bishop from Barnwell*, 80–83.

59. For Brown's cooperation with Moody, see Reed et al., *Savannah River Site at Fifty*, 97–103.

60. For Southern California and defense-related growth, see Nash, *American West Transformed*; McGirr, *Suburban Warriors*, chapter 1. In *The Rise of the Gunbelt*," Markusen et al., note that as defense-related activity has grown since World War II, "interregional per capita incomes have converged, with spectacular gains by the southern states" (21). Carlton takes a somewhat different position regarding the impact of defense spending. Although he acknowledges that since 1945, the South has received an increasing proportion of its income from defense spending, the actual mix of spending has not benefited the region as much as other parts of the country. In particular, he argues, the South has lagged other regions in its receipt of prime contracts. See David L. Carlton, "The American South and the U.S. Defense Economy," in *South, the Nation, and the World*, ed. Carlton and Coclanis, 152–53.

61. Hooks, "Guns and Butter," 265.

62. Schulman, *From Cotton Belt to Sunbelt*, 136; Markusen et al., *Rise of the Gunbelt*; "Southern Militarism," 61.

63. Cole Blease Graham Jr., "James Francis Byrnes," in *South Carolina Encyclopedia*, ed. Edgar, 114–15.

64. Lee, "South Carolina's Cold Warrior."

65. Huntley, "Mendel Rivers."

66. Bleser, *Hammonds of Redcliffe*, 307; JSB Diary, 32:37–38, JSB/FWB Papers.

67. JSB Diary, 32:39.

68. Reed et al., *Savannah River Site at Fifty*, 134.

69. E. C. Thomas, interview.

70. Reed et al., *Savannah River Site at Fifty*, 134.

71. SHS, Confidential Memorandum, November 28, 1950, Personal File: Savannah River Plant, SHS Papers.

72. *ASR*, November 29, 1950.

73. Reed et al., *Savannah River Site at Fifty*, 138.

74. Ronnie Bryant, interview.

75. *ASR*, November 29, 1950.

76. Ibid., December 8, 1950.

77. Lenwood Melton, interview.

78. *ASR*, May 11, 1951.

Chapter Two. A Varied Landscape

1. Stokes, *Savannah*, 14–16.

2. Kovacik and Winberry, *South Carolina*, 18.

3. Ibid., 18, 41.

4. Ibid., 18, 44.

5. Ibid., 18; Burton, *In My Father's House*, 18.

6. Downey, *Planting a Capitalist South*, 15; Kovacik and Winberry, *South Carolina*, 41.

7. Edgar, *South Carolina*, 52.

8. Burton, *In My Father's House*, 19.

9. Vandervelde, *Aiken County*, 56; Downey, *Planting a Capitalist South*, 13, 19.

10. Faust, *James Henry Hammond*, 61.

11. Ibid., 70, 132; Bleser, *Hammonds of Redcliffe*, vii.

12. Bleser, *Hammonds of Redcliffe*, vii.

13. Faust, *James Henry Hammond*, 107–16.

14. Ibid., 105, 129–30, 274–75, 278–82.

15. Ibid., chapter 5.

16. Vandervelde, *Aiken County*, 61–63.

17. Tom Downey, "Hamburg," in *South Carolina Encyclopedia*, ed. Edgar, 415.

18. Hayne, "Aiken, South Carolina," 623; Downey, *Planting a Capitalist South*, 94.

19. Aaron Marrs, "South Carolina Railroad," in *South Carolina Encyclopedia*, ed. Edgar, 903.

20. Downey, *Planting a Capitalist South*, 93.

21. Hayne, "Aiken, South Carolina," 623.

22. James Farmer Jr., "Aiken," in *South Carolina Encyclopedia*, ed. Edgar, 12.

23. *ASR*, July 22, 1958.

24. Henderson, *Short History*, 2; Farmer, "Aiken," 12.

25. *ASR*, July 22, 1958; Farmer, "Aiken," 10. Aiken's son, William Jr., later became governor of South Carolina.

26. Hayne, "Aiken, South Carolina," 624.

27. Ibid., 625; *Aiken Remembers.*

28. Hayne, "Aiken, South Carolina," 625.

29. *Aiken, South Carolina as a Health and Pleasure Resort,* 4–5.

30. Downey, *Planting a Capitalist South,* 123–31.

31. Ibid., 133–35.

32. Ibid., 138–44.

33. Henderson, *Short History,* 18.

34. Farmer, "Playing Rebels," 50.

35. Edgar, *South Carolina,* 377; Robeson, "'Ominous Defiance,'" 67.

36. Downey, "Hamburg," 415.

37. Kantrowitz, *Ben Tillman,* 50.

38. Hyman S. Rubin III, "Reconstruction," in *South Carolina Encyclopedia,* ed. Edgar, 780.

39. Kantrowitz, *Ben Tillman,* 50.

40. Edgar, *South Carolina,* 398; Rubin, "Reconstruction," 780.

41. Edgar, *South Carolina,* 402–3.

42. Robert K. Ackerman, "Wade Hampton III," in *South Carolina Encyclopedia,* ed. Edgar, 422.

43. Kantrowitz, *Ben Tillman,* 65.

44. Ibid., 67–70; Edgar, *South Carolina,* 403.

45. Mark M. Smith, "'All Is Not Quiet"; Richard Zuczek, "Ellenton Riot," in *South Carolina Encyclopedia,* ed. Edgar, 295.

46. Kantrowitz, *Ben Tillman,* 76–77.

47. Burton, *In My Father's House,* 30; Downey, "Hamburg," 415.

48. Somerville, *States through Irish Eyes,* 28.

49. Ibid., 29.

50. Harry Worcester Smith, *Life and Sport,* 6–7; MacDowell, *Aiken Scrapbook.* Joye Cottage is located at the corner of Easy Street and Whiskey Road.

51. Lang, "Our Far-Flung Correspondents," 40.

52. *South Carolina: WPA Guide,* 159.

53. See, for example, ASR, June 16, 1952.

54. Register, Willcox Hotel, Aiken County Historical Museum, Aiken, South Carolina.

55. *Aiken Remembers.*

56. Clarence Mitchell, "NAACP Report on the 'H' Bomb Project in South Carolina," February 5, 1951, 1951 SRP File, Box A134, NUL-SRO.

57. Willar Hightower to author, March 22, 2012; Gallman, interview; Key, interview.

58. Robeson, "'Ominous Defiance,'" nn. 4, 5; Sampson, "Rise," 103; Key, interview.

59. Robeson, "'Ominous Defiance,'" 68.

60. Conroy, "Horses Don't Eat Moon Pies," 47, 49.

61. Ibid., 52.

62. Sylvia Bryant, interview.

63. Esther Melton, interview.

Chapter Three. "A Land Doomed and Damned"

1. Lang, "Our Far-Flung Correspondents," 47–48; McMillan, "H-Bomb's First Victims," 18; ASR, December 6, 1950; Louise Cassels, *Unexpected Exodus*, 3.

2. Stephen Harley, interview, in Browder and Brooks, *Memories of Home*, 164.

3. JSB Diary, 32:39, JSB/FWB Papers.

4. Ibid., 32:46.

5. WDW, typescript for broadcast, "Inside South Carolina," December 3, 1950, Topical File: Energy, Nuclear, SRP, Box 29, WDW Papers.

6. McMillan, "H-Bomb's First Victims," 18; Reed et al., *Savannah River Site at Fifty*, 140.

7. WDW, "Notes on Ellenton Meeting, December 6, 1950," Topical File: Energy, Nuclear, Savannah River Plant, Articles by WDW, Box 29, WDW Papers.

8. McMillan, "H-Bomb's First Victims," 19; ASR, December 8, 1950.

9. Lang, "Our Far-Flung Correspondents," 48.

10. Browder and Brooks, *Memories of Home*, vii. In the initial days after the announcement, the towns of Jackson and Snelling were likewise targeted for evacuation. They eventually fell outside the plant's boundaries and were spared. See ASR, January 12, 1951.

11. Lang, "Our Far-Flung Correspondents," 42.

12. JSB Diary, 32:38.

13. ASR, February 9, 1951.

14. Eubanks quoted in Booton Herndon, "That Others May Live," *Redbook*, March 25, 1951, 80.

15. E. I. Du Pont de Nemours and Company, *Savannah River Plant Construction History*, 35–36.

16. Ellenton was officially incorporated on December 24, 1880. See Browder and Brooks, *Memories of Home*, vii, 3, 6.

17. Browder and Brooks, *Memories of Home*, 38. It was apparently more cost-effective to leave the lights on than to turn them off at daylight and on at dark.

18. Browder and Brooks, *Memories of Home*, 11.

19. Ibid., 12.

20. Ibid., 14.

21. Ibid., 21.

22. Ibid., 14.

23. Ibid.

24. Ibid., 62.

25. Ibid., 13.

26. Ibid., 12.

27. McMillan, "H-Bomb's First Victims," 19.

28. O'Berry, *Ellenton, S.C.*, 134.

29. Ibid., 156 n. 91.

30. Ibid.

31. Browder and Brooks, *Memories of Home*, 43.

32. Ibid., 44; Louis Cassels and Cassels, *Inquiry*, 1.

33. Browder and Brooks, *Memories of Home*, 50.

34. Louise Cassels, *Unexpected Exodus*, 4.

35. Louis Cassels and Cassels, *Inquiry*, 1–2. According to county deed records, Ellen G. Cassels was the first in the family to purchase property—a quarter acre in Ellenton for fifty dollars in 1900. See Direct Index to Titles, A–Mc, 1872–1913, and Title Book Di, 376, Register of MESNE Conveyances, Aiken County, Aiken County Government Complex, Aiken, South Carolina. H. M. Cassels first appears in the deed books in 1903. See Direct Index to Titles, A–Mc, 1872–1913, and Title Book LI, 342.

36. O'Berry, *Ellenton, S.C.*, 142 n. 57; Louis Cassels and Cassels, *Inquiry*, 1.

37. Louis Cassels and Cassels, *Inquiry*, 1; Fielding Foreman, interview.

38. Louis Cassels and Cassels, *Inquiry*, 2.

39. Fielding Foreman, interview. The records of the dissolution of the corporation list thirty-two separate properties and businesses owned in common by the Cassels/Foreman family. See Title Book 127, 292–97.

40. Louis Cassels, *Coontail Lagoon*, 79, 80.

41. Louis Cassels and Cassels, *Inquiry*, 3; *Shorter College Alumni Directory*, 23; Browder and Brooks, *Memories of Home*, 93.

42. Louise Cassels, *Unexpected Exodus*.

43. Browder and Brooks, *Memories of Home*, 63, 64.

44. Louise Cassels, *Unexpected Exodus*, 8; Reed et al., *Savannah River Site at Fifty*, 133.

45. Browder and Brooks, *Memories of Home*.

46. McMillan, "H-Bomb's First Victims," 18.

47. "The Atom: The Displaced," 22.

48. William Stephen Harley, quoted in Browder and Brooks, *Memories of Home*, 160; Louise Cassels, *Unexpected Exodus*, 28.

49. ASR, December 13, 1950; Louise Cassels, *Unexpected Exodus*, 35.

50. Louise Cassels, *Unexpected Exodus*, 28.

51. JSB Diary, 32:47.

52. R. M. Evans to Walter J. Williams, December 1, 1950, File 3, Box 9, Subseries A, Series III, SRPP.

53. M. W. Boyer to H. F. Brown, December 5, 1950, File 4, Box 9, Subseries A, Series III, in ibid.

54. R. M. Evans to M. W. Boyer, December 20, 1950, Boyer to Evans, December 29, 1950, File 3, Box 9, Subseries A, Series III, in ibid.

55. Reed et al., *Savannah River Site at Fifty*, 147.

56. South Atlantic Division, Corps of Engineers, Information Bulletin 5, January 15, 1951, Atomic Plant B General Information File, BRM Papers.

57. Chapin, et al., "In the Shadow," 68; ASR, January 31, 1951.

58. South Atlantic Division, Corps of Engineers, Information Bulletin 1, December 13, 1950, Atomic Plant—General Information File, BRM Papers.

59. Louise Cassels, *Unexpected Exodus*, 93–94.

60. See South Atlantic Division, Corps of Engineers, Information Bulletin 6,

January 19, 1951, Atomic Plant—General Information File, BRM Papers; Information Bulletin 11, n.d., Atomic Plant—Land Investigation File, BRM Papers; Louise Cassels, *Unexpected Exodus*, 16.

61. Reed et al., *Savannah River Site at Fifty*, 147.

62. Dick Richardson to BRM, March 18, 1951, Atomic Plant—Land Investment File, BRM Papers.

63. Louis Cassels, *Coontail Lagoon*, 73.

64. See, for example, HH to JSB, January 21, 1951, File 348, Box 6, JSB/FWB Papers.

65. Louise Cassels, *Unexpected Exodus*, 46–47.

66. Reed et al., *Savannah River Site at Fifty*, 154. Not all property disputes went to trial. Property often was included in a Complaint in Condemnation and Declaration of Taking when a clear title could not readily be established. Once clear title was established, many of these property owners accepted the government's offer. See for example, *U.S. v. 5139.5 Acres of Land, More or Less, Situate in Aiken and Barnwell Counties, South Carolina, and A. H. Corley et al., and Unknown Owners*, Civil Action 2758, Tract A-52, Order and Judgment, December 23, 1953, Box 267, District Court of the United States for the Eastern District of South Carolina, Aiken Division, Record Group 21, National Archives and Records Administration, Southeast Region, Morrow, Georgia. In August 1951, "a ruling . . . replaced a jury trial with three judges who would go direct to a Claimant's lot in order to make the final decision" (Reed et al., *Savannah River Site at Fifty*, 152–53).

67. See *U.S. v. 6945.3 Acres of Land, More or Less, Situate in Aiken and Barnwell Counties, South Carolina, Ida B. Smith, et al., and Unknown Owners*, Civil Action 2834, Tract C-201, Order, November 6, 1952, Record Group 21, Eastern District of South Carolina, Aiken Division. The judge ordered the government pay the defendant an additional $79,550; Thurmond's and Busbee's firms split $28,551.79.

68. Louis Cassels, *Coontail Lagoon*, 72.

69. For Strom Thurmond's pre-senatorial career, see Frederickson, *Dixiecrat Revolt*.

70. *U.S. v. 5139.5 Acres of Land*, Tract A-60.

71. Ibid., Testimony, October 1–3, 1951, 96.

72. Ibid., 97.

73. Ibid., 97–98.

74. Ibid., 98.

75. Ibid., 100.

76. *United States v. 6945.3 Acres of Land*, Tract C-201, Property of the Harley Estate, Testimony, April 7–9, 1952, 11, 28–29, 41–46.

77. *U.S. v. 5139.5 Acres of Land, Tract A-60, Known as Sleepy Hollow Farms*, October 1–3, 1951, Transcript, 8-39, Box 269, District Court of the United States for the Eastern District of South Carolina, Aiken Division.

78. *Barnwell People-Sentinel*, October 4, 1951, Series VIII, Scrapbook 1, Reel 110, AED Records.

79. *United States v. 5139.5 Acres of Land*, Tracts A-45, A-63, Dr. A. H. Corley and A. H. Corley Jr., Landowners, Testimony, September 27–28, 1951.

80. JSB Diary, 32:81, 82. See also HH to JSB, December 21, 1950, File 347, Box 6, JSB/FWB Papers. Billings received a Notice of Condemnation on December 28, 1950. See J. B. Barker to JSB, December 28, 1950, File 347, JSB/FWB Papers.

81. HH to JSB, December 26, 1950, Gordon Britton to JSB, December 21, 1950, File 347, Box 6, JSB/FWB Papers.

82. HH to JSB, January 13, 1951, South Carolina State Highway Department to JSB, "Notice of Condemnation," December 28, 1950, File 348, Box 6, JSB/FWB Papers.

83. HH to JSB, January 21, 1951, in ibid.

84. Henry C. Hammond to JSB, January 31, 1951, in ibid.; HH to JSB, January 26, 1951, File 349, Box 6, JSB/FWB Papers.

85. HH to JSB, February 8, 1951, File 350, Box 6, JSB/FWB Papers.

86. JSB Diary, 32:212.

87. *United States v. 5139.5 Acres of Land*, Tract A-60, Sleepy Hollow Farms, Testimony, October 1–3, 1951, 19.

88. Fielding Foreman, interview; Louise Cassels, *Unexpected Exodus*, 66.

89. *United States v. 6945.3 Acres of Land*, Tract H-748, Order and Judgment, August 16, 1951.

90. Ibid., Tract H-709, Order and Judgment, August 8, 1951. Bush, received $21,442 for the 151.5 acre plot; the government's original offer was $17,500 (Final Judgment, October 13, 1952).

91. *United States v. 5139.5 Acres of Land*, Tract A-60, Order and Judgment, June 21, 1951.

92. Chapin et al., "In the Shadow," 69.

93. McMillan, "H-Bomb's First Victims," 20.

94. Louise Cassels, *Unexpected Exodus*, 66.

95. "The Atom: The Displaced," 22.

96. Lang, "Our Far-Flung Correspondents," 48.

97. McMillan, "H-Bomb's First Victims," 17.

98. Ibid., 19.

99. *Charleston News and Courier*, September 27, 1951.

100. Reed et al., *Savannah River Plant at Fifty*, 154.

101. Browder and Brooks, *Memories of Home*, 162.

102. See, for example, *United States v. 5139.5 Acres of Land*, Tract D-308, Photographic Exhibits. See also Reed et al., *Savannah River Site*, 155–56; Cabak and Inkrot, *Old Farm, New Farm*, 23–25.

103. Louise Cassels, *Unexpected Exodus*, 87.

104. Chapin et al., "In the Shadow," 67.

105. Holland, "Steward of World Peace," 51.

106. Chapin et al., "In the Shadow, 67.

107. WDW, typescript of broadcast, "Inside South Carolina."

108. Chapin et al., "In the Shadow," 75–76.

109. Ibid., 146.

110. Ibid.

111. Holland, "Steward of World Peace," 57.

112. Chapin et al., "In the Shadow," 146.

113. Holland, "Steward of World Peace," 55.

114. Chapin et al., "In the Shadow," 106.

115. Holland, "Steward of World Peace," 56.

116. Alexander, interview.

117. ASR, April 2, 1958.

118. U.S. Atomic Energy Commission, Press Releases, June 4, 1953, October 10, 1954, Energy, Nuclear, SRP, Press Releases, SRP Operations Office File (2 of 3), Box 30, WDW Papers.

119. Caroll M. Eaddy, "A Town Dies," ASR, March 24, 1952.

Chapter Four. "Bigger'n Any Lie"

1. *Augusta Herald*, October 19, 1951, Series VIII, Scrapbook 1, Reel 110, AED Records.

2. *Greenville News*, October 24, 1951, in ibid.

3. Reed et al., *Savannah River Site at Fifty*, 167–69; *Augusta Herald*, October 19, 1951, Series VIII, Scrapbook 1, Reel 110, AED Records.

4. History of Negotiation of Contract AT(07-2)-1, n.d., n.p., File 1, Box 5, Subseries A, Series II, SRPP; U.S. Department of Labor, *Bulletin*, 2.

5. R. M. Evans to CAN, August 9, 1950, File 7, Box 6, Subseries C, Series II, SRPP; SHS, "Effects of the Savannah River H-Plant Project on the Local Economy, and on Graniteville Company in Particular," June 30, 1952, SHS Papers.

6. U.S. Atomic Energy Commission, SROO, "Facts on the SRP of the USAEC in Aiken, Barnwell, and Allendale Counties, S.C.," January 23, 1953, Topical File: Energy, Nuclear, SRP, Correspondence, 1951–1980, Box 30, WDW Papers.

7. CAN to SHS, October 20, 1953, SHS Papers.

8. "Wizards of Wilmington," 94.

9. HH to JSB, January 28, 1951, File 349, Box 6, JSB/FWB Papers.

10. "Deserted Village," 28.

11. HH to JSB, February 15, 1951, File 350, Box 6, JSB/FWB Papers.

12. HH to JSB, April 29, 1951, File 354, Box 6, JSB/FWB Papers.

13. Henry C. Hammond to JSB, February 20, 1951, File 350, Box 6, JSB/FWB Papers.

14. *New York Times*, October 3, 1951.

15. WDW, typescript, Topical File: Energy, Nuclear, SRP, Box 29, WDW Papers.

16. *New York Times*, October 3, 1951.

17. U.S. Department of Labor, *Bulletin*, 5.

18. HH to JSB, January 13, 1951, File 348, Box 6, JSB/FWB Papers.

19. HH to JSB, May 8, 1951, File 355, Box 6, JSB/FWB Papers.

20. G. O. Robinson Jr. to WDW, May 7, 1951, Topical File: Energy, Nuclear, SRP, Correspondence, 1951–1980, Box 30, WDW Papers; CAN, Testimony, in *Employment Practices at Savannah River Project, Hearings*, 10

21. CAN, Testimony, in *Employment Practices at Savannah River Project, Hearings*, 8–9.

22. U.S. Department of Labor, *Bulletin*, 3; CAN, Testimony, in *Employment Practices at Savannah River Project, Hearings*, 27.

23. U.S. Department of Labor, *Bulletin*, 8.

24. *ASR*, January 19, 1951.

25. HH to JSB, July 29, 1951, File 358, Box 6, JSB Papers.

26. R. K. Mason, Testimony, in *Employment Practices at Savannah River Project, Hearings*, 45.

27. See, for example, CAN to SHS, October 20, 1953, October 19, 1954, SHS Papers.

28. U.S. Department of Labor, Press Release, February 11, 1951, Atomic Plant—General Information File, BRM Papers; *Greenville News*, October 20, 1951, Series VIII, Scrapbook 1, Reel 110, AED Records.

29. "SRP Wage Rates/Bacon-Davis Determination," January 22, 1959, File 13, Box 10, Subseries A, Series III, SRPP.

30. WDW, typescript, December 31, 1952, typescript, [ca. 1951], Topical File: Energy, Nuclear, SRP, Box 29, WDW Papers.

31. SHS to R. C. Blair, December 1, 1960, Personal File: Savannah River Plant, SHS Papers; SHS, "Effects of the Savannah River H-Plant Project."

32. SHS, "Notes on Telephone Conversation with Mr. A. G. Heinsohn, President of Cherokee Textile Mill, December 17, 1950," December 21, 1950, Personal File: Savannah River Plant, SHS Papers.

33. See, for example, *Augusta Herald*, June 4, 1951.

34. *ASR*, February 29, 1952.

35. SHS, "Effects of the Savannah River H-Plant Project."

36. See "Comparison—Hourly Wage Rates," February 12, 1952, SHS Papers.

37. SHS to James F. Byrnes, February 2, 1951, ibid.

38. G. H. Sumarau to SHS, November 4, 1955, Personal File, SHS Papers.

39. G. H. Seigler to BRM, April 1, 1952, Misc. 1952—Atomic Plant File, BRM Papers.

40. "Resolution," January 4, 1951, in ibid.

41. U.S. Department of Labor, *Bulletin*, 4, 9.

42. Ibid., 6.

43. Clarence Mitchell, "NAACP Report on 'H' Bomb Project in South Carolina," February 5, 1951, 1951 SRP File, Box A134, NUL-SRO.

44. JAT to NUL Administration, February 2, 1951, 1951 January–March Correspondence File, Box A134, NUL-SRO.

45. "Tin-Hat-Topped Workmen Distinguish H-Bomb Area," *Atlanta Constitution*, October 6, 1951, Series VIII, Scrapbook 1, Reel 110, AED Records.

46. *New York Times*, October 3, 1951.

47. U.S. Department of Labor, *Bulletin*, 5, 12–21; Reed et al., *Savannah River Site at Fifty*, 186. See also CAN, Testimony, in *Employment Practices at Savannah River Project, Hearings*, 18.

48. *Augusta Herald*, October 3, 1951; *Augusta Chronicle*, October 9, 1951, Series VIII, Scrapbook 1, Reel 110, AED Records.

49. Reed et al., *Savannah River Site at Fifty*, 191.

50. McCoy, *Presidency of Harry S. Truman*, 98–99.

51. *Augusta Chronicle*, October 9, 1951, Series VIII, Scrapbook 1, Reel 110, AED Records.

52. Leslie Gould and Emanuel Doernberg, "Unions Control Atomic Energy Commission Plant Hiring," *New York Journal American*, October 19, 1951, File 1, Box 13, Subseries C, Series III, SRPP.

53. Transcript, radio broadcast, September 21, 1951, in ibid.

54. W. M. Tanner to W. M. Wheeler, September 17, 1951, copy in ibid.

55. "Notes on Wheeler Incident," September 17, 1951, in ibid.

56. W. A. Monihan to R. K. Mason, October 10, November 1, 1951, File 4, Box 13, Subseries C, Series III, SRPP.

57. W. A. Monihan, "Information for Wheeler Files," September 17, 1951, File 1, Box 13, Subseries C, Series III, SRPP.

58. *Augusta Chronicle*, November 4, 1951, Series VIII, Scrapbook 1, Reel 110, AED Records.

59. *Employment Practices at Savannah River Project, Hearings*, 32, 35.

60. Ibid., 6, 7, 14; Granville M. Read quoted in *Greenville News*, November 7, 1951, *Augusta Chronicle*, November 8, 1951, Series VIII, Scrapbook 1, Reel 110, AED Records; *Augusta Chronicle*, November 7, 1951, File 2, Box 13, Subseries C, Series III, SRPP.

61. *Employment Practices at Savannah River Project, Hearings*, 15, 60, 62, 68, 71.

62. *Employment Practices at Savannah River Project, Report*, 12, 14.

63. *Greenville News*, October 20, 1951, Series VIII, Scrapbook 1, Reel 110, AED Records.

64. *Columbia State*, October 28, 1951, in ibid.

65. Holland, "Steward of World Peace," 72.

66. HOD to NUL Administration, May 15, 1951, 1951 SRP Reports File, Box A134, NUL-SRO; Holland, "Steward of World Peace," 72.

67. Holland, "Steward of World Peace," 4, 83; *New York Times*, October 11, 1951.

68. ASR, December 12, 1950; Eugene Montgomery to NCJ, n.d., 1951 SRP January–March Correspondence File, Box A134, NUL-SRO.

69. See "Executive Order 9980: Regulations Governing Fair Employment Practices within the Federal Establishment," at www.trumanlibrary.org/executiveorders.

70. JAT to NUL Administration, February 2, 1951, 1951 SRP January–March Correspondence File, Box A134, NUL-SRO.

71. Olwell, *At Work in the Atomic City*, 23, 92–93.

72. Findlay and Hevly, *Atomic Frontier Days*, 27.

73. Clarence Mitchell quoted in NUL report, JAT to NUL Administration, February 2, 1951, UCDS February–October File, Box A135, NUL-SRO.

74. JAT to NCJ, February 2, January 15, 1951, 1951 SRP January–March Correspondence File, Box A134, NUL-SRO.

75. Eugene Montgomery to NCJ, n.d., Robert A. Brooks to NCJ, February 18, 1951, in ibid.

76. Quoted in Holland, "Steward of World Peace," 77.

77. ASR, January 31, 1951.

78. JAT to NUL Administration, February 2, 1951, 1951 SRP January–March Correspondence File, Box A134, NUL-SRO.

79. JAT to NCJ, February 2, 1951, in ibid.

80. Holland, "Steward of World Peace," 78–79.

81. Eugene Montgomery to NCJ, n.d., 1951 SRP January–March Correspondence File, Box A134, NUL-SRO; Holland, "Steward of World Peace," 105–6.

82. JAT to NUL Administration, March 15, 1951, 1951 January–March Correspondence File, Box A134, NUL-SRO.

83. HOD to NUL Administration, May 15, 1951, 1951 SRP Reports File, Box A134, NUL-SRO.

84. James Hinton to Clarence Mitchell, May 15, 1951, 1951 SRP April–June Correspondence File, Box A134, NUL-SRO.

85. HOD to NCJ, June 19, 1951, in ibid.

86. HOD to NUL Administration, May 15, 1951, 1951 SRP Reports File, Box A, NUL-SRO.

87. JAT to NUL Administration, March 15, 1951, 1951 SRP January–March Correspondence File, Box A134, NUL-SRO. See also HOD to NCJ, June 13, 1951, 1951 April–June Correspondence File, Box A134, NUL-SRO.

88. HOD to NCJ, June 19, 1951, 1951 April–June Correspondence File, Box A134, NUL-SRO.

89. HOD to NUL Board Members and Staff, June 6, 1951, in ibid.

90. See, for example, advertisements in *Augusta Herald*, May 6, 11, 1951.

91. JAT to NUL Administration, March 15, 1951, 1951 SRP January–March Correspondence File, Box A134, NUL-SRO.

92. HOD to NCJ, June 19, 1951, 1951 April–June Correspondence File, Box A134, NUL-SRO.

93. JAT to NUL Administration, March 15, 1951, 1951 SRP January–March Correspondence File, Box A134, NUL-SRO.

94. Notes Deborah Holland, "Blacks comprised between 75–80% of the unskilled and semi-skilled labor market and were welcomed into unions with jurisdiction over such work" ("Steward of World Peace," 93, 97–100).

95. HOD to NUL Administration, May 15, 1951, 1951 SRP Reports File, Box A134, NUL-SRO.

96. HOD to NCJ, May 29, 1951, 1951 April–June Correspondence File, Box A134, NUL-SRO.

97. HOD to NUL Administration, May 15, 1951, 1951 SRP Reports File, Box A134, NUL-SRO.

98. HLA to NCJ, September 4, 1951, in ibid.

99. Holland, "Steward of World Peace," 99, 104.

100. Ibid., 90.

101. HOD to NCJ, May 21, 1951, 1951 SRP April–June Correspondence File, Box A134, NUL-SRO.

102. U.S. Department of Labor, *Bulletin*, 7; U.S. Department of Labor, Bureau of Employment Security, *Bimonthly Summary*, 18.

103. U.S. Department of Labor, *Bulletin*, 9.

104. DeWitt identified the employment of female workers as a critical issue (HOD to NUL Board Members and Staff, June 6, 1951, 1951 April–June Correspondence File, Box A134, NUL-SRO).

105. Strom, *Beyond the Typewriter*, 299–303, 369, 372.

106. The nearest urban daily, the *Augusta Herald*, most regularly carried advertisements for these positions; see, for example, May 5, 1951.

107. Brattain, "Gender, Race, and the Construction of the 'Southern Worker,'" 10.

108. Davies, *Woman's Place*, 154–56, 168.

109. HOD to NUL Administration, May 15, 1951, 1951 SRP Reports File, Box A134, NUL-SRO.

110. Ibid.

111. HOD to NUL Board Members and Staff, June 6, 1951, April–June Correspondence File, Box A134, NUL-SRO.

112. HOD to NUL Administration, May 15, 1951, 1951 SRP Reports File, Box A134, NUL-SRO.

113. HOD to NCJ, June 19, 1951, 1951 April–June Correspondence File, Box A134, NUL-SRO; unidentified clipping, July 7, 1951, 1951 SRP Reports File, Box A134, NUL-SRO.

114. Lester B. Granger to Harry S. Truman, July 5, 1951, File 413, Box 1235, White House Central Files, Official File, HST Papers.

115. Lester H. Persells to Harry S. Truman, July 27, 1951, File 526-B, Box 1381, White House Central Files, Official File, HST Papers.

116. American Veterans Committee, Press Release, July 29, 1951, NCJ, Reports, June–December 1951 File, Box A128, NUL-SRO.

117. William Benton to Harry S. Truman, October 20, 1951, File 526-B, Box 1381, White House Central Files, Official File, HST Papers.

118. "Statement by the President," December 3, 1951, "Executive Order," December 3, 1951, File 526-B, Box 1381, White House Central Files, Official File, HST Papers.

119. "Statement by the President," December 3, 1951, "Executive Order," December 3, 1951, File 526-B, Box 1381, White House Central Files, Official File, HST Papers; *Augusta Chronicle*, December 4, 1951, Series VIII, Scrapbook 1, Reel 110, AED Records.

120. Walter White and A. Philip Randolph to Harry S. Truman, November 11, 1951, File 413, Box 1235, White House Central Files, Official File, HST Papers. White and Randolph reviewed a draft of the bill and sent their thoughts to the president.

121. McCoy and Ruetten, *Quest and Response*, 275.

122. NCJ to JAT, May 31, 1951, 1951 April–June Correspondence File, Box A134, NUL-SRO.

123. Ibid.

124. HLA to NCJ, March 17, 1953, SRP 1953 File, Box A157, NUL-SRO.

125. HLA to NCJ, February 26, 1954, SR-AEC Project 1954 January–March File, Box A165, NUL-SRO.

126. Holland, "Steward of World Peace," 120.

127. HLA to NCJ, April 20, 1953, SRP 1953 File, Box A157, NUL-SRO.

128. HLA to CAN, July 15, 1953, in ibid.

129. HLA to Jacob Seidenberg, April 22, 1954, HLA to NCJ, May 20, 1954, April–September 1954 SRP File, Box A165, NUL-SRO.

130. Julian Lee to HLA, August 20, 1954, in ibid.; HLA to NCJ, April 22, 1956, Alston Reports, April–June 1956 File, Box A174, NUL-SRO.

131. Holland, "Steward of World Peace," 135, 306.

132. Hightower, interview; *Newsday*, January 22, 2000; Rivera, "Aiken, South Carolina," 8; *Augusta Chronicle*, November 28, 2001.

133. Willar Hightower to author, March 17, 2012.

Chapter Five. Rejecting the Garrison State

1. For population influx estimates, see Holland, "Steward of World Peace," 61–62. Estimates are based on peak employment figures of forty-six thousand and include accompanying family members as well as merchants and service providers.

2. U.S. Department of Labor, *Bulletin*, iii, 1.

3. Statement by L. W. Dunbar, Community Relations Officer, Office of the Manager, AEC, Savannah River, UCDS, Minutes, Meeting on the Savannah River Area H-Bomb Plant, Atomic Energy Commission, April 4, 1952, UCDS April–June 1952 File, Box A148, NUL-SRO.

4. While Goldfield notes that "most southern cities began plotting their urban-planning strategies during" World War II, the same cannot be said for smaller towns such as Aiken (*Region, Race, and Cities*, 254).

5. *ASR*, December 1, 1950.

6. Lang, "Our Far-Flung Correspondents," 44.

7. Ibid., 45.

8. Ibid., 46.

9. *ASR*, December 1, 1950; "New Atomic Bomb Plant Hits Augusta," 90; *New York Times Magazine*, November 30, 1952, 10–11; Turner, "Aiken for Armageddon," 54; U.S. Atomic Energy Commission, Press Release, January 23, 1952, Atomic Plant—General Information File, BRM Papers; Ben E. Douglas to BRM, December 4, 1950, Atomic Plant—Miscellaneous File, BRM Papers. Maybank was inundated with requests from people and companies seeking to open businesses in the area. See, for example, George W. Dunlap to BRM, December 12, 1950, Misc.—Atomic Plant File 1951, BRM Papers.

10. Pere Seward, Testimony, in *Hearing before the Joint Committee*, 21. New employees came from all regions of the United States, with only 20 percent coming from South Carolina. See Chapin et al., "In the Shadow," xiii, 36, 93.

11. For information on the Oak Ridge and other Manhattan Project facilities and related resident problems, see Olwell, *At Work in the Atomic City*; Hales, *Atomic Spaces*. No government town had been constructed at the Arco, Idaho, AEC project; however, the SRP project dwarfed Arco in size and construction schedule. See U.S. Department of Labor, *Bulletin*, 22.

12. Findlay and Hevly, *Atomic Frontier Days*, 107.

13. Henry D. Smyth, Statement, in *Hearing before the Joint Committee on Atomic Energy*, 1; Schoch-Spana, "Reactor Control and Environmental Management, 154.

14. Lang, "Our Far-Flung Correspondents," 42.

15. E. I. Du Pont de Nemours and Company, *Savannah River Plant Construction History*, 358–59; Chapin et al., "In the Shadow," 21–24.

16. Reed et al., *Savannah River Site at Fifty*, 223; *Augusta Herald*, November 5, 1951, Series VIII, Scrapbook 1, Reel 110, AED Records.

17. U.S. Department of Labor, *Bulletin*, 22.

18. Typescript notes, n.d., Atomic Plant File, BRM Papers.

19. Walter J. Williams, Testimony, in *Hearing before the Joint Committee on Atomic Energy*, 2.

20. Raymond M. Foley, Testimony, in ibid., 9.

21. Ibid., 14.

22. ASR, December 20, 1950. See also HH to JSB, March 13, 1951, File 352, Box 6, JSB/FWB Papers.

23. ASR, December 13, 1950.

24. "New Atomic Bomb Plant Hits Augusta," 92.

25. Chapin et al., "In the Shadow," 47; Turner, "Aiken for Armageddon"; Glenwood J. Sherrard to James F. Byrnes, July 2, 1953, Rent Stabilization File, General Subject File, James F. Byrnes Papers, South Carolina Department of Archives and History, Columbia. Rent control was discontinued as of July 31, 1953.

26. "New Atomic Bomb Plant Hits Augusta," 92. See also *Time*, December 11, 1950, 22.

27. Leonard R. Holley to BRM, February 26, 1951, Atomic Plant—Miscellaneous File, BRM Papers; John E. Forsythe to W. Price Fallaw, December 26, 1951, Orion Whatley to Charles M. Hammond, January 5, 1952, General Correspondence File, Aiken County Sheriff Papers, South Carolina Department of Archives and History.

28. U.S. Department of Labor, *Bulletin*, 23.

29. HH to JSB, July 24, 1951, File 358, Box 6, JSB/FWB Papers.

30. JAT to NCJ, February 2, 1951, 1951 SRP January–March Correspondence File, Box A134, NUL-SRO.

31. Mary Jane Willett, Southern Region, YWCA, "Report on Visit to Savannah River Project, May 21–24, 1951," United Community Defense Services File, February–October 1951, Box A135, NUL-SRO.

32. Chapin et al., "In the Shadow," 102, 107–10.

33. Sylvia Bryant, interview; Juanita Thomas, interview.

34. Chapin et al., "In the Shadow," 110–11, 187. Social scientists from the University of North Carolina determined that only a "negligible number" of blacks had moved to South Carolina to work in the new plant. The five thousand African Americans eventually employed at the plant came from the surrounding area, thus negating the need for segregated housing. See Holland, "Steward of World Peace," 63.

35. ASR, December 29, 1950; ACC Minutes, October 8, 1951.

36. Pere Seward, Testimony, in *Hearing before the Joint Committee on Atomic Energy*, 18.

37. "New Atomic Bomb Plant Hits Augusta," 94. The developer eventually applied to the federal government for a two-million-dollar grant to cover creation and maintenance of water and sewer lines in these new developments. It received grants from the Housing and Home Finance agency in June 1952. See ACC Minutes, January 8, June 9, 1952.

38. Pere Seward, Testimony, in *Hearing before the Joint Committee on Atomic Energy*, 20–21.

39. Winchester Smith to BRM, October 15, 1951, Atomic Plant—Waterworks File, BRM Papers.

40. Pere Seward, Testimony, in *Hearing before the Joint Committee on Atomic Energy*, 21. Goldfield notes that even in "good times," most southern cities did not willingly provide adequate services (Goldfield, *Cotton Fields and Skyscrapers*, 181; Goldfield, *Region, Race, and Cities*, 250–51).

41. "New Atomic Bomb Plant Hits Augusta," 92; H. E. Bailey to BRM, July 18, 1951, Housing File, BRM Papers; *Columbia State*, July 18, 1951.

42. Reed et al., *Savannah River Site at Fifty*,. See also "Statement of McClellan Ratchford, Director, Aiken Office, Housing and Home Finance Agency," in UCDS, Minutes, Meeting on the Savannah River Area H-Bomb Plant, Atomic Energy Commission, April 4, 1952, UCDS April–June 1952 File, Box A148, NUL-SRO.

43. Raymond Foley, Testimony, in *Hearing before the Joint Committee on Atomic Energy*, 12.

44. ASR, June 11, 1951, J. Strom Thurmond Scrapbooks, vol. 12, reel 3, J. Strom Thurmond Papers, Clemson University Libraries, Clemson University, Clemson, South Carolina.

45. Reed et al., *Savannah River Site at Fifty*, 223; ASR, May 7, 1951.

46. Chapin et al., "In the Shadow," 195.

47. Ibid., chapter 6.

48. Mary Jane Willett, YWCA, "Report on Visit to Savannah River Project," 1951 SRP File, Box A134, NUL-SRO.

49. Clarence Mitchell, "NAACP Report on 'H' Bomb Project in South Carolina," February 5, 1951, 1951 SRP File, Box A134, NUL-SRO.

50. Olwell, *At Work in the Atomic City*, 21.

51. WDW to G. O. Robinson, May 23, 1952, Robinson to WDW, May 29, 1952, Topical File: Energy, Nuclear, SRP, Correspondence, 1951–1980, Box 30, WDW Papers.

52. HOD to NCJ, June 13, 1951, 1951 April–June Correspondence File, Box A134, NUL-SRO.

53. HLA to NCJ, September 4, 1951, 1951 SRP Reports File, ibid.

54. "Statement of H. O. Weeks, Mayor, Aiken, S.C., Accompanied by Sarah H. Busch, Executive Secretary, Chamber of Commerce; John A. May, Member, House of Representatives, South Carolina; A. J. Rutland, Superintendent of Education, Aiken County; and Mr. Jimmie Sundy, Citizen," in *Defense Housing Act*, 324–32.

55. Raymond Foley, Testimony, in *Hearing before the Joint Committee on Atomic Energy*, 13, 14.

56. Chapin et al., "In the Shadow," 49.

57. See *Defense Housing Act*; Chapin et al., "In the Shadow," 47–48; Defense Housing and Community Facilities and Services Act (Public Law 139, 82nd Congress). Public Law 94, passed during the 83rd Congress, extended the 1953 deadline (Press Release, September 24, 1951, File 1282 (1950–1953), Box 1591, Official File, HST Papers).

58. Chapin et al., "In the Shadow," 48.

59. BRM to Quincy Kennedy, October 22, 1951, Atomic Plant—Waterworks File, BRM Papers. See also statement of McClellan Ratchford, Director of Aiken Housing and Home Finance Agency, UCDS, Minutes, Meeting on the Savannah River Area H-Bomb Plant, Atomic Energy Commission, April 4, 1952, UCDS April–June 1952 File, Box A148, NUL-SRO.

60. Reginald A. Johnson to Lester Granger et al., October 19, 1951, UCDS February–October 1951 File, Box A135, NUL-SRO. This memorandum lists forty-one critical housing areas.

61. Chapin et al., "In the Shadow," 50.

62. "New Atomic Bomb Plant Hits Augusta," 94. Specifically, the new legislation provided for the designation of critical defense housing areas, and with such areas required (1) relaxation of credit controls invoked on residential construction shortly after the Korean conflict broke out in 1950, (2) special FHA mortgage insurance terms on certain types of new sale and rental housing to be "programmed" by Housing and Home Finance Agency for these areas, and (3) special FNHA mortgage purchase assistance. See Defense Housing and Community Facilities and Services Act (Public Law 139, 82nd Congress); Reed et al., *Savannah River Site at Fifty*, 224–25.

63. Reed et al., *Savannah River Site at Fifty*, 225.

64. See Atomic Plant—Waterworks File, BRM Papers.

65. Sarah Busch, Testimony, in *Defense Housing Act*, 331.

66. Winchester Smith to BRM, October 15, 1951, Atomic Plant—Waterworks File, BRM Papers.

67. A. A. Foreman and H. L. McClain to BRM, July 1, 1953, Atomic Plant—Waterworks File, BRM Papers.

68. A. A. Foreman and H. L. McClain to Albert Cole, July 1, 1953, in ibid.

69. Mrs. W. T. Phillips to BRM, September 18, 1952, in ibid.

70. Mrs. Mack Foreman to BRM, September 12, 1952, in ibid.

71. Mrs. B. D. Brinkley to BRM, September 17, 1952, in ibid.

72. Reed et al., *Savannah River Site at Fifty*, 236–40.

73. Savannah River Operations Office, "Economic Impact on Communities near the Savannah River Plant," May 1963, 6, File 7, Box 6, Subseries C, Series II, SRPP.

74. CAN to John A. May, March 25, 1953, Savannah River Project File, General Subject File, Box 9, Byrnes Papers; Chapin et al., "In the Shadow," 83. The population figure accounts for some city annexation and new neighborhoods receiving city services.

75. Chapin et al., "In the Shadow," 193.

76. ASR, December 20, 1950, January 5, 1951; "New Atomic Bomb Plant Hits Augusta," 92; Chapin et al., "In the Shadow," 59.

77. Chapin et al., "In the Shadow," 194.

78. ASR, December 8, 1950; Reed et al., *Savannah River Site at Fifty*, 238.

79. ACC Minutes, April 27, May 11, 1953.

80. Reed et al., *Savannah River Site at Fifty*, 229.

81. Chapin et al., "In the Shadow," 4, 194.

82. Ibid., 194.

83. Ibid., January 19, 1951.

84. ACC Minutes, January 8, June 11, 1951, January 14, February 11, May 11, October 13, 1952, April 27, 1953.

85. R. K. Mason to CAN, October 22, 1952, File 7, Box 6, Subseries C, Series II, SRPP.

86. HLA to NCJ, April 15, 1952, Harry Alston Reports, April–June 1952 File, Box A136, NUL-SRO.

87. HLA to NCJ, April 3, 1952, United Community Defense Services 1952, April–June File, Box A148, NUL-SRO.

88. HLA to NCJ, April 15, 1952, Harry Alston Reports, April–June 1952 File, Box A136, NUL-SRO.

89. See City of Aiken Police Department Reports for January 1951–September 1953, in ACC Minutes, February 1951–October 1953; "New Atomic Bomb Plant Hits Augusta," 96.

90. *ASR*, February 16, 1951.

91. ACC Minutes, March 12, 1951, January 22, May 12, August 11, 1952.

92. Ibid., October 13, 1952.

93. Ibid., September 8, 1952.

94. Ibid., February 8, May 7, June 7, July 2, August 3, September 6, October 4, 1951, March 7, 1952. Courtney also complained of impromptu garbage dumps and unsanitary boardinghouses.

95. Phyllis F. Beal to HLA, October 15, 1951, SRP August–December 1951 Correspondence File, Box A134, NUL-SRO.

96. Statement of Mrs. J. L. Bell, District Supervisor, South Carolina Department of Public Welfare, UCDS, Minutes, Meeting on the Savannah River Area H-Bomb Plant, Atomic Energy Commission, April 4, 1952, UCDS April–June 1952 File, Box A148, NUL-SRO.

97. Cathryn S. Guyler to Committee Members, May 20, 1952, SRP May–July 1952 File, Box A147, NUL-SRO.

98. UCDS, Minutes, Meeting on the Savannah River Area H-Bomb Plant, Atomic Energy Commission, April 4, 1952, UCDS April–June 1952 File, Box A148, NUL-SRO.

99. "History of Negotiation of Contract AT(07-2)-1," n.d., File 1, Box 5, Subseries A, Series II, SRPP.

100. Chapin et al., "In the Shadow," 137; Reed et al., *Savannah River Site at Fifty*, 238, 245, 246. For growth in Aiken County generally, see Aiken County Commission, Minutes, vol. 3, 1951–1955, South Carolina Department of Archives and History.

Chapter Six. "Better Living"

1. Ronnie Bryant, interview.

2. A. R. Luedecke to R. C. Blair, "Cooperation in Industrial Development Efforts

of Communities: The Problem Facing the Savannah River Plant and Surrounding Communities, with Particular Reference to the City of Aiken," January 11, 1963, 2, File 7, Box 6, Subseries C, Series II, SRPP.

3. O'Mara, *Cities of Knowledge*, 17.

4. Ndiaye, *Nylon and Bombs*, 3.

5. O'Mara, *Cities of Knowledge*, 19–21.

6. Boyer, *By the Bomb's Early Light*, 49, 51.

7. Sherry, *In the Shadow of War*, 203.

8. *Time*, January 2, 1961.

9. Du Pont "established its first formal research and development laboratory in 1902." Beginning around 1940, "the company was an intensively research-driven, technology-driven enterprise, depending on the commercial development of its own research ideas for its sustenance" (David A. Hounshell, "Du Pont and the Management of Large-Scale Research and Development," in *Big Science: The Growth of Large-Scale Research*, ed. Galison and Hevly, 236).

10. Grams, *Official Guide*, n.p.

11. Ndiaye, *Nylon and Bombs*, 123.

12. Zilg, *Du Pont*, 346, 388.

13. "New Products Spark Company's Growth," *Better Living*, September–October, 1951, 4.

14. "Why We Eat Better: Industrial Advances in U.S. Open the Way to Rich, Varied Diet," *Better Living*, November–December 1951, 2–8.

15. "New Americans: European Joining Du Pont Finds Material Well-Being Only One Facet of Rich U.S. Life," *Better Living*, March–April 1952, 9–14.

16. Brinkley, *End of Reform*, 65–85.

17. Zilg, *Du Pont*, 14–19.

18. *Savannah River News*, April 15, 1955, May 29, September 4, 1953.

19. "Wizards of Wilmington," 95; *Uncommon Man*; Albert E. Conway, "In Memoriam: Crawford H. Greenewalt," *The Auk* 111 (January 1994): 188–89.

20. "Wizards of Wilmington," 95; *Uncommon Man*.

21. Greenewalt, *Slow and Steady Way*, 2.

22. Ibid., 3.

23. Greenewalt, *Human Achievement*,

24. See, for example, Greenewalt, *Philosophy of Business Leadership*, 10–11.

25. For examples of Greenewalt's views on science and society, see Greenewalt, *Uncommon Man*; Greenewalt, *How Much Freedom—Or How Little?*; Greenewalt, *Research, the Great Reformer*. Throughout the 1950s, Greenewalt maintained a close albeit at times contentious relationship with the Eisenhower administration. For scientists as public policy gurus, see Bird and Sherwin, *American Prometheus*.

26. "Recruitment of Technical Personnel for Operations," ca. 1952, File 1, Box 5, Subseries A, Series II, SRPP.

27. McKibben, interview; Walt Joseph, interview.

28. McKibben, interview; Walt Joseph, interview.

29. Ronnie Bryant, interview.

30. "Memo for Housewives," *Savannah River News*, May 28, 1954.

31. Quoted in Reed et al., *Savannah River Site at Fifty*, 1.

32. Walt Joseph, interview.

33. Arthur W. Rich, interview.

34. Clary, interview.

35. *ASR*, March 11, 1954.

36. Ibid., March 13, 20, 1956.

37. Ibid., January 15, 1954.

38. Heckendorn, interview.

39. Mart A. Stewart argues that landscapes represent cultural values—in this case, the primacy of efficiency ("Southern Environmental History," in *Companion*, ed. Boles, 414–15).

40. Reed et al., *Savannah River Site at Fifty*, 109.

41. Du Pont noted that by 1963, 61.3 percent of the total SRP workforce resided in and around Aiken. See Savannah River Operations Office, "Economic Impact on Communities near the Savannah River Plant," May 1963, 2, File 7, Box 6, Subseries C, Series II, SRPP.

42. Ibid., 3.

43. O'Mara, *Cities of Knowledge*, 39, 44.

44. *ASR*, February 22, 1952.

45. Reed et al, *Savannah River Site at Fifty*, 229.

46. For annexation of suburban areas, see ACC Minutes, October 24, 1955, April 9, July 9, 1956, July 14, 1958, December 1, 1959, March 23, 1960.

47. Esther Melton, interview.

48. Otis Melton, interview.

49. Perhaps the one exception to this would be the Kalmia subdivision, which was named for William Gregg's estate.

50. E. C. Thomas, interview.

51. Clary, interview.

52. Quoted in Reed et al., *Savannah River Site at Fifty*, 294–95. See also Holland, "Steward of World Peace," 105, 120–21.

53. *ASR*, January 23, February 4, 1953.

54. Savannah River Operations Office, "Economic Impact on Communities near the Savannah River Plant," May 1963, 1, File 7, Box 6, Subseries C, Series II, SRPP.

55. Findlay and Hevly, *Atomic Frontier Days*, 119–27.

56. Savannah River Operations Office, "Economic Impact on Communities near the Savannah River Plant," May 1963, 6, File 7, Box 6, Subseries C, Series II, SRPP.

57. Chapin et al., "In the Shadow," 134.

58. *ASR*, April 20, 1953; Arthur D. Rich, interview; Arthur W. Rich, interview.

59. *ASR*, June 20, 1952.

60. ACC Minutes, April 25, 1966, includes proposal for Kalmia Shopping Plaza to accommodate the city's expansion.

61. *ASR*, February 18, 1952.

62. A. R. Luedecke to R. C. Blair, "Cooperation in Industrial Development Efforts

of Communities: The Problem Facing the Savannah River Plant and Surrounding Communities, with Particular Reference to the City of Aiken," January 11, 1963, 3, File 7, Box 6, Subseries C, Series II, SRPP.

63. Esther Melton, interview; Browder and Brooks, *Memories of Home*, 63–64.

64. Esther Melton interview; Clary, interview; Juanita Thomas, interview; Lenwood Melton, interview; Sylvia Bryant, interview.

65. Lenwood Melton, interview.

66. *ASR*, November 30, 1951.

67. ACC Minutes, November 9, December 7, 1953; *ASR*, April 15, 1953.

68. *ASR*, June 6, 1956.

69. Ibid., January 20, 1954.

70. ACC Minutes, August 27, December 10, 1956, October 12, 1964.

71. Ibid., June 25, 1956.

72. Ibid., January 8, 1962.

73. Conroy, "Horses Don't Eat Moon Pies," 50.

74. Don and Jean Roth, interview.

75. Reed et al., *Savannah River Site at Fifty*, 244–45, 246.

76. "Aiken's Answer to Town Problems," 188; *Aiken, South Carolina*, ca. 1960s, Brochure File, Subject Files, Aiken Chamber of Commerce, Aiken, South Carolina; *ASR*, October 10, 1967.

77. *ASR*, September 13, 1967.

78. *Charm and Progress*, ca. 1960, Brochure File, Subject Files, Aiken Chamber of Commerce.

79. Aiken Chamber of Commerce, *Commemorating the 125th Anniversary of the City of Aiken*, 1960, Aiken County History File, Historical Files, Aiken Chamber of Commerce.

Chapter Seven. Shifting Landscapes

1. "Frederick Cannon Brinkley," in Bailey, Morgan, and Taylor, *Biographical Directory*, 1:189.

2. ACC Minutes, 1953–61.

3. ACC Minutes, April 27, May 11, 1953.

4. Crosland Park Civic Association, Resolution, March 5, 1955, included in ACC Minutes, March 8, 1955.

5. ACC Minutes, May 23, 1955; "Aiken's Answer to Town Problems," 188.

6. Zuczek, *State of Rebellion*; Mark M. Smith, "'All Is Not Quiet"; Key, *Southern Politics*, chapters 7, 13; Kalk, *Origins*, xviii.

7. Tindall, *Disruption of the Solid South*, 47.

8. Frederickson, *Dixiecrat Revolt*.

9. Sampson, "Rise," 18; Perry and Watkins, *Rise of the Sunbelt Cities*; Gifford, "'Dixie,'" 208; Strong, *Urban Republicanism*.

10. Gifford, "'Dixie,'" 208.

11. *Survey of Aiken County Schools*, 3.

12. Sampson, "Rise," chapter 2.

13. Ibid., 21.

14. Ibid., 277.

15. Gifford, "'Dixie,'" 211.

16. Sampson, "Rise," 279.

17. Ibid., 277.

18. Kalk, *Origins*, 30.

19. Clary, interview.

20. Sampson, "Rise," 278.

21. Gifford, "'Dixie,'" 209.

22. *ASR*, October 28, 1960.

23. Ibid., November 18, 1960.

24. Ibid., September 7, 1960.

25. MacClaren, interview.

26. Joseph quoted in Reed et al., *Savannah River Site at Fifty*, 251–52.

27. *ASR*, December 8, 1959; MacClaren, "Aiken County Republican History."

28. *ASR*, December 12, 1961.

29. Ibid., February 12, 1960.

30. Ibid., December 1, 1959.

31. Ibid., December 11, 1961.

32. Ibid., December 7, 1961.

33. Ibid., March 22, 1961.

34. Ibid., April 25, 1963. The Republicans did not offer candidates for Aiken City Council in 1963. See *ASR*, October 3, 1963.

35. Ibid., February 26, 1962.

36. For information on Johnston's career, see Simon, *Fabric of Defeat*; Frederickson, *Dixiecrat Revolt*.

37. WDW to Barry Goldwater, January 14, 1962, Campaign Files, 1962, Box 4, WDW Papers.

38. *ASR*, November 7, 1962.

39. Workman, *Case for the South*, 59, 162–63.

40. WDW to Barry Goldwater, April 30, 1962, Campaign Files, 1962, Box 4, WDW Papers.

41. WDW, Speech, October 2, 1962, Campaign Files, 1962, Box 5, in ibid.

42. WDW, Acceptance Speech, Republican State Convention, March 17, 1962, in ibid.

43. WDW, Speech, August 25, 1962, in ibid.

44. *ASR*, July 15, October 26, 1952.

45. WDW, Acceptance Speech, Republican State Convention, March 17, 1962, Campaign Files, 1962, Box 5, WDW Papers.

46. WDW, Speech, October 2, 1962, in ibid.

47. Gus Robinson to WDW (with typed notes from WDW), January 4, 1962, in ibid.

48. J. Bradford Hays to WDW, [March 1962], "Aiken County Newsletter for Workman-Spence," September 27, 1962, in ibid.

49. WDW to Frank, August 21, 1962, in ibid.

50. Merritt, "Senatorial Election."

51. "Aiken County Vote Tallies," n.d., Campaign Files, 1962, Box 5, WDW Papers.

52. W. W. Wannamaker Jr., "1962 2nd District Congressional Race," in ibid.

53. ASR, April 25, 1963.

54. Frederickson, *Dixiecrat Revolt*, 234.

55. ASR, June 25, September 17, 1964.

56. Merritt, "Senatorial Election," 289; Cohodas, *Strom Thurmond*, 358.

57. ASR, March 4, 1964.

58. Ibid., November 4, 1964.

59. Ibid., August 31, September 10, 1965.

60. Ibid., September 1, 1965.

61. Ibid., September 14, December 14, 1965.

62. MacClaren, interview.

63. ASR, November 15, 1967.

64. Ibid., April 22, 1969.

65. MacClaren, interview.

66. "Gilbert Edward McMillan," in Bailey, Morgan, and Taylor, *Biographical Directory*, 2:1020.

67. ASR, November 13, 1969.

68. Ibid., November 9, 1966.

69. Ibid., November 8, 10, 1966.

70. MacClaren, "Aiken County Republican History." The county commission replaced a system whereby the county was administered by a supervisor and three road commissioners. See *Aiken Standard*, March 20, November 8, 1972.

71. Roberson et al., *Over a Hundred Schoolhouses*, 13.

72. Ibid., 276, 280; ASR, August 12, 1964.

73. Roberson et al., *Over a Hundred Schoolhouses*, 13.

74. Law, *Forever Flourishing*.

75. *Survey of Aiken County Schools*, 11.

76. *Columbia State*, January 25, 1951.

77. Riddick, *Aiken County Schools*, 186.

78. Ibid., 189–90.

79. ASR, September 2, 1964.

80. Ibid., September 20, 1965.

81. Ibid., August 17, 1967.

82. Gallman, interview.

83. Roberson et al., *Over a Hundred Schoolhouses*, 133.

84. ASR, November 30, 1967.

85. Ibid., 134.

86. Roberson et al., *Over a Hundred Schoolhouses*, 135.

87. ASR, August 21, 1967.

88. Ibid., April 26, 1968.

89. Ibid., May 28, 1968.

90. Ibid., February 12, 1969.

91. Ibid., March 25, 1969.

92. Ibid., March 26, 1969.

93. Ibid., July 4, 1969.

94. Ibid., July 17, August 11, 1969.

95. Ibid., August 5, 1969; Gallman, interview; *102nd Annual Report of the State Superintendent of Education, State of South Carolina, 1970–1971* (Columbia: State Budget and Control Board, 1971).

96. Gallman, interview.

97. Hightower, interview.

98. Gallman, interview.

99. Hightower, interview. See also *Aiken Standard*, April 11, June 9, 1975.

100. *The Hornet* (Aiken High School yearbook), 1975.

101. Gallman, interview.

102. *Survey of Aiken County Schools*, 7. By 1980, all elementary schools in Aiken had white majorities. See *Aiken Standard*, October 17, 1980.

103. Davis, *Race against Time*, argues that in Natchez, Mississippi, the defense of segregation was based heavily on whites' perceptions of blacks' cultural differences.

104. Willar Hightower to author, March 22, 2012.

105. Hightower, interview; Clary, interview; Gallman, interview.

106. Ndiaye, *Nylon and Bombs*, 181.

107. Hightower, interview.

108. Gallman, interview.

109. Willar Hightower to author, March 22, 2012.

110. *Aiken Standard*, November 7, 1973.

111. Ibid., November 4, 9, 1977.

112. Ibid., April 15, 1981.

113. Ibid., November 9, 1986.

114. www.scstatehouse.gov/member.

115. *Aiken Standard*, July 31, 2011.

Epilogue

1. Carlisle and Zenzen, *Supplying the Nuclear Arsenal*, 180–82.

2. Reed et al., *Savannah River Site at Fifty*, 484–511.

3. Lutz, *Homefront*, 106.

4. Findlay and Hevly, *Atomic Frontier Days*, 205.

5. *Charleston Post and Courier*, April 4, 1995; Reed et al., *Savannah River Site at Fifty*, 500–501.

6. *Atlanta Journal-Constitution*, September 26, 2006.

7. *Augusta Chronicle*, August 28, 2005; *Atlanta Journal-Constitution*, July 9, 2007.

8. *Jacksonville Florida Times-Union*, March 2, 1999.

9. *Atlanta Journal-Constitution*, April 13, 2000.

10. *Augusta Chronicle*, January 25, May 27, June 14, 2000; *Washington Post*, May 12, 2007.

11. *New York Newsday*, January 22, 2000.

12. Reed et al., *Savannah River Site at Fifty*, 461; *Atlanta Journal-Constitution*, May 31, 2007.

13. Gibbons, interview.

14. *Aiken Standard*, September 5, 2010; *Savannah River Heritage Foundation Newsletter*, September 2010.

BIBLIOGRAPHY

Primary Sources

Archives and Collections

Aiken, South Carolina
  Aiken County Government Complex
    City Council, Minutes
    Chamber of Commerce Files
    Plat Books, Deed Books, Register of MESNE Conveyances
  University of South Carolina at Aiken, Gregg-Graniteville Library
    E. I. du Pont de Nemours and Company, Inc., Atomic Energy Division Records
    Graniteville Bulletin
    Samuel H. Swint Papers
  Aiken County Historical Museum
    Register, Willcox Hotel
Charleston, South Carolina
  Special Collections, Marlene and Nathan Addlestone Library, College of
    Charleston
    Burnet R. Maybank Papers
Clemson, South Carolina
  Clemson University Libraries
    Edgar G. Brown Papers
    James F. Byrnes Papers
    J. Strom Thurmond Papers
Columbia, South Carolina
  South Carolina Department of Archives and History
    County Records
      Aiken County Sheriff Department Papers
      Aiken County Council, Minutes
      Aiken County Council, General Correspondence
    Manuscripts
      James F. Byrnes Papers
    Municipal Records
      Aiken, City Council Minutes, 1950–1980
      Aerial Surveys of City of Aiken, 1951–1952

State Agencies
    South Carolina Development Board
    South Carolina Department of Research, Planning, and Development
South Caroliniana Library, University of South Carolina at Columbia
    Manuscripts
        John Shaw Billings and Frederika Wade Billings Papers
        John Shaw Billings Scrapbooks
    Modern Political Collections
        William D. Workman Papers
        Solomon Blatt Papers
        Olin D. Johnston Papers
Independence, Missouri
  Harry S. Truman Library
    Harry S. Truman Files
        President's Secretary's Files
        White House Central Files: Official File
Morrow, Georgia
  National Archives and Records Administration, Southeast Region
    Records of the Atomic Energy Commission, Record Group 326
    Records of the District Courts of the United States, Record Group 21
Washington, D.C.
  Library of Congress
    Papers of the NAACP
    Papers of the Urban League
    Papers of the National Urban League—Southern Regional Office
  National Archives and Records Administration
    Atomic Energy Commission Papers, Record Group 236
    President's Committee on Contract Compliance, Record Group 325
    Farmers Home Administration, Record Group 96
Wilmington, Delaware
  Hagley Museum and Library
    E. I. du Pont de Nemours and Company, Atomic Energy Division, Savannah
        River Plant Papers, Accession 1957
    Crawford H. Greenewalt Diaries, Accession 1889
    Crawford H. Greenewalt Papers, Accession 1814

Government Documents

SOUTH CAROLINA

South Carolina Development Board. *Four Reasons Why South Carolina Believes the
    New National Accelerator Laboratory Should be Located in the Aiken-Augusta Area
    on the Savannah River.* 1965.
———. *South Carolina on the March: Ten Years of Progress.* 1954.
South Carolina Research, Planning, and Development Board. *General Statistics on
    South Carolina.* 1948, 1950, 1953, 1958.

———. *Know South Carolina*. [195?].

———. *Second Annual Report, Fiscal Year 1946–1947*. 1947.

———. *South Carolina Servicemen after the War*. 1945.

———. *Welcome to South Carolina*. [1952?].

UNITED STATES

Buck, Alice L. *A History of the Atomic Energy Commission*. U.S. Department of Energy. DOE/ES-0003/1. 1983.

Defense Housing Act, Hearing before the Committee on Banking and Currency, United States Senate, 82nd Congress, First Session, on S. 349, A Bill to Assist the Provision of Housing and Community Facilities and Services Required in Connection with the National Defense, Part 2B, *Hearing in Aiken, South Carolina, February 28, 1951*. 1951.

Discrimination and Full Utilization of Manpower Resources: Hearings before the Subcommittee on Labor and Labor-Management Relations of the Committee on Labor and Public Welfare, United States Senate, 82nd Congress, Second Session, on S.1732 and S.551, April 7, 8, 16, 17, 18, and 21, 1952. 1952.

Employment Practices at Savannah River Project: Hearings before a Special Subcommittee of the Committee on Education and Labor, House of Representatives, 82nd Congress, First Session, Hearings held at Augusta, Georgia, November 5, 6, 7, 8, and 9, 1951. 1952.

Employment Practices at Savannah River Project: Report of Special Subcommittee on Labor Relations to the Committee on Economic and Labor Pursuant to H. Res. 73. 1952.

Foreign Relations of the United States, 1950. Vol. 1, *National Security Affairs: Foreign Economic Policy*. 1977.

Hearing before the Joint Committee on Atomic Energy, Congress of the United States, 82nd Congress, First Session, on Housing for Savannah River and Paducah Sites, February 16, 1951. 1951.

U.S. Bureau of the Census. *Sixteenth Census of the United States: 1940*.

———. *Seventeenth Census of the United States: 1950*.

———. *Eighteenth Census of the United States: 1960*.

U.S. Department of Energy. *Facts and Data on the U.S. Atomic Energy Commission's Savannah River Plant in South Carolina*. N.d.

———. *The Savannah River Plant*. 1980.

U.S. Department of Labor. *Bulletin of the Bureau of Labor Statistics*. No. 1100, *Labor and the Savannah River AEC Project*. 1952.

U.S. Department of Labor, Bureau of Employment Security. *Bimonthly Summary of Labor Market Developments in Major Areas*. 1951.

U.S. Statutes at Large Containing the Laws and Concurrent Resolutions Enacted during the First Session of the Eighty-Second Congress of the United States of America, 1951, and Reorganization Plans and Proclamations. Vol. 65. 1952.

U.S. Statutes at Large Containing the Laws and Concurrent Resolutions Enacted during the First Session of the Eighty-Third Congress of the United States of America, 1953, and Reorganization Plans and Proclamations. Vol. 67. 1953.

Reports

Chapin, F. Stuart, Jr., Theodore W. Wirths, Alfred M. Denton Jr., and John C. Gould. "In the Shadow of a Defense Plant: A Study of Urbanization in Rural South Carolina; A Final Report of the Savannah River Urbanization Study." Institute for Research in Social Science, University of North Carolina at Chapel Hill, June 1954.

"State of South Carolina Industrial Development Analysis," prepared for South Carolina Development Board, [1966?].

E. I. Du Pont de Nemours and Company Publications and Audiovisual Materials

Better Living Employee Magazine. 1949–52. Hagley Museum and Library, Wilmington, Delaware.

Builders of Tomorrow. Videotape A41. 1954. Hagley Museum and Library, Wilmington, Delaware.

Building for Atomic Energy. Videotape A41. Engineering Division, Savannah River Operations Office, [1954?]. Hagley Museum and Library, Wilmington, Delaware.

Company and Community: The Responsibilities of Business in Society. 1967. Rubenstein Library, Duke University, Durham, North Carolina.

The Du Pont Story. Videotape. 1950. Hagley Museum and Library, Wilmington, Delaware.

Facts and Figures: The Savannah River Plant of the U.S. Atomic Energy Commission. 1952. South Caroliniana Library, University of South Carolina at Columbia.

The Savannah River Laboratory, Atomic Energy Commission. Videotape. n.d. Hagley Museum and Library, Wilmington, Delaware.

The Savannah River Plant: The Tradition, the Commitment, the Facts. 1989. Hagley Museum and Library, Wilmington, Delaware.

Savannah River Plant Construction History. Vol. 1, *Administration.* 1957. Department of Energy Documents Collection, University of South Carolina at Aiken.

Savannah River Plant History: Plantwide Activities, July 1954 through December 1972." N.d. Department of Energy Documents Collection, University of South Carolina at Aiken.

The Savannah River Plant of the U.S. Atomic Energy Commission. 1963. South Caroliniana Library, University of South Carolina at Columbia.

The Story of the Atomic Energy Commission's Savannah River Plant. Videotape A41. [1955?]. Hagley Museum and Library, Wilmington, Delaware.

Books

Public Papers of the Presidents of the United States: Harry S. Truman: Containing the Public Messages, Speeches, and Statements of the President, January 1 to December 31, 1949. Washington, D.C.: U.S. Government Printing Office, 1964.

Pamphlets and Speeches

Aiken, South Carolina as a Health and Pleasure Resort. Charleston, S.C.: Walker, Evans, and Cogswell, 1889.

Greenewalt, Crawford H. *How Much Freedom—Or How Little?* Speech, November 17, 1952. Widener Library, Harvard University, Cambridge, Massachusetts.

———. *Human Achievement and the Free Society*. Speech, June 25, 1958. Widener Library, Harvard University, Cambridge, Massachusetts.

———. "A Philosophy of Business Leadership." Speech, September 13, 1956. Central Library, Southern Methodist University, Dallas, Texas.

———. *Research, the Great Reformer*. Speech, May 10, 1951. Hagley Museum and Library, Wilmington, Delaware.

———. *The Slow and Steady Way of Progress*. Speech, December 5, 1951. Pamphlet Collection, Duke University Library, Durham, North Carolina.

Newsletter

Savannah River Heritage Foundation, 2009–11.

Yearbook and Directory

The Hornet, Aiken High School, 1972, 1975.

Shorter College Alumni Directory, 1999. Livingston Library, Shorter College, Rome, Georgia.

Articles

"Atomic Blowup." *Business Week*, September 19, 1953, 179–80.

"The Atom: The Displaced." *Time*, December 11, 1950, 21–22.

"Deserted Village." *Time*, March 10, 1952, 28.

Hayne, Paul H. "Aiken, South Carolina." *Appleton's Journal*, December 2, 1871, 623–26.

"The H-Bomb Town." *New York Times Magazine*, November 30, 1952, 10–11.

Herndon, Booton. "That Others May Live." *Redbook*, March 25, 1951, 25, 80–84.

"How to Make a Buck." *Time*, November 6, 1950, 93.

Lang, Daniel. "Our Far-Flung Correspondents: Camellias and Bombs." *New Yorker*, July 7, 1951, 40, 42–49.

Lipton, Howard. "The H-Bomb Hits the South." *New Republic*, June 30, 1952, 9.

"Mobilization." *Time*, March 10, 1952, 28.

"New Atomic Bomb Plant Hits Augusta with a Bang." *Business Week*, November 10, 1951, 88–90, 92, 94, 96.

"Obituary of Ms. Augusta Cassels." *Augusta Chronicle*, July 8, 1999.

"The Pure Savannah." *Time*, December 25, 1950, 48.

"The Wizards of Wilmington." *Time*, April 16, 1951, 94–102.

Newspapers

Aiken Standard and Review
Atlanta Journal Constitution
Columbia State
New York Times

Interviews by Author

Georgianna Alexander, New Ellenton, South Carolina, December 22, 2008.
Cy Banick, Aiken, South Carolina, August 2005.
Ronnie Bryant, Graniteville, South Carolina, May 2003; telephone, March 7, 2007.
Sylvia Bryant, Graniteville, South Carolina, May 2003; telephone, November 6, 2006.
Owen Clary, telephone, October 26, 2005, November 2, 2009.
Bret Crawford, Aiken, South Carolina, March 14, 2007.
Todd Crawford, Aiken, South Carolina, December 2004, March 14, 2007.
Vernon Dunbar, New Ellenton, South Carolina, March 13, 2007.
Jim Duncan, telephone, October 26, 2005.
Arthur Ashley Foreman III, telephone, October 24, 2005.
Fielding Foreman, telephone, November 18, 2005.
James Gallman, telephone, October 20, 2009.
Whit Gibbons, Tuscaloosa, Alabama, November 11, 2011.
L. C. Green, New Ellenton, South Carolina, March 13, 2007.
Frank M. Heckendorn, telephone, April 20, 2007.
Willar Hightower, Aiken, South Carolina, March 17, 2011.
Paula Joseph, Aiken, South Carolina, March 14, 2007.
Walt Joseph, Aiken, South Carolina, December 2004, March 14, 2007.
Janie Key, telephone, February 3, 2010.
Carl Langley, telephone, April 11, 2007.
Harber "Mac" MacClaren, Aiken, South Carolina, December 2004.
Sonya Mazzell, telephone, November 15, 2005.
Mal McKibben, Aiken, South Carolina, December 2004.
Esther Melton, Graniteville, South Carolina, May 3, 2002; telephone, November 6, 2006.
Lenwood Melton, Graniteville, South Carolina, May 2003.
Otis Melton, Graniteville, South Carolina, May 2003.
Sue Pack, New Ellenton, South Carolina, March 13, 2007.
Arthur D. Rich, Aiken, South Carolina, October 15, 2005.
Arthur W. Rich, Aiken, South Carolina, October 15, 2005.
Allen Riddick, Aiken, South Carolina, March 14, 2011.
Don and Jean Roth, Aiken, South Carolina, August 2005.
Ken Stephens, interview, April 22, 2007.
E. C. Thomas, Graniteville, South Carolina, May 2003.
Juanita Thomas, Graniteville, South Carolina, May 2003.

Secondary Sources

Aiken Remembers. Scrapbook Productions, 2006.

"Aiken's Answer to Town Problems: Citizen, Chamber of Commerce, City Hall Teamwork." *American City* 71 (September 1956): 188, 190.

Ashley, Franklin, ed. *Faces of South Carolina: Essays on South Carolina in Transition*. Columbia, S.C.: Ashley, 1974.

Bailey, N. Louise, Mary L. Morgan, and Carolyn R. Taylor. *Biographical Directory of the South Carolina Senate, 1776–1985*. Columbia: University of South Carolina Press, 1986.

Bebbington, William P. *History of Du Pont at the Savannah River Plant*. Wilmington, Del.: Du Pont, 1990.

Bird, Kai, and Martin J. Sherwin. *American Prometheus: The Triumph and Tragedy of J. Robert Oppenheimer*. New York: Knopf, 2005.

Black, Earl, and Merle Black. *Politics and Society in the South*. Cambridge: Harvard University Press, 1989.

———. *The Rise of Southern Republicans*. Cambridge: Belknap Press of Harvard University Press, 2003.

Bleser, Carol, ed. *The Hammonds of Redcliffe*. New York: Oxford University Press, 1981.

Boles, John, ed. *A Companion to the American South*. Hoboken, N.J.: Wiley-Blackwell, 2004.

Boyer, Paul. *By the Bomb's Early Light: American Thought and Culture at the Dawn of the Atomic Age*. Chapel Hill: University of North Carolina Press, 1985.

Brattain, Michelle. "Gender, Race, and the Construction of the 'Southern Worker.'" Paper presented at Gender and Work Series, Kennesaw State University, Kennesaw, Georgia, 2008.

Brinkley, Alan. *The End of Reform: New Deal Liberalism in Recession and War*. New York: Knopf, 1995.

Brooks, Jennifer E. *Defining the Peace: World War II Veterans, Race, and the Remaking of Southern Political Tradition*. Chapel Hill: University of North Carolina Press, 2004.

Browder, Tonya Algerine, and Richard David Brooks. *Memories of Home: Dunbarton and Myers Mill Remembered*. Savannah River Archaeological Research Heritage Series 1. Columbia: Savannah River Archaeological Research Program, Community History Project, South Carolina Institute of Archaeology and Anthropology, University of South Carolina, 1993.

———. *Memories of Home: Reminiscences of Ellenton*. Savannah River Archaeological Research Heritage Series 2. Columbia: Savannah River Archaeological Research Program, Community History Project, South Carolina Institute of Archaeology and Anthropology, University of South Carolina, 1996.

Building Bombs. Lightfoot Films, 1989.

Bull, Emily. *Eulalie*. Columbia, S.C.: Bryan, 1973.

Burton, Orville Vernon. *In My Father's House Are Many Mansions: Family and Com-*

munity in Edgefield, South Carolina. Chapel Hill: University of North Carolina Press, 1985.

Cabak, Melanie A., and Mary M. Inkrot. *Old Farm, New Farm: An Archaeology of Rural Modernization in the Aiken Plateau, 1875–1950*. With contributions by Elizabeth J. Abel, Mark D. Groover, and George L. Wingard. Savannah River Archaeological Research Papers 9. Columbia: Savannah River Archaeological Research Program, South Carolina Institute of Archaeology and Anthropology, University of South Carolina, 1997.

Carlisle, Rodney P., and Joan M. Zenzen. *Supplying the Nuclear Arsenal: American Production Reactors, 1942–1992*. Baltimore: Johns Hopkins University Press, 1996.

Carlton, David L., and Peter Coclanis, eds. *The South, the Nation, and the World*. Charlottesville: University of Virginia Press, 2003.

Carson, Clayborne. *In Struggle: SNCC and the Black Awakening of the 1960s*. Cambridge: Harvard University Press, 1995.

Carter, Dan T. *From George Wallace to Newt Gingrich: Race in the Conservative Counterrevolution, 1963–1994*. Baton Rouge: Louisiana State University Press, 1999.

———. *The Politics of Rage: George Wallace, the Origins of the New Conservatism, and the Transformation of American Politics*. Baton Rouge: Louisiana State University Press, 1996.

Cassels, Louis. *Coontail Lagoon: A Celebration of Life*. Philadelphia: Westminster, 1974.

Cassels, Louis, and Charlotte Cassels. *An Inquiry into the Origins of the Cassels Family of Ellenton, South Carolina*. Washington, D.C.: privately published, 1971.

Cassels, Louise. *The Unexpected Exodus: How the Cold War Displaced One Southern Town*. 1971; Columbia: University of South Carolina Press, 2007.

Chafe, William H. *Civilities and Civil Rights: Greensboro, North Carolina, and the Black Struggle for Freedom*. New York: Oxford University Press, 1981.

Cirincione, Joseph. *Bomb Scare: The History and Future of Nuclear Weapons*. New York: Columbia University Press, 2007.

Cobb, James C. *The Selling of the South: The Southern Crusade for Industrial Development, 1936–1990*. 2nd ed. Urbana: University of Illinois Press, 1993.

Cohodas, Nadine. *Strom Thurmond and the Politics of Southern Change*. Macon, Ga.: Mercer University Press, 1994.

Cole, Will. *The Many Faces of Aiken: A Pictorial History*. Norfolk/Virginia Beach: Donning, 1986.

Conroy, Pat. "Horses Don't Eat Moon Pies." In *Faces of South Carolina: Essays on South Carolina in Transition*, ed. Franklin Ashley, 47–79. Columbia, S.C.: Ashley, 1974.

Craig, Campbell, and Fredrik Logevall. *America's Cold War: The Politics of Insecurity*. Cambridge: Belknap Press of Harvard University Press, 2009.

Davies, Margery W. *Woman's Place Is at the Typewriter: Office Work and Office Workers, 1870–1930*. Philadelphia: Temple University Press, 1982.

Davis, Jack E. *Race against Time: Culture and Separation in Natchez since 1930*. Baton Rouge: Louisiana State University Press, 2001.

Dillon, Kimberly Ann. "Reconstructing Aiken: Resort Development in Aiken, S.C., 1830–1900." Master's thesis, University of South Carolina at Columbia, 1997.

Dittmer, John. *Local People: The Struggle for Civil Rights in Mississippi.* Champagne: University of Illinois Press, 1995.

Donovan, Robert J. *Tumultuous Years: The Presidency of Harry S. Truman, 1949–1953.* 1982; Columbia: University of Missouri Press, 1996.

Dorian, Max. *The Du Ponts: From Gunpowder to Nylon.* Trans. Edward B. Garside. Boston: Little, Brown, 1962.

Downey, Tom. *Planting a Capitalist South: Masters, Merchants, and Manufacturers in the Southern Interior, 1790–1860.* Baton Rouge: Louisiana State University Press, 2009.

Dudziak, Mary L. *Cold War Civil Rights: Race and the Image of American Democracy.* Princeton: Princeton University Press, 2001.

Edgar, Walter. *Sleepy Hollow: The Study of a Rural Community.* A Report Prepared for the Savannah River Laboratory. Columbia, SC: Institute for Southern Studies, University of South Carolina, 1981.

———. *South Carolina: A History.* Columbia: University of South Carolina Press, 1998.

———, ed. *The South Carolina Encyclopedia.* Columbia: University of South Carolina Press, 2006.

Egerton, John. *Speak Now against the Day: The Generation before the Civil Rights Movement in the South.* Chapel Hill: University of North Carolina Press, 1995.

Farmer, James O. "Playing Rebels: Reenactment as Nostalgia and Defense of the Confederacy in the Battle of Aiken." *Southern Cultures* 11 (Spring 2005): 46–73.

Faust, Drew Gilpin. *James Henry Hammond and the Old South: A Design for Mastery.* Baton Rouge: Louisiana State University Press, 1982.

Fernlund, Kevin, ed. *The Cold War American West, 1945–1989.* Albuquerque: University of New Mexico Press, 1998.

Findlay, John M., and Bruce Hevly. *Atomic Frontier Days: Hanford and the American West.* Seattle: Center for the Study of the Pacific Northwest and University of Washington Press, 2011.

Fischer, Phyllis. *Los Alamos Experience.* New York: Japan, 1985.

Fishbine, Glenn. *Children of Usher: Growing Up in Los Alamos.* Columbus, Ohio: Gom, 2004.

Flank, Lenny, ed. *Hell's Fire: A Documentary History of the American Atomic and Thermonuclear Weapons Programs: From Hiroshima to the Cold War and the War on Terror.* St. Petersburg, Fla.: Red and Black, 2008.

Frederickson, Kari. *The Dixiecrat Revolt and the End of the Solid South, 1932–1948.* Chapel Hill: University of North Carolina Press, 2001.

Gaddis, John Lewis. *The Cold War: A New History.* New York: Penguin, 2005.

———. *We Now Know: Rethinking Cold War History.* Oxford: Oxford University Press, 1997.

Galison, Peter, and Bruce Hevly, *Big Science: The Growth of Large-Scale Research.* Stanford: Stanford University Press, 1992.

Gerber, Michele Stenehjem. *On the Home Front: The Cold War Legacy of the Hanford Nuclear Site*. Lincoln: University of Nebraska Press, 1992.

Gifford, Laura Jane, "'Dixie Is No Longer in the Bag': South Carolina Republicans and the Election of 1960." *Journal of Policy History* 19 (2007): 207–33.

Gilmore, Glenda Elizabeth. *Defying Dixie: The Radical Roots of Civil Rights, 1919–1950*. New York: Norton, 2008.

Goldfield, David R. *Cotton Fields and Skyscrapers: Southern City and Region, 1670–1980*. Baton Rouge: Louisiana State University Press, 1982.

———. *Region, Race, and Cities: Interpreting the Urban South*. Baton Rouge: Louisiana State University Press, 1997.

Grams, Martin, Jr. *The Official Guide to the History of the Cavalcade of America*. Kearney, Neb.: Morris, 1998.

Greenewalt, Crawford H. *The Uncommon Man: The Individual in the Organization*. New York: McGraw-Hill, 1959.

Hales, Peter Bacon. *Atomic Spaces: Living on the Manhattan Project*. Urbana: University of Illinois Press, 1997.

Hamer, Fritz. *The Homefront and the Beginning of Change: World War II and South Carolina, 1941–1945*. Columbia: Palmetto Conservation Foundation, 1997.

Henderson, P. F. *A Short History of Aiken and Aiken County*. Columbia: Bryan, 1951.

Hevly, Bruce, and John M. Findlay, eds. *The Atomic West*. Seattle: University of Washington Press, 1998.

Hogan, Michael J. *A Cross of Iron: Harry S. Truman and the Origins of the National Security State, 1945–1954*. Cambridge: Cambridge University Press, 1998.

Holland, Deborah J. "Steward of World Peace, Keeper of Fair Play: The American Hydrogen Bomb and Civil Rights, 1945–1954." PhD diss., Northwestern University, 2002.

Hooks, Gregory. "Guns and Butter, North and South: The Federal Contribution to Manufacturing Growth, 1940–1990." In *The Second Wave: Southern Industrialization from the 1940s to the 1970s*, ed. Philip Scranton, 255–85. Athens: University of Georgia Press, 2001.

Hounshell, David A., and John Kenly Smith Jr. *Science and Corporate Strategy: Du Pont R&D, 1902–1980*. New York: Cambridge University Press, 1988.

Hunner, Jon. *Inventing Los Alamos: The Growth of an Atomic Community*. Norman: University of Oklahoma Press, 2004.

Huntley, William. "Mendel Rivers and the Expansion of the Charleston Naval Station." *Proceedings of the South Carolina Historical Association* (1995): 31–33.

Johnson, Charles W., and Charles O. Jackson. *City behind a Fence: Oak Ridge, Tennessee, 1942–1946*. Knoxville: University of Tennessee Press, 1981.

Johnson, Leland, and Daniel Schaffer. *Oak Ridge National Laboratory: The First Fifty Years*. Knoxville: University of Tennessee Press, 1994.

Kalk, Bruce H. *The Origins of the Southern Strategy: Two-Party Competition in South Carolina, 1950–1972*. Lanham, Md.: Lexington, 2001.

Kantrowitz, Stephen. *Ben Tillman and the Reconstruction of White Supremacy*. Chapel Hill: University of North Carolina Press, 2000.

Key, V. O., Jr. *Southern Politics in State and Nation*. New York: Knopf, 1949.

Kovacik, Charles F., and John J. Winberry. *South Carolina: The Making of a Landscape*. Columbia: University of South Carolina Press, 1989.

Kruse, Kevin. *White Flight: Atlanta and the Making of Modern Conservatism*. Princeton: Princeton University Press, 2007.

Kruse, Kevin M., and Stephen Tuck, eds. *Fog of War: The Second World War and the Civil Rights Movement*. New York: Oxford University Press, 2012.

Lander, Ernest M., Jr. "The Decline and Resurrection of South Carolina: An Overview." *Proceedings of the South Carolina Historical Association* (1984): 96–104.

Lanier, Sidney. *Florida: Its Scenery, Climate, and History: With an Account of Charleston, Savannah, Augusta, and Aiken*. 1876; Gainesville: University of Florida Press, 1973.

Lassiter, Matthew D. *The Silent Majority: Suburban Politics in the Sunbelt South*. Princeton: Princeton University Press, 2006.

Law, Donald M. *Forever Flourishing: The History of Aiken Preparatory School*. N.p., 1992.

Lee, Joseph Edward, "South Carolina's Cold Warrior: James P. Richards, Captain of America's International 'Fire Department' during the 1950s." *Proceedings of the South Carolina Historical Association* (1993): 14–16.

Leffler, Melvyn P. *A Preponderance of Power: National Security, the Truman Administration, and the Cold War*. Stanford: Stanford University Press, 1992.

Litchman, Kirstin Embry. *Secrets of a Los Alamos Kid, 1946–1953*. Los Alamos, N.M.: Los Alamos Historical Society, 2001.

Lotchin, Roger W. *Fortress California, 1910–1961: From Warfare to Welfare*. New York: Oxford University Press, 1992.

Lotchin, Roger W., and David R. Long. "World War II and the Transformation of Southern Urban Society: A Reconsideration," *Georgia Historical Quarterly* 58 (Spring 1999): 29–57.

Lumpkin, Katherine Du Pre. *The Making of a Southerner*. 1946; Athens: University of Georgia Press, 1991.

Lutz, Catherine. *Homefront: A Military City and the American Twentieth Century*. Boston: Beacon, 2001.

MacClaren, Harber. "Aiken County Republican History: A Partial Chronicle." Unpublished manuscript in author's possession, 2004.

MacDowell, Dorothy Kelly. *An Aiken Scrapbook: A Picture Narrative of Aiken and Aiken County, South Carolina*. 2 vols. Aiken, S.C.: MacDowell, 1982.

Markusen, Ann, Peter Hall, Scott Campbell, and Sabina Deitrick. *The Rise of the Gunbelt: The Military Remapping of Industrial America*. New York: Oxford University Press, 1991.

Martin, Jessica E. "Corporate Cold Warriors: American Business Leaders and Foreign relations in the Eisenhower Era." PhD diss., University of Colorado, Boulder, 2006.

McCoy, Donald R. *The Presidency of Harry S. Truman*. Lawrence: University Press of Kansas, 1984.

McCoy, Donald R., and Richard T. Ruetten. *Quest and Response: Minority Rights and the Truman Administration*. Lawrence: University Press of Kansas, 1973.

McCullough, David G. *Truman*. New York: Simon and Schuster, 1993.

McGirr, Lisa. *Suburban Warriors: The Origins of the New American Right*. Princeton: Princeton University Press, 2002.

McMillan, George. "The H-Bomb's First Victims." *The Reporter*, March 6, 1951, 17–20.

McMillen, Neil R., ed. *Remaking Dixie: The Impact of World War II on the American South*. Jackson: University Press of Mississippi, 1997.

Merritt, Russell. "The Senatorial Election of 1962 and the Rise of Two-Party Politics in South Carolina." *South Carolina Historical Magazine* 98 (July 1997): 281–301.

Mitchell, Broadus. *William Gregg: Factory Master of the Old South*. 1928; New York: Octagon, 1966.

Moore, Winfred B., Jr., and Orville Vernon Burton, eds. *Toward the Meeting of the Waters: Currents in the Civil Rights Movement of South Carolina during the Twentieth Century*. Columbia: University of South Carolina Press, 2008.

Mosley, Leonard. *Blood Relations: The Rise and Fall of the Du Ponts of Delaware*. New York: Atheneum, 1980.

Myers, Andrew H. *Black, White, and Olive Drab: Racial Integration at Fort Jackson, South Carolina, and the Civil Rights Movement*. Charlottesville: University of Virginia Press, 2006.

Nash, Gerald D. *The American West Transformed: The Impact of the Second World War*. Bloomington: Indiana University Press, 1985.

———. *The Federal Landscape: An Economic History of the Twentieth-Century West*. Tucson: University of Arizona Press, 1999.

Ndiaye, Pap A. *Nylon and Bombs: Du Pont and the March of Modern America*. Trans. Elborg Forster. Baltimore: Johns Hopkins University Press, 2007.

O'Berry, Lucius Sidney. *Ellenton, S.C.: My Life . . . Its Death*. Ed. Richard David Brooks and Tonya Algerine Browder. Columbia: Savannah River Archeological Research Program, South Carolina Institute of Archaeology and Anthropology, University of South Carolina, 1999.

O'Brient, Tim, Jodee Stallo, and the *Aiken Standard*. *Portraits of the Past: A Pictorial History of Aiken County*. Marceline, Mo.: D-Books, 2002.

Olwell, Russell B. *At Work in the Atomic City: A Labor and Social History of Oak Ridge, Tennessee*. Knoxville: University of Tennessee Press, 2004.

———. "Help Wanted for Secret City: Recruiting Workers for the Manhattan Project at Oak Ridge, Tennessee, 1942–1946." *Tennessee Historical Quarterly* 58 (Spring 1999): 52–69.

O'Mara, Margaret Pugh. *Cities of Knowledge: Cold War Science and the Search for the Next Silicon Valley*. Princeton: Princeton University Press, 2005.

Parsons, Elsie Worthington Clews. "Folklore from Aiken, S.C." *Journal of American Folklore* 34 (January–March 1921): 1–39.

Payne, Charles. *I've Got the Light of Freedom: The Organizing Tradition and the Mississippi Freedom Struggle*. Berkeley: University of California Press, 1995.

Perry, David C., and Alfred J. Watkins, eds. *The Rise of the Sunbelt Cities*. Beverly Hills, Calif.: Sage, 1977.

Phillips, Jonathan F. "Building a New South Metropolis: Fayetteville, Fort Bragg, and the Sandhills of North Carolina." PhD diss., University of North Carolina at Chapel Hill, 2002.

Reed, Mary Beth, Mark Swanson, Steve Gaither, J. W. Joseph, and William R. Henry. *Savannah River Site at Fifty*. Washington, D.C.: U.S. Department of Energy; Stone Mountain, Ga.: New South Associates, 2002.

Rivera, Elaine. "Aiken, South Carolina: High Tension in a Company Town." *Time*, June 15, 1998, 8.

Rhodes, Richard. *Dark Sun: The Making of the Hydrogen Bomb*. New York: Simon and Schuster, 1995.

Riddick, Allen. *Aiken County Schools: A Pictorial History and More*. Aiken, S.C.: Rocket, 2003.

———. *Memories of Growing Up and Living in Aiken, S.C.* Aiken, S.C.: Rocket, 2011.

Roberson, Frank G., John B. Bradley, William A. Gallman, and Jack Hunter. *Over a Hundred Schoolhouses: A Historical Account of Public Education in Aiken County before and after Consolidation and Integration*. N.p., 2000.

Robertson, Evermae Broughton. "The Effect of the Savannah River Project Migrant Population on the Williston Elementary School up to June 1953." Master's thesis, University of South Carolina at Columbia, 1953.

Robeson, Elizabeth. "An 'Ominous Defiance': The Lowman Lynchings of 1926." In *Toward the Meeting of the Waters: Currents in the Civil Rights Movement of South Carolina during the Twentieth Century*, ed. Winfred B. Moore Jr. and Orville Vernon Burton, 65–92. Columbia: University of South Carolina Press, 2008.

Robinson, Gus O. *And What of Tomorrow?* New York: Comet, 1956.

Rosenberg, David Alan. "American Atomic Strategy and the Hydrogen Bomb Decision." *Journal of American History* 66 (June 1979): 62–87.

Sampson, Gregory B. "The Rise of the 'New' Republican Party in South Carolina, 1948–1974: A Case Study of Political Change in a Deep South State." Ph.D. diss., University of North Carolina at Chapel Hill, 1984.

Sanger, S. L. *Working on the Bomb: An Oral History of World War II Hanford*. Portland, Ore.: Portland State University Continuing Education Press, 1995.

Schoch-Spana, Monica. "Reactor Control and Environmental Management: A Cultural Account of Agency in the U.S. Nuclear Weapons Complex." PhD diss., Johns Hopkins University, 1988.

Schulman, Bruce. *From Cotton Belt to Sunbelt: Federal Policy, Economic Development, and the Transformation of the South, 1938–1980*. Durham: Duke University Press, 1994.

Scribner, Christopher MacGregor. *Renewing Birmingham: Federal Funding and the Promise of Change, 1939–1979*. Athens: University of Georgia Press, 2002.

Shafer, Byron E., and Richard Johnston. *The End of Southern Exceptionalism: Class, Race, and Partisan Change in the Postwar South*. Cambridge: Harvard University Press, 2006.

Sherry, Michael S. *In the Shadow of War: The United States since the 1930s*. New Haven: Yale University Press, 1995.

Shroyer, Jo Ann. *Secret Mesa: Inside Los Alamos National Laboratory*. New York: Wiley, 1998.

Siddons, Anne Rivers. *King's Oak*. New York: HarperCollins, 1999.

Simon, Bryant. *A Fabric of Defeat: The Politics of South Carolina Millhands, 1910–1948*. Chapel Hill: University of North Carolina Press, 1998.

Smith, Harry Worcester. *Life and Sport in Aiken and Those Who Made It*. New York: Derrydale, 1935.

Smith, Mark M. "'All Is Not Quiet in Our Hellish County': Facts, Fiction, Politics, and Race—The Ellenton Riot of 1876." *South Carolina Historical Magazine* 95 (April 1994): 142–55.

Somerville, Edith Oeone Anna. *The States through Irish Eyes*. Boston: Houghton Mifflin, 1930.

South Carolina: The WPA Guide to the Palmetto State. 1941; Columbia: University of South Carolina Press, 1988.

"Southern Militarism." *Southern Exposure* 1 (Spring 1973).

Stewart, Mart A. *"What Nature Suffers to Groe": Life, Labor, and Landscape on the Georgia Coast, 1680–1920*. Athens: University of Georgia Press, 2002.

Stokes, Thomas L. *The Savannah*. 1951; Athens: University of Georgia Press, 1982.

Strom, Sharon Hartman. *Beyond the Typewriter: Gender, Class, and the Origins of Modern American Office Work, 1900–1930*. Urbana: University of Illinois Press, 1992.

Strong, Donald S. *Urban Republicanism in the South*. 1960; Westport, Conn.: Greenwood, 1977.

Sullivan, Patricia. *Days of Hope: Race and Democracy in the New Deal Era*. Chapel Hill: University of North Carolina Press, 1996.

Survey of Aiken County Schools. Nashville: George Peabody College for Teachers, 1964.

Tindall, George B. *The Disruption of the Solid South*. Athens: University of Georgia Press, 1972.

———. *The Emergence of the New South, 1913–1945*. Baton Rouge: Louisiana State University Press, 1967.

Toole, Gasper Loren. *Ninety Years in Aiken County*. Charleston, S.C.: Walker, Evans, and Cogswell, 1957.

Turner, Jobie Shay. "Aiken for Armageddon: The Savannah River Site and Aiken, S.C., 1950–1955." Master's thesis, University of Georgia, 1997.

Tyson, Timothy B. *Radio Free Dixie: Robert F. Williams and the Roots of Black Power*. Chapel Hill: University of North Carolina Press, 1999.

The Uncommon Man: Crawford H. Greenewalt." Atomic Heritage Foundation, 2008.

Vandervelde, Isabel. *Aiken County: The Only South Carolina County Founded during Reconstruction*. Spartanburg, S.C.: Reprint Company, 1999.

Wang, Jessica. *American Science in an Age of Anxiety: Scientists, Anticommunism, and the Cold War*. Chapel Hill: University of North Carolina Press, 1999.

Wells, Samuel F., Jr. "Sounding the Tocsin: NSC 68 and the Soviet Threat." *International Security* 4 (August 1979): 116–58.

Woods, Annie Laurie. "Aiken: The Winter Newport." *Metropolitan Magazine*, April 1899, 369–74.

Woods, Jeff. *Black Struggle, Red Scare: Segregation and Anticommunism in the South, 1948–1968*. Baton Rouge: Louisiana State University Press, 2004.

Workman, William D. *The Bishop from Barnwell: The Political Life and Times of Senator Edgar A. Brown*. Columbia, S.C.: Bryan, 1963.

———. *The Case for the South*. New York: Devin-Adair, 1960.

York, Herbert F. *The Advisors: Oppenheimer, Teller, and the Superbomb*. Stanford: Stanford University Press, 1976.

Zilg, Gerard Colby. *Du Pont: Behind the Nylon Curtain*. Englewood Cliffs, N.J.: Prentice-Hall, 1974.

Zuczek, Richard. *State of Rebellion: Reconstruction in South Carolina*. Columbia: University of South Carolina Press, 1996.

INDEX

Nelson, Curtis A., 49; Du Pont employment policies, 89; fair hiring at SPR, 103

New Ellenton, 71; creation of, 71–73; housing problems and, 120; impact of SRP on, 140; racial segregation in, 72–73

New Windsor, 32

Nixon, Richard M., 164; support in South Carolina, 153

North Augusta, S.C., 158; impact of SRP on, 140

NSC-68, 108

NUL. *See* National Urban League

Nye Committee, investigation of Du Pont, 17, 18–19

Oak Ridge National Laboratory, 5, 28, 75, 154; employee housing and, 110; fair hiring practices and, 92–93; housing for African American workers, 115–16

Orangeburg County, 39

Port Royal-Augusta Railroad, 50

Public Law 815, 118

Public Law 874, 118

Redcliffe, 25, 49, 67–68

Red Shirts, 40

Republican Party: Aiken, S.C., and, 160–61; Aiken County and, 8, 39–41, 147–48, 149, 152–55, 158–61; South Carolina and, 147, 148, 149–52, 153, 155–61; southern states and, 147, 148, 150–51, 152; Strom Thurmond and, 158–60, 161; suburbanization and, 151, 160

Richards, James P., 24

Richmond County, Ga., 117

Riley, John J., 49–50

Rivers, L. Mendel, 24–25

Roosevelt, Franklin D., 92, 150

Savannah River, 34, 47, 50; Clarks Hill Project and, 23; environmental impact of SRP on, 173, 174–75; natural attributes of, 30, 31; water purity of, 23

Savannah River Ecological Laboratory, 175

Savannah River Heritage Foundation, 176

Savannah River News, 131–32, 158

Savannah River Plant (SRP), 1, 5, 147, 170; African American employment and, 7–8, 79, 91–106; announcement of, 26–27, 49, 123; construction of, 80–102; consumption and, 6, 124, 131–32, 141, 142; creation of middle class and, 124; cultural impact of, 122, 144–46; economic impact of, 6, 28, 79, 84, 112, 123–24, 138–40, 144, 175, 176; employee housing problems and, 110–20; environmental legacy of, 171–75; impact on community services, 108, 117–18; impact on Korean War, 75, 80; impact on landscape, 1, 7, 70–71, 78, 125, 137–38, 143; neutrino detection and, 176; new mission in 1980s, 171; political impact of, 8, 79, 90–91, 105, 169; removal of resident population and, 48–74; renamed Savannah River Site, 171; rural transformation and, 50; school desegregation and, 167–68, 169; size of, 75; social impact of, 136–37; specific natural attributes of plant site, 20–21, 23; suburbanization and, 6, 113–14, 119–20, 124, 138–46; worker health and, 173–74

Savannah River Site. *See* Savannah River Plant

Savannah River Valley, 23; cotton cultivation in, 33–34; impact of Civil War and Reconstruction on, 37–41; kaolin extraction, 34; landscape of, 31–32; racial slavery in, 30–31, 34; as site of innovation, 30; tobacco cultivation in, 33

Savannah Town, 32

school desegregation: in Aiken County, 163–68; in Horse Creek Valley, 163

POLITICS AND CULTURE IN THE TWENTIETH-CENTURY SOUTH

A Common Thread: Labor, Politics, and Capital Mobility in the Textile Industry
by Beth English

"Everybody Was Black Down There": Race and Industrial Change in the Alabama Coalfields
by Robert H. Woodrum

Race, Reason, and Massive Resistance: The Diary of David J. Mays, 1954–1959
edited by James R. Sweeney

The Unemployed People's Movement: Leftists, Liberals, and Labor in Georgia, 1929–1941
by James J. Lorence

Liberalism, Black Power, and the Making of American Politics, 1965–1980
by Devin Fergus

Guten Tag, Y'all: Globalization and the South Carolina Piedmont, 1950–2000
by Marko Maunula

The Culture of Property: Race, Class, and Housing Landscapes in Atlanta, 1880–1950
by LeeAnn Lands

Marching in Step: Masculinity, Citizenship, and The Citadel in Post–World War II America
by Alexander Macaulay

Rabble Rousers: The American Far Right in the Civil Rights Era
by Clive Webb

Who Gets a Childhood: Race and Juvenile Justice in Twentieth-Century Texas
by William S. Bush

Alabama Getaway: The Political Imaginary and the Heart of Dixie
by Allen Tullos

The Problem South: Region, Empire, and the New Liberal State, 1880–1930
by Natalie J. Ring

The Nashville Way: Racial Etiquette and the Struggle for Social Justice in a Southern City
by Benjamin Houston

Cold War Dixie: Militarization and Modernization in the American South
by Kari Frederickson

CPSIA information can be obtained
at www.ICGtesting.com
Printed in the USA
FFOW01n1651280214
3937FF